THE POETICS OF INSECURITY

The Poetics of Insecurity turns the emerging field of literary security studies upside down. Rather than tying the prevalence of "security" to a culture of fear, Johannes Voelz shows how American literary writers of the past two hundred years have mobilized insecurity to open unforeseen and uncharted horizons of possibility for individuals and collectives. In a series of close readings of works by Charles Brockden Brown, Harriet Jacobs, Willa Cather, Flannery O'Connor, and Don DeLillo, Voelz brings to light a cultural imaginary in which conventional meanings of security and insecurity are frequently reversed, so that security begins to appear as deadening and insecurity as enlivening. Timely, broad-ranging, and incisive, Johannes Voelz's study intervenes in debates on American literature as well as in the interdisciplinary field of security studies. It fundamentally challenges our existing explanations for the pervasiveness of "security" in American cultural and political life.

JOHANNES VOELZ is Professor of American Studies, Democracy, and Aesthetics at Goethe-Universität Frankfurt, Germany. In 2016, he was awarded a Heisenberg-Professorship by the German Research Foundation. He is the author of *Transcendental Resistance: The New Americanists and Emerson's Challenge* (2010) and has edited several books and special issues, among them "Security and Liberalism," a theme issue of *Telos* (Spring 2015) and "Chance, Risk, Security: Approaches to Uncertainty in American Literature," a theme issue of *Amerikastudien / American Studies* (Fall 2015).

CAMBRIDGE STUDIES IN AMERICAN
LITERATURE AND CULTURE

Editor
Ross Posnock, *Columbia University*

Founding Editor
Albert Gelpi, *Stanford University*

Advisory Board
Robert Levine, *University of Maryland*
Wai Chee Dimock, *Yale University*
Tim Armstrong, *Royal Holloway, University of London*
Walter Benn Michaels, *University of Illinois, Chicago*
Kenneth Warren, *University of Chicago*

RECENT BOOKS IN THIS SERIES

165. JOHANNES VOELZ
 The Poetics of Insecurity: American Fiction and the Uses of Threat

164. JOHN HAY
 Postapocalyptic Fantasies in Antebellum American Literature

163. PAUL JAUSSEN
 Writing in Real Time

162. CINDY WEINSTEIN
 Time, Tense, and American Literature: When Is Now?

161. STACEY MARGOLIS
 Fictions of Mass Democracy in Nineteenth-Century America

160. PAUL DOWNES
 Hobbes, Sovereignty, and Early American Literature

159. CODY MARRS
 Nineteenth-Century American Literature and the Long Civil War

158. DAVID BERGMAN
 The Poetry of Disturbance: The Discomforts of Postwar American Poetry

157. MARK NOBLE
 American Poetic Materialism from Whitman to Stevens

(*continued after Index*)

THE POETICS OF INSECURITY

American Fiction and the Uses of Threat

JOHANNES VOELZ
Goethe-Universität Frankfurt

CAMBRIDGE
UNIVERSITY PRESS

University Printing House, Cambridge CB2 8BS, United Kingdom

One Liberty Plaza, 20th Floor, New York, NY 10006, USA

477 Williamstown Road, Port Melbourne, VIC 3207, Australia

314-321, 3rd Floor, Plot 3, Splendor Forum, Jasola District Centre, New Delhi - 110025, India

103 Penang Road, #05-06/07, Visioncrest Commercial, Singapore 238467

Cambridge University Press is part of the University of Cambridge.

It furthers the University's mission by disseminating knowledge in the pursuit of education, learning and research at the highest international levels of excellence.

www.cambridge.org
Information on this title: www.cambridge.org/9781108407861
DOI: 10.1017/9781108291408

© Johannes Voelz 2018

This publication is in copyright. Subject to statutory exception and to the provisions of relevant collective licensing agreements, no reproduction of any part may take place without the written permission of Cambridge University Press.

First published 2018
First paperback edition 2021

A catalogue record for this publication is available from the British Library

ISBN 978-1-108-41876-8 Hardback
ISBN 978-1-108-40786-1 Paperback

Cambridge University Press has no responsibility for the persistence or accuracy of URLs for external or third-party internet websites referred to in this publication, and does not guarantee that any content on such websites is, or will remain, accurate or appropriate.

To Magda

Contents

Acknowledgments		*page* xi
1	Introduction: Security and the Uncertain Worlds of Fiction	1
2	The Virtue of Uncertainty: Securing the Republic in *Arthur Mervyn*	34
3	Harriet Jacobs's Imagined Community of Insecurity	65
4	Willa Cather and the Security of Radical Contingency	96
5	Cold War Liberalism and Flannery O'Connor's "The Displaced Person"	128
6	In the Future, Toward Death: Finance Capitalism and Security in DeLillo's *Cosmopolis*	156
	Epilogue	181
Notes		189
Bibliography		225
Index		243

Acknowledgments

This book grew out of my *Habilitationsschrift* at Goethe-Universität Frankfurt, titled "Fictions of Security: American Literature and the Uses of Uncertainty." I am, first of all, deeply grateful to Christa Buschendorf. Her unwavering support allowed me to turn my initial idea into a completed book during the duration of my contract as a junior faculty member in the American Studies department at Frankfurt. I also wish to thank my other colleagues at Frankfurt for creating an atmosphere at once relaxed, amiable, and encouraging. The members of my *habilitation* committee – Christa Buschendorf, Heinz Drügh, Julika Griem, Susanne Opfermann, and Michael C. Williams of the University of Ottawa – provided insightful comments that greatly helped me during the revision process. Achim Geisenhanslüke, Bernd Herzogenrath, Stefanie Müller, Birgit Spengler, Simon Wendt, and Jan Wilm read individual chapters, swapped ideas, or brought unfamiliar texts to my attention.

The largest part of the manuscript emerged during a two-year stint, from 2012 to 2014, as Visiting Fellow at Stanford University, which was graciously funded by a Feodor-Lynen-Fellowship of the Alexander von Humboldt-Foundation. Despite working in a different field, Russell Berman, my host at Stanford, gave me his time, attention, and ideas, and collaborated with me on a special issue I edited for *Telos* (on *Security and Liberalism*) during my stay. I am also grateful to friends and colleagues at Stanford's English department and the Center for the Comparative Study of Race and Ethnicity, particularly to Paula Moya and Ramón Saldívar, Nancy Ruttenburg, Sianne Ngai, Mark McGurl, Jose-David Saldívar, Vaughn Rasberry, Gavin Jones, and David Palumbo-Liu. Colleagues from other Californian universities were also vital interlocutors, in particular Jeff Hole and Devin Zuber.

Over the years, I have given numerous talks on the subject of this book. At these occasions, and in subsequent email exchanges, I have particularly benefited from the feedback of Branka Arsić, Laura Bieger, Michael

Boyden, Dustin Breitenwischer, Lawrence Buell, Birgit Däwes, Thomas Dikant, Elena Esposito, Winfried Fluck, Astrid Franke, Paul Grimstad, Andrew Gross, Karin Höpker, Alfred Hornung, Gerd Hurm, Gordon Hutner, Heinz Ickstadt, Frank Kelleter, Christian Klöckner, Maurice S. Lee, Claus Leggewie, Günter Leypoldt, Philipp Löffler, Ruth Mayer, Timothy Melley, Donald Pease, Carla Peterson, and Joel Pfister. I am fortunate that so many of the above have offered not just their guidance but their friendship. Thanks also go to Ross Posnock, who sensed the potential of the book to be part of his series at Cambridge University Press. I also thank Ray Ryan and Thomas Haynes for the support from the side of the press, Fred Goykhman for copyediting, and Ramesh Karunakaran for steering the project through production. I'm moreover grateful to the two anonymous reviewers. For their help in preparing the manuscript and index, I thank Refika Cömert, Maren Emde, Tom Freischläger, and Garry Zettersten.

Some of the material of this book appeared in earlier form elsewhere. A shortened version of Chapter 6 appeared as "In the Future, Toward Death: Finance Capitalism and Security in DeLillo's *Cosmopolis*" in *Amerikastudien / American Studies* 60.4 (2015): 505–526, published by Winter Verlag, Heidelberg, and reprinted here with permission. The introduction to the same issue ("Chance, Risk, Security: Approaches to Uncertainty in American Literature. An Introduction," *Amerikastudien / American Studies* 60.4 [2015]: 385–402) contained small portions from Chapter 1 of this book, also reprinted with permission.

Magda Majewska has been my most formative conversation partner while this book came into being. She has provided me with that most elusive experience – a sense of security – and has led me to understand how to inhabit it: not as an end, but as a beginning.

CHAPTER 1

Introduction
Security and the Uncertain Worlds of Fiction

If we had to predict the label that will serve as a shorthand description for the early twenty-first century, "The Age of Security" would seem like a safe choice. Not that the political, social, and cultural prevalence of "security" is new. During the Cold War era, security was one of the instrumental concepts in the attempt to subsume life in its entirety under a bipolar geopolitical conflict. But since the late twentieth century, security has increasingly emancipated itself from its geopolitical frame. While "the terrorist" has to some extent been placed in the ideological position of "the communist," the worry about security goes beyond the fear of terrorism. Security has come to seem of existential importance because all aspects of life appear to be fundamentally insecure.[1]

Clearly, the ramifications of the contemporary reign of security are deeply troublesome. These concerns, it should be admitted openly at the outset, form the initial motivation for this book. Security, particularly in the United States, has earned its bad reputation: it serves as a catchall legitimation for state violence and the abrogation of human and civil rights; the private sector exploits its profitability, providing security services for a wide variety of state and nonstate costumers; finally, we, the people: private consumers of security goods, who turn our homes into high-tech fortresses, fret about computer viruses, credit card fraud, and identity theft, try to ensure our children's safety, and monitor each of our steps to optimize our well-being. Who could blame us? We can't let anything happen to our lives.

This book, however, is not an exploration of the politically disconcerting realities of the Age of Security. Rather, it takes a step back and asks: How can the prevalence of the category of security be explained? How could security become so influential in modern culture? How do we account for the apparent appeal of security? To address these questions, *The Poetics of Insecurity* undertakes a series of close readings of more or less canonical works of American literature from roughly the past two hundred years.

Literary criticism, I maintain, has a significant contribution to make to the study of security. Literature turns our attention to aspects of security that remain difficult to perceive as long as it is analyzed, the way it is usually done, within the parameters of political and social theory. As I will make clear in the course of this introductory chapter, my larger argument contends that it is these aspects revealed by literature that help explain the pervasiveness of the category of security in America's cultural and political life.

1.1 Aiming for Insecurity

In much of U.S. literature, security appears remarkably different from the way we have come to think of it. Political theorists, social scientists, critical humanists, and journalists largely agree that people begin to worry about, and care for, security whenever they feel threatened. Facing insecurity, the argument goes, people are willing to stomach all kinds of odious measures if only these measures promise to make them feel secure once more. The concern with security, from this vantage point, is all about the effort to undo insecurity.[2]

An important strand in American literature, I argue in this book, makes the opposite point. Across different genres and periods, American writers from the early republic to the present have shared an unspoken conviction: the concern with security allows us to explore, experience, make use of, and even take pleasure in insecurity. In the worlds created by this literature, insecurity is much more than a fearful encounter with threat. Being insecure creates new possibilities and opens up spaces. The writings of Charles Brockden Brown, Harriet Jacobs, Willa Cather, Flannery O'Connor, and Don DeLillo suggest a broad (if necessarily incomplete) range of such emerging possibilities.

To be sure, there are plenty of other writers who would have allowed me to explore the reevaluation of insecurity equally well. James Fenimore Cooper, Herman Melville, Henry James, Jack London, and Thomas Pynchon are only a few of the alternatives I have considered as suitable focal points for a chapter. All of them share a double-edged attitude toward security that runs through American fiction: on the one hand, they are acute to the magnitude of threats that beleaguer life in modern America. On the other hand, they are deeply skeptical, if not averse, to the very idea of creating a life around security so long as security is defined as safety, predictability, and orderliness. In the literature I consider in this study, this ambivalence leads to alternative articulations of security and insecurity. "Nothing is secure but life, transition, the energizing spirit,"

Ralph Waldo Emerson writes in "Circles" (189) – a Transcendentalist and proto-pragmatist credo that is remarkable in that it does not outright reject the ideal of security, but rather strives to identify security with the unsettling forces that are usually understood as the very essence of insecurity. Without wanting to subsume the authors discussed in this book under the umbrella of an Emersonian tradition, all of my chapters bring to light literary strategies that unsettle the meaning of security by re-valorizing insecurity in one way or another.

Throughout this study I inquire into the philosophical and aesthetic implications of the logic of security, and I reconstruct the different imaginative appeals of security and insecurity as they take shape in literature of different periods and genres. This is an agenda that is decidedly not historicist: though I embed each literary text in its historical context, the reason I do so is not that the texts I have chosen are meant to stand in for the time period of American (literary) history from which they emerged. In other words, I have not settled on Brown, Jacobs, Cather, O'Connor, and DeLillo because they are the most representative authors for their respective moment. Rather, in my readings, historical contextualization matters for an understanding of what made the imagination of security and insecurity in these literary texts possible. I inquire into the specific literary strategies my authors use for turning insecurity and threat into openings for new possibilities, and I explore the nuances and details that define and structure the imagination of those new possibilities.

For the most part, what it is that emerges in the face of threat is not self-evident but needs to be teased out of the texts, precisely by paying close attention to each author's poetics of insecurity. This is also the reason why I devote my chapters to one text each, rather than showing how the texts I analyze illuminate others. Unfolding how threat is put to use in literature requires slowing down, developing a sensibility for the finely wrought texture of each of the imaginary engagements with scenarios of insecurity, and tracing out the temporal trajectory of each of the narrative responses to threat. What hopefully emerges from this book, then, is not a linear history of security through literature, not a coherent narrative of the development of the literary appropriation of (in)security, say, through the lens of a particular genre such as melodrama or the jeremiad, but rather an account of how over the course of two hundred years the logic of security has brought forth widely diverging variations of imaginary uses of threat.

Because I am convinced that in the cultural imagination security and insecurity are multifaceted in ways that go far beyond today's political discourse of security, I have refrained from putting at the center of my study literary works that are primarily concerned with such topics as terrorism, international conflict, or war. As I already suggested, the logic of security has come to pervade virtually all areas of life. To get to the varieties of how this logic plays out in the literary imagination, it is helpful not to linger on topics that are prestructured by how we have come to talk about security habitually. For this reason, the reader will not find chapters on such novels as William Dean Howells's *The Hazards of New Fortune*, Henry James's *Princess Casamassima*, Jack London's *The Assassination Bureau, Ltd.*, or other literary treatments of terrorism from the high tide of turn-of-the-century anarchist violence or from the rich body of the so-called 9/11 novel.[3]

Each of the texts on which I focus engages at least one security threat of its time. Arising from historically specific conditions, these security threats differ significantly from each other. But they are all equally formidable in that they ultimately point back to macro-level transformations that endanger a whole way of life. Not all of the writers use the language of "security" and "insecurity," and a glance at the history of the concept tells us that they indeed could not: Although the term *securitas* reaches back all the way to Cicero, and "security" has stood at the center of modern political thought since Hobbes, in the United States, as in other Western countries, it was not until the 1930s that "security" became a word used self-reflexively, as a value-laden term with an ideological ring to it, akin to "freedom," "liberty," and "prosperity." But the idea of security is not intrinsically tied to the word, even if the appearance of the word in a given text necessarily shapes the idea.[4]

In Charles Brockden Brown's *Arthur Mervyn* (1799/1800), no less than the future of the young republic is at stake. It is threatened by the corruption encapsulated by fraudulent transnational merchants and, more immediately, by a yellow fever epidemic raging in Philadelphia. In Harriet Jacobs's *Incidents in the Life of a Slave Girl* (1861), insecurity becomes a most pressing issue for the runaway slave who is threatened with recapture, but insecurity moreover arises from slavery's "reign of terror" (as Jacobs puts it; see *Incidents* 933) that threatens to tear down civilization in its entirety. In *The Professor's House* (1925) – as well as in her other works – Willa Cather takes up the great modernist topos of modernity's melting all that is solid into air; a melting pot so hot that one can only join what Cather called "the backward" and seek refuge in a nostalgic past. For Flannery O'Connor, too, modernity is the cause of insecurity, but in her fictional works, the good life is not threatened by the evaporation of tradition so much as by the blind belief in secular rationality. Don DeLillo, finally, thematizes the terror threats directed at the nation's – and indeed, as the title of his novel *Cosmopolis* (2003) suggests, the world's – power elite, specifically at finance capitalists. But the insecurity is so grave that it hardly stops at a few powerful individuals: it endangers the entire edifice that makes up what postmodern novelists like to describe as "the system." And not only is the system the target; it is also, simultaneously, the source of threat.

Staggering as these types of insecurity are, they by no means induce stifling fear or even the wish to return to the order of normalcy. Threat, instead, becomes an enabling condition. Entering Philadelphia in the midst of the yellow fever epidemic of 1793, Brown's hero Arthur Mervyn believes he is meeting his personal disaster. He is convinced – wrongly, as it will turn out – that he has contracted the disease and will imminently perish. In this situation of extreme insecurity, Arthur suddenly experiences a liberating burst of energy: "This incident, instead of appalling me, tended rather to invigorate my courage. The danger which I feared had come. I might enter with indifference, on this theater of pestilence" (*Arthur Mervyn* 111). Arthur presents himself as driven by desperate courage: having been doomed to death, he has nothing to lose. Insecurity, he implies, has given way to the certainty of death. In truth, however, neither is Arthur sick (at least not at this point in the novel), nor is he less determined to act once he realizes that he is in perfect health and the future is once again open. Insecurity sets him free as an agent. Moreover, the hero who thought his fate had been sealed finds with relief that he remains vulnerable to the raging plague. Insecurity, it suddenly appears, is the essence of life.

In Harriet Jacobs's *Incidents* – the autobiographical rendition of a female slave's ordeal – it would seem that there can be no tolerance of, and certainly no gain from, insecurity. And indeed, Jacobs sets up a happy ending that promises the conversion of insecurity into freedom: "Reader, my story ends with freedom; not in the usual way, with marriage. I and my children are now free!" (*Incidents* 944). But what follows is a significant qualification: "We are as free from the power of slaveholders as are the white people at the north. And though that, according to my ideas, is not saying a great deal, it is a vast improvement in my condition" (944–945). Former slaves and whites, Jacobs insists, are equally insecure vis-à-vis slaveholders, who seem to be gaining the upper hand in national politics. As the North seems to fall under the rule of slavocracy, freedom – the foundation of everything the North stood for – is diminished to relative improvement. Over the course of *Incidents*, a new community is imagined into existence. Its common trait is insecurity, and no one is in a better position to certify its existence than the former slave herself. If insecurity cannot be removed, at least Jacobs finds a way to put it to use for a new political imaginary of a North transracially united in threat.

Whereas a good number of "fictions of security" follow Brown's and Jacobs's template of aspiring to security and, in doing so, discovering unexpected advantages slumbering in insecurity, Willa Cather's characters nostalgically recreate a time-space of security in the ruins of the past. Surrounded by the forgotten relics of what was once a safe haven for a people of Southwestern pueblo dwellers, Cather's youthful hero Tom Outland for a brief moment experiences the "unalloyed" happiness of perfect security (*Professor's House* 253). But what is it that turns the fulfillment of security into, what he calls, a "religious emotion"? (253). Like an heir of Thoreau's, Tom Outland "simplifies" his surroundings until, "a close neighbour to the sun, I seemed to get the solar energy in some direct way" (253). What happens in this moment of perfect security is in fact similar to what other texts describe as *insecurity*: bathing in sunlight, freed from any material and social clutter, the world opens up to him in its radical contingency. Nothing actual has restricted the range of the possible; all options of the future are open. Perfect security becomes perfect potentiality.

In Flannery O'Connor's work we encounter a religiously oriented variation of Cather's association of security with radical uncertainty. As she phrased it in her essay "The Fiction Writer and His Country," "the novelist with Christian concerns will find in modern life distortions which are repugnant to him, and his problem will be to make these appear as distortions to an audience which is used to seeing them as natural; and he may well be forced to take ever more violent means to get his vision across to this hostile audience" (805). The violent destruction of her characters becomes her preferred means of shocking her readers out of their dangerous complacency induced by the secular Enlightenment. The only way to handle the insecurity arising from modernity's catastrophic commitment to instrumental rationality is to up the ante and create a state of physical insecurity of the most brutal kind. Ideally, her characters and readers end up like the chastened farm owner of "The Displaced Person," who becomes a stranger on her land and to her own body and who ends her days displaced in isolation: "She felt she was in some foreign country" ("Displaced Person" 326). In O'Connor's apocalyptic imagination, violent insecurity has become the only imaginable form of security.

None of the novelists studied in this book is as adamant about the invigorating and thrilling effect of confronting insecurity as Don DeLillo. In *Cosmopolis*, the financial tycoon Eric Packer has become numbed by the abstractions of the virtual world of speculation. Only when he focuses on the prospects of losing his enormous fortune and on the security threats to his person does he momentarily feel that he is returning to the real. Watching "prices spiral into lubricious plunge," he registers an effect that "was sexual, cunnilingual in particular" (106). This orgiastic "joy at all misfortune, in the swift pitch of markets down," is only topped by the sensation of physical insecurity: "it was the threat of death at the brink of night that spoke to him most surely about some principle of fate he'd always known would come clear in time. Now he could begin the business of living" (107). For DeLillo's characters, really living one's life requires a keen sense of one's mortality, and this sense of personal finitude is made available by insecurity. Whereas O'Connor identifies security with a type of insecurity that can be fully realized only in death, for DeLillo the concern with security stages an encounter with threat that recovers a sense of being alive.

Eric Packer's invigoration caused by "the threat of death," in fact, comes closest to Arthur Mervyn's emancipation through pestilential dangers. From the perspective of security, the gothic novel of the early republic and the late postmodern novel of the early twenty-first century meet as two ends of a long arch that spans some two hundred years. Along the way, insecurity enables individual action and self-development; it allows people to sharpen their sensibilities about the counterfactual and merely potential; it provides an arena for the cultivation of aggressive impulses; it permits reflection about our existential condition regarding mortality, finitude, and survival; it equips the most vulnerable subjects with resources for generating social and political authority; and it mobilizes political solidarity among emerging communities unified by no more than threat.

These imaginary experiences triggered by the confrontation with insecurity are principally of two kinds: they either foster the imaginary construction of worlds that differ from present reality, or they facilitate the sense of recovering an aspect of existence that is perceived as having become unavailable. To put it succinctly, security generates stories of discovery and recovery. Brown and Jacobs embody the first case: here the emphasis is on the openness and uncertainty of the future, which allows for imagined scenarios in which individuals forage into unknown realms or modes of existence, or in which new communities take shape. In the second category we find the works of Cather, O'Connor, and DeLillo: acts of recovery in which the imminence of existential threat allows individuals to regain an awareness of their own embeddedness in history, of the prevalence of the otherworldly, or of their existential finitude; in theses cases, security – meaning, again, the confrontation with insecurity – enables the individual to reconstruct a greater depth of meaning for his or her life by putting the self in perspective.

1.2 The Concept of Security

This brief overview begins to suggest how I employ the term "security" throughout this book. Security becomes a matter of concern when, first of all, there is a perception of a malevolent threat that creates a sense of insecurity. The threat may appear as imminent or removed, concrete or vague, but in any case it exists as a potential of a future that has yet to arrive. All threats are in this sense merely possible threats, however dangerous they may appear.

On this level, the concern with security is deeply bound up with fear. But in the critical literature on security, the role of fear is most often conceptualized in a one-dimensional way. Most of the security theories that emphasize the role of fear hold that the political class has teamed up with the news media and the entertainment industry to create a "culture of fear."[5] In such a culture, the population is constantly afraid. It isn't so much that everyone is incessantly ready to run from an immediate threat, but, according to the argument, low-intensity fear has come to structure the habitual orientation to the world.[6] The immediate connection with security seems irrefutable: a population that constantly experiences the world through the lens of fear will crave security in all realms of life. Individuals will organize their lives around the eradication of contingency. And in their roles as political subjects, people will welcome authoritarian regimes or truncated forms of liberal democracy, in which an inflated executive branch and a legislative ruled by lobbyists obstructs collective will formation. According to the culture-of-fear thesis, these types of government manage to garner consent because they make the most persuasive claims for answering the population's fears. We find at work here a political mechanism that is as ingenious as it is pernicious, for the fear that makes people desire protective leadership is the result of the fearmongering by the political class.[7]

From a theoretical perspective, however, the culture-of-fear thesis rests on problematic assumptions that can best be shown by taking a closer look at the work of Brian Massumi, a leading proponent of affect theory, who has written on the politics of fear in a series of essays and books going back to the early 1990s. In his article "Fear (the Spectrum Said)," from 2005, Massumi argues that threat and fear are not situated on the level of ideas but need to be regarded as affects. After September 11, 2001, the Bush administration found ways of directing the population affectively through such means as the color alert system, which comprised five threat levels, ranging from green (threat level "low") to red ("severe"). The US government, Massumi effectively claims, created a remote control for the body politic: "Addressing bodies from the dispositional angle of their affectivity, instead of addressing subjects from the positional angle of their ideations, shunts government function away from the mediations of adherence or belief and toward direct activation" (34). To bolster his theory of "direct activation," Massumi enlists the support of William James. James famously insisted, in his essay "What is an Emotion?," that we do not act in response to an emotion, but rather feel an emotion as a consequence of our action. Thus, according to James, we do not start to run because we feel fear, but we feel fear because we start to run. James's larger argument is that the process in which an emotion arises must be reconstructed in three steps: first, we have a sense perception (e.g., we see a bear), next we react bodily (we run), and finally we sense the emotion (we feel fear).

In Massumi's reading, the Jamesian model provides the basis for the argument that emotions like fear can be externally triggered in a controlled manner by devices like the color alert system. All we need is the trigger for fear, and that trigger is threat: "Threat is the cause of fear in the sense that it triggers and conditions fear's occurrence" (36). James, however, is far from insinuating that his theory opens the door to calculable manipulation. (The exception is self-manipulation: smile, James suggests, and you really will feel happy.) The relation between the initial sense perception and the ensuing corporeal and mental reactions cannot be fixed. It is for this reason that emotions like fear and pride take on significance in social life. As James explains, "the most important part of my environment is my fellow-man. The consciousness of his attitude towards me is the perception that normally unlocks most of my shames and indignations and fears.... What the action itself may be [James here means: whether someone scolds me, ignores me, etc.] is quite insignificant, so long as I can perceive in it intent or *animus*. *That* is the emotion-arousing perception" ("What" 195–196). For James, then, in everyday life, the three-step sequence leading to the experience of emotions does not begin with an unmediated external impulse that can be reproduced at will, but with the processes of consciousness of our social embeddedness. Fear is usually not triggered by color codes. What elicits our fear is rather our mental construction of what others may think of us. Jamesian emotions, including the "emotion-arousing perception," are thus part of humans' intersubjective relationality.

Massumi's theorization of "direct activation" in fact has been belied by his very example. The advisory system soon turned out to serve as an excellent case study for the failure of generalized, unmediated affect management. Even the Department of Homeland Security had to concede this. In its 2009 report, the "Homeland Security Advisory System Task Force" came to the conclusion that "at its best, there is currently indifference to the Homeland Security Advisory System and, at worst, there is a disturbing lack of public confidence in the system" (1). The color-coding system was consequently phased out in 2011.

Besides the fact that the affect theory approach to the culture of fear problematically minimizes the intersubjective dimension of the affective life of security, a further problem arises from the way in which this approach theorizes fear itself (or fails to). In particular, proponents of the culture-of-fear thesis tend to neglect fear's temporal structure. The Swedish philosopher Lars Svendsen makes the useful observation that "fear always contains a protention, a future projection, concerning pain, injury or death.... The core of fear is the assumption of a negative future situation. Although not every negative future situation gives rise to fear, something has to be at stake" (39). Svendsen (here implicitly echoing Heidegger) points our attention away from the sheer feeling of fear (imagined as a bodily, non-cognitive state) to the cognitive operations at work in it. Whether we are dealing with an imminent danger (say, by a car coming straight at us) or a remote situation (say, the spread of a contagious disease in a different part of the world), fear is always future-oriented and can thus be described as a varying set of attitudes toward a future that is seen as harmful.[8] But fear is also inherently dialectic. Time is not merely structured around a future of loss, but also by the wish or desire to retain whatever is threatened. Fear is thus an essentially temporal emotion, a way of relating to the future torn between the possibility of loss and the wish to retain what might be lost – a struggle over whose outcome we are not in control.

To slightly rephrase this idea, we can think of fear as bound up with desire; both fear and desire are reliant on time and, in turn, help structure time. Recently, philosopher and literary critic Martin Hägglund has sharpened this thought by coining a pair of terms – *chronophilia* and *chronophobia* – that give expression to the dialectic entanglement of fear and desire against the horizon of time:

> The key argument here concerns the co-implication of *chronophobia* and *chronophilia*. The fear of time and death does not stem from a metaphysical desire to transcend temporal life. On the contrary, it is generated by the investment in a life that can be lost. It is because one is attached to a

temporal being (chronophilia) that one fears losing it (chronophobia). Care in general, I argue, depends on such a double bind. On the one hand, care is necessarily chronophilic, since only something that is subject to the possibility of loss – and hence temporal – can give one a reason to care. On the other hand, care is necessarily chronophobic, since one cannot care about something without fearing what may happen to it. (*Dying* 9–10)

Without spelling it out, Hägglund provides a crucial connection for the link between fear and security. His explication of our double bind to time – we experience the projection of the future as both fearful (the passing of time presupposes loss) and full of desire (in wishing to prevent loss, we desire our continuing bond to the temporal unfolding of the future) – provides the structure of the experience of "care." Etymologically and conceptually, care lies at the core of the notion of security (*securitas*), which Cicero introduced as a neologism derived from *sine*/*se* and *cura* and which he initially comprehended as a mental state of calm (literally a state "without care"), to be distinguished from *salus*, which denoted physical safety.[9] As John Hamilton has pointed out in his recent encompassing philological exploration of the term, classical *securitas*, drawing on the Epicurean *ataraxia* (freedom from disturbances) and the Stoic *apatheia* (freedom from passions), conceptualizes the removal of care (or fear) as bound up with the same kind of dialectical co-implication we see at work in chronophilia and chronophobia: if security is to protect life, rather than usher in a death-like state of lifelessness, *sine cura* cannot be located outside of time and contingency (cf. *Security* 53). The fearlessness of *sine cura* can only benefit life if it remains within time, but this means that the care-free life of *securitas* is unthinkable without the continuing need for care. From its earliest theorizations, we can reconstruct security as complementing fear: together, both terms give expression to the double bind of an open future (to our twofold being bound to it) in which the threat of death and the wish for life meet and mingle.

But the future projection operative in the emotion of fear does not merely indicate that the future is insecure; the future is furthermore revealed to be uncertain. The difference between uncertainty and insecurity is crucial. Uncertainty neutrally refers to the fact that the future has yet to actualize and that it may do so in different ways. Insecurity, on the other hand, regards the future as harmful and thus constitutes one particular scenario constructed from the uncertainty of the future.

It is the uncertainty of the future that makes possible a second dimension of security: it consists in the belief that the threats looming in the uncertain future can be answered, that there are, in fact, alternative future courses. From this follows the emancipating potential of security's concern with the potentially harmful uncertainty of the future. In finding a response to insecurity, the subject of security turns the uncertainty of the future to its own favor. Security promises that up to a certain point the uncertain future can be rationally designed and controlled.

In the simplest version security disarms insecurity and sets the orderly course of events back on track. But in the imagination of security found in American literature, this notion of security is generally dismissed as an idle – and ultimately dystopian – fantasy. "A great power has to act. We were struck hard. We need to retake the future," Richard Elster, the protagonist in Don DeLillo's 2010 novel *Point Omega*, pronounces. Elster is a "defense intellectual" whose career climaxed when he advised the Pentagon on the second Iraq war. And indeed, his philosophy of security is about as sagacious as Donald Rumsfeld's. With a relish reminiscent of O'Connor, DeLillo spends the rest of his short novel disorienting his protagonist until he is thoroughly disabused of his belief in the possibility to take possession of the future. In disassembling his character's convictions, in exposing him to his own perplexity, DeLillo expresses a view about security that is implicit in much of American literature: any attempt to control the future relies on the power of insecurity to wrest the future from human control and reassert its contingency. The concern with security becomes enabling only on the condition that it does not triumph once and for all over insecurity. For such an all-out triumph would not only master looming threats, it would liquidate uncertainty itself and thus render impossible any active engagement with the future. Under such circumstances, life would lose its vitality. As Henry David Thoreau puts it acerbically in *Walden* (1854): "If man is alive, there is always *danger* that he may die, though the danger must be allowed to be less in proportion as he is dead-and-alive to begin with" (444). If life under the conditions of a future fully mastered would come to resemble death, the mastered future itself would paradoxically turn into its opposite. For a future fully brought under control would turn into a *fait accompli*. Put differently, the future would convert back into fate and any active care about the things to come would have to terminate. With insecurity and uncertainty vanquished, the dystopic potential of the care-free life of *securitas* comes into full view.

My conception of security, then, highlights the interplay, articulated in much of modern American letters, of the fearful encounter of threat and the possibility to respond to it. This interplay is complex in the sense that both dimensions battle with, but also sustain, each other. Security, then, relates to a distinctly modern grammar of agency, according to which rationality appears as bound up with, and conditioned by, what exceeds its reach.[10]

As I have already indicated, what makes this grammar of agency particularly modern is the understanding of time that underlies it. If security, as Hägglund and Hamilton suggest, is driven by the aim to remain within time – which means not merely to survive, but also to remain exposed to uncertainty and even insecurity – security amounts to a concern which the premoderns would have hardly understood. As Charles Taylor and others have pointed out, in premodern thought the temporal realm stood in opposition to varying versions of higher time. The temporal existence of the *saeculum* was generally viewed as a transitional stage to be followed by the entry into eternity – no matter whether eternity was thought of, in the Platonic tradition, as the realm of the unchanging, full being of Ideas, or, in the Christian belief pattern first expressed fully by Augustine, as the "gathered time" that draws together the past and the future into the divine present (cf. Taylor, *Secular Age* 54 ff.).

To think in terms of "security" is dependent on a worldview in which the future is temporal and secular, rather than spiritual and eternal, and thus becomes a matter of human care or concern. If the future is the object of care and concern, it thereby becomes open to being shaped by human rationality. At the same time, the fact that the future is construed as an open-ended contingency structured by fear and desire indicates, once again, that attempts to take care of the future are predicated on the impossibility of fully bringing it under control.[11]

Conceptualized in these terms, security is a symptom of secularization (in the sense that the *saeculum* gains priority over eternity), but this should not be misunderstood as suggesting the disappearance of religious belief. What changes are rather the conceptual problems to be handled by belief. If in the Age of Security, broadly conceived, futurity is reconfigured as immanent, this creates new problems, and religion provides one possible resource for making sense of them. Most crucially, perhaps, religious vocabularies become helpful where the tasks to be taken over by humans – particularly the care for the future – outstrip capacities of foresight and control. One might think here, for instance, of the strong resonance of the problem of evil in modern times: in matters of theodicy, religion gets invoked *following* the encounter of dreadful consequences of human action. It is not coincidental that Augustine's theodicy, premodern though it is, explains the existence of evil by pointing to God's granting humans *free will* – a gift that enabled humans to turn away from God.[12] By the same token, religious vocabularies provide an idiom for cultural critique and allow for culturally resonant articulations of insecurity that locate the source of threat inside of the body politic – the genre of the Jeremiad is the best example here.[13] As the uses of religious language in a good number of my texts attest – including those by Harriet Jacobs, Willa Cather, Don DeLillo, and most of all Flannery O'Connor – religious discourse has been instrumental in giving weight to the concern with security, even if that concern has arisen in its modern form only with the dawn of what Taylor calls "the Secular Age."

1.3 Security and Risk

The modern conception of time brings forth a concern not only with security but also with risk. Niklas Luhmann has remarked that "since the seventeenth century the topics of security and risk have matured in a process of mutual interaction" (*Risk* 20), and indeed, I treat security and risk as interrelated, though diverging, strategies of confronting a future conceptualized as contingent. Etymologically, the word "risk" betrays its economic origins: *rischio* or *rischiare* contains the Greek *rhiza*, which denotes both root and cliff. *Rischiare* thus originally meant sailing around cliffs, or entering waters full of cliffs, and by extension, consciously accepting the danger of shipwreck because of a potential for pecuniary gain (see "Risiko" in Ritter, *Wörterbuch* vol. 8, column 1045). Indeed, economic historians have detailed how closely the rise of the concept of risk has been tied to the emergence of capitalism and particularly trade by sea. Jonathan Levy, for instance, has noted that in nineteenth-century America, "the image of the ship on stormy waters became a powerful metaphor for the perils and possibilities of life under capitalism" (*Freaks of Fortune* 2). Capitalism thrives on uncertainty and is thus deeply invested in its ambiguity of opportunity and danger. Risk itself is a sign of this ambiguity. On the one hand, the history of risk is the history of attempts to manage it through various kinds of insurance and hedging. But on the other hand there is also, as Levy puts it, "the existential thrill of taking a risk. That tension was at the very operational and moral heart of both capitalism and a rising liberal order" (2).[14]

It is this ambiguity that marks the key difference in my conception of risk and security. Risk describes an active stance of seeking out uncertainty for the possible gains contained in it. Security, by contrast, provides unexpected possibilities of transformation (whether individual or collective) under the condition of a malevolent threat. In the case of risk, action is enabled by uncertainty, and harm is a potential result of the action taken. In the case of security, action becomes *necessitated* by an uncertainty that has already turned into a threat. The keyword here is "necessity" because it suggests an existential dimension. Think of security in relation to computers: we habitually use metaphors such as "viruses" and "Trojans" that evoke mortal danger.[15]

In the logic of security, in other words, it is necessity that creates openings and opportunities, whereas in the logic of risk it is the potential of gain that motivates the action. It is true, however, that once a social environment becomes structured by risk, risk-taking is no longer purely optional: not acting creates risks of its own.[16] We need only think of the world of finance: here, not acting may quickly result in the depreciation of one's assets. In a sense, risk-taking can thus become a necessity as well. But there is a difference to the type of necessity created by threat. In risk societies, not acting is still an option; it is merely necessary to comprehend not acting as one possible behavior among others to choose from. In other words, not acting is an action, too. The choice of action is guided by the calculation, formalized or intuitive, of probable outcomes, and the goal remains to choose the option that is the most advantageous. When under threat, however, acting is – at least figuratively – a matter of life and death. Calculation of the greatest gain is no longer necessary, or even possible, since the objective is single-mindedly modest: survival. Gain and survival thus mark the two different kinds of telos that set risk and security apart.

In most theoretical accounts, risk and security differ much more drastically than I have just suggested. Political theorist Herfried Münkler, for instance, distinguishes between risk and security on the basis of their tolerance for uncertainty. In his view, the logic of risk recognizes its dependence on uncertainty and therefore aims to merely manage it, rather than resolve it. Security, on the other hand, aims to convert uncertainty (more precisely, the malevolent type of uncertainty that is insecurity) into order. Or, as Münkler puts it, "dangers [his term for the harms emanating from risk] ... can be controlled and mastered by dividing and separating them, whereas threats ... which arise neither accidentally nor unintentionally but are backed by an opposing will, must be kept out of a secured zone [whether physical or symbolic] by means of barriers and blockades" ("Strategien" 28). In my own conception, by contrast, security is significantly closer to risk: both share a high tolerance for the harmful potential of uncertainty. For the risk-taker, uncertainty provides the resource for gain. The subject of security, on the other hand, needs uncertainty in order to bind himself or herself to the future, i.e., to remain within time. In either logic, uncertainty becomes a generative force.

This conceptual proximity of security and risk is borne out by many of the texts explored in this book. Both logics frequently interact, either in complementary fashion or by way of contradistinction. They come closest to each other in Charles Brockden Brown's republican fictions. In *Arthur Mervyn*, insecurity enables actions that are properly described as risk-taking. Turning humans into agents under distress, insecurity allows them to assess, and morally value, the possibly harmful consequences their actions will have on themselves and others. Risk and insecurity are cornerstones of a republican morality of virtue and valor in which taking risks to one's own life for the benefit of others is considered the epitome of virtue: "Why should you risk your safety for the sake of one whom your kindness cannot benefit, and who has nothing to give in return?," Arthur, sick with the yellow fever, asks his saviors (*Arthur Mervyn* 7). He can only accept their disinterested risk-taking on his behalf on the condition that he declare his own interest in their help to be subordinate to his interest in their safety. Risk is virtuous when undertaken for another, and a sign of vice when undertaken with material self-interest in mind. Risk moves to the center of republican concern because it is in the ability to assume the risk of one's life that the individual becomes a modern subject, endowed with the responsibility over her actions and the moral capacity to act virtuously, or not.

For Harriet Jacobs, on the other hand, risk and (in)security capture two different stages of the slave's tribulations. Like many other slave narrators, she uses the language of risk to describe the momentous decision to flee from her master. The contemplation of this step is an existential risk calculation: if she succeeds, she will gain freedom; if she fails, she will be punished. And even if her punishment will not be death, her chances for another attempt at freedom will greatly diminish. Again, in taking this risk, the slave assumes the ability to plan the future events of her life. In assuming her risk, the slave performatively lays claim to her freedom. However, once fled to the North, Jacobs describes her situation – again in consonance with other slave narrators – as "insecure." While risk referred to a moment of decision over the future of her life, insecurity captures the fugitive's permanent condition after her flight. If, for Arthur Mervyn, the threatened state of insecurity opened a space for risky action, for Jacobs the assumption of the risk over her life is expected to inaugurate freedom, but leads to insecurity instead.

DeLillo develops yet another variant of the relation between security and risk. His protagonist thrives on, and suffers from, the world of finance capitalism, in which the technologies of risk management seem to have mastered the future. Risk management has become so intricate that there is not a trace of thrill left in risk. The uncertainty of the future has given way to stasis. To liberate himself, Eric Packer must regain a sense of temporal progression, history, and mortality, which becomes available only when the managed future of risk is confronted with the unwieldy futurity addressed by the concern with security. While in Brown's novel insecurity enabled risky action and in Jacobs's narrative insecurity usurped the place of freedom that was to follow the assumption of risk, in DeLillo's text insecurity counteracts the efforts of risk management: tamed chance is returned to its wild nature. Though DeLillo's novel overtly contrasts security and risk, it is a poignant example of the close alliance between both logics: the concern with security restores to risk its full spectrum of hedging and opening.

The specimens of literature examined in this book display a remarkable tolerance for uncertainty. In my reading, this stance toward the uncertain future is a symptom of a democratic culture and society. Democracy here does not primarily denote a political system, but a particular kind of culture linked to a post-rank social order. In such an order, the individual is no longer born into a fixed social hierarchy. With the prefixed orders of rank society having collapsed, individuals are formally set on equal footing. As Alexis de Tocqueville, in the second volume of *Democracy in America* (1840), sagaciously pointed out, the result is a preoccupation of the democratic citizen with the prospects of rise and fall: "When … ranks are mingled and privileges destroyed, when patrimonies divide and enlightenment and liberty spread, the desire to gain well-being occurs to the imagination of the poor, and the fear of losing it to the mind of the rich" (933). In Tocqueville's view, the "conditions of equality" do not produce economic equality – far from it. They rather fixate the democrat on future changes in his or her position, whether for the better or worse. This, Tocqueville contends, is reflected in the literature produced in democratic countries in that it is concerned with the future rather than with the past: "Democratic peoples hardly worry about what has been, but they readily dream about what will be, and their imagination has no limits in this direction; it expands and grows without measure. This offers a vast opening to poets and allows them to move their portrayal far away from what is seen. Democracy, which closes the past to poetry, opens the future" (836).

What we can take away from Tocqueville's still valid observation is that because the place of individuals in post-rank society is not determined by birth, the responsibility for the individual's future becomes shouldered on the individual. Again, this points to the proximity of risk and security. From one perspective, the individual becomes a risk-taker, or an entrepreneurial self deeply invested in the uncertain future.[17] But from another perspective, the fluidity of the social structure and the need to take care of the future expose the individual to situations that appear as vital threats and that simultaneously open spaces of opportunity.

Consider once more the threat scenarios imagined by my group of authors: in each case, insecurity results from a de-hierarchized social structure and the (often paradoxical) consequences of having to take care of the future. In particular, insecurity arises from: a type of upward mobility that leads from poverty to extraordinary wealth, made possible by the virtualization of the world, which, in turn, leads to a general loss of the reality principle and the self-destabilization of the system of global capital (DeLillo); the hubristic rationality of secularism, which creates the illusion that the world and the future may be designed in such a way that the individual can reach worldly self-realization (O'Connor); a gross materialism that is oblivious to the values enshrined in civilization and relinquishes what makes life worth living (Cather). The most illustrative examples are provided by Brown and Jacobs. The world depicted in *Arthur Mervyn* is populated by fraudulent merchants, confidence men, sharpers, shady social climbers ("nabobs"), thieves, and murderers. The republic is shaken to its foundations by the fluidity of a social world, which provides no means to assess the status of an individual other than judging his or her sincerity – which requires putting blind faith in people's "face value." For this very reason, Arthur Mervyn hovers between embodying the threat to the republic and fighting for the restoration of virtue. Insecurity becomes a zone of indistinction, and the only possible way to secure the republic is to elevate uncertainty into a virtue of its own.[18]

Harriet Jacobs's slave narrative is another case in point. As a fugitive in the North, she inhabits a liminal position between enslavement and freedom. For her, insecurity is tied to her "social formlessness" (to use Karen Halttunen's term), which, in her case, is also a legal formlessness. Her position in the North (particularly before the 1850 Fugitive Slave Act) attests to the uncertain and contested reach of slavery into the North. The fugitive makes apparent that at its historical highpoint, slavery – the closest equivalent to a system of firmly fixed rank in the antebellum United States – is an order not without gaps and holes: due to its geographic concentration in the South, it resists easy categorization at its northern fringes. For Jacobs, this uncertainty proves characteristically ambiguous, exposing her to threat and insecurity, but also considerably improving her situation over her enslavement in North Carolina.

The case of Harriet Jacobs helps clear up a possible misunderstanding: saying that security as it appears in the texts discussed in this book is a problem particularly urgent in democracies is not at all to suggest that the United States is, or ever was, an egalitarian society, nor that the fact that the individual is chiefly responsible for his or her future means that "you can get it if you really want." It simply means that the individual, newly burdened with responsibility, has to navigate through the power structures that emerge in place of the old order of ranks. And while everyone is required to steer, only some obtain access to navigable routes.

The concern with security that I reconstruct throughout my chapters is peculiar to American literature insofar as the consequences of a democratic post-rank social order are particularly pronounced here. But of course, the concern with security is not therefore absent in modern literature from other national traditions. De-hierarchizing tendencies have been a hallmark of modern society in general. And on top of that, modern literature is not merely linked to the complex of security and insecurity via content. As I want to explore in the remaining pages of this introduction, literature intersects with the modern preoccupation with security by means of two formal features: fictionality and narrativity. These two formal dimensions enable us to argue that literature can provide insights about security that are relevant beyond the world of literature.

1.4 Fictionality and Security

From the late eighteenth through the nineteenth century, American literature provides a view on what Catherine Gallagher, in a justly influential essay, has termed "the rise of fictionality" ("Rise"). The early chapters of *The Poetics of Insecurity* show this rise in mid-process. Brown's novels paid tribute to, but also chafed against, the reservations against fiction prevalent at his time: they purported to provide guidance for virtuous behavior, yet they activated the reader's imagination in ways that, once released, could no longer be harnessed to the sanctioned purposes of morality. Jacobs's slave narrative, on the other hand, is part of a mid-century constellation in which fictional and nonfictional texts jointly committed themselves to reform efforts such as abolitionism. This agenda relied on aesthetic strategies aimed to create politically desirable emotional effects, above all sympathy. To this end, a writer like Jacobs used a number of novelistic techniques, ranging from dramatic chapter titles to melodramatic plots, a differentiated amplitude between foreground and background, and the variation of narrative pace and rhythm. The permeability of fiction and nonfiction typical for this time period is the chief reason why I have included a chapter on Jacobs's slave narrative in a book that primarily discusses fiction. But since that permeability indicates that nonfictional texts, like fictional ones, aimed at the readers' affective experience, nonfictional genres came under the suspicion of being fictional, and fictional texts like *Uncle Tom's Cabin* were frequently accused of lying. The roughly sixty years between the writings of Brown and Jacobs thus capture a transitional phase of American letters in which literature exerted pressure on its established functions while the modern understanding of fictionality had yet to achieve cultural dominance.[19]

We are familiar with the strong resentments toward novelistic fictionality in the United States well into the 1820s. Novels had such a bad reputation in the early republic that authors had to deny their fictionality in order to bypass the severest censure. As Harrison Orians writes in a classic article on the subject, "Fully fifteen of the first hundred American novels italicized on their title pages a declaration of their foundation on truth. These varied from blunt asseverations of 'Founded on Fact,' 'Founded in Truth,' 'A Tale of Truth,' to explanatory comments such as 'interspersed with many surprising incidents in the life of the late Count Pulaski' and 'founded on Recent Facts which have transpired in the Course of the late Revolution of Moral Principles in France'" (204). The invented worlds created in literature had to appear as anchored in reality – "founded in truth" – in order to assure that the fictional doublings of reality served the demands of republican virtue. The claim to veracity was key for this purpose: in order for literature to be able to instruct, the imagination had to be kept from running wild. As Gallagher has shown with respect to English literature, until the modern understanding of fictionality became firmly established, literary genres and texts had to make clear that the worlds they represented were not lies. This could be achieved either by highlighting the fantastic character of their invented worlds or, alternatively, by claiming that these invented worlds referred to actually existing reality. Defoe, for instance, claimed that Robinson Crusoe was a real person. Until the novel became an established genre, literature got into trouble whenever it presented a story that was plausible enough to be true, yet that was a mere invention: "in the early eighteenth century," Gallagher writes, "a likely fiction was still considered a lie by the common [English] reader" ("Rise" 339).

As the novel was struggling for acceptance, there emerged a new understanding of what it meant for a story to be fictional. Gallagher points out that British eighteenth-century novelists routinely invoked Aristotle's definition of poetry. As Aristotle famously explains in the *Poetics*, while history relates particular facts (what actually happened), poetry presents to the reader what might happen and what is therefore probable. Charles Brockden Brown invokes precisely this Aristotelian argument in his essay "The Difference between History and Romance" (published in 1800, about six months prior to part II of *Arthur Mervyn*). He characterizes the romance as fulfilling a desire for curiosity and the romancer (who here is synonymous with the poet) as adept in the art of speculation. "Curiosity is not satisfied with viewing facts in their disconnected state in natural order, it is prone to arrange them anew, and to deviate from present and sensible objects, into speculations on the past or future; it is eager to infer from the present state of things, their former and future condition" ("Difference" 341).

Devoting itself to speculation on the past and the future, the romance pushes toward a new understanding of fictionality: the invented world of the romance creates scenarios that must be probable enough to be given credit. Two different meanings of probability, or likelihood, come together here: the represented world must be made likely, or plausible, by way of inference – a cognitive requirement – but it must also be likely in the sense that it must be *like* the known world – a requirement of verisimilitude located on the level of representation.[20] This combination allows the literary text to create a world that might be true without making a referential truth claim in doing so. As Gallagher points out, this requires the reader to adopt a particular attitude: the reader of novels must approach "a narrative as credible while thinking it affirms nothing" ("Rise" 345).

The rise of fictionality does not merely describe a development internal to literature, but also places literature at the center of an emerging cultural practice based on the mental operation of granting credibility to scenarios while freeing them from the responsibility of affirming a particular truth. This practice grows out of the ability to take a stance toward representations of the world located between the poles of belief and disbelief. Gallagher speaks of a "disposition of ironic credulity enabled by optimistic incredulity; one is dissuaded from believing the literal truth of a representation so that one can instead admire its likelihood and extend enough credit to buy into the game" (346).[21] Such "flexible mental states," she continues, "were the sine qua non of modern subjectivity" (346).

This mental attitude, essential to literary fiction, is also the basis of both security and risk, the two primary techniques of confronting modern uncertainty. In other words, I argue that the rise of modern fictionality explains why literature is a cultural practice that is intimately connected to the rise of security (and risk) in modern society.

Gallagher draws on examples from the risk economy in order to buttress her argument that along with the rise of fictionality in literature there emerged, what she calls, an "expedient fictionality": "One thinks immediately of merchants and insurers calculating risks, or of investors extending credit on small collateral and reasoning that the greater the risk the higher the profit, but no enterprise could prosper without some degree of imaginative play" (346). Risk involves imaginative play as well as calculated planning. It insists that guessing the future is not a matter of mere luck. Risk-taking requires the modern subject to act under conditions of uncertainty as if one acted with certainty, while remaining aware that such certainty is not in fact obtainable.

In many cases, the modern mind even has to be able to act on premises whose truth value is not only known to be unknown, but is in fact known to be false. Paper money is the best example: after the introduction of bank notes, ordinary people had to come to terms with the fact that banks could not sufficiently back up the disseminated bills with specie, although bank notes, as Stephen Mihm reminds us, were nothing but "'promises to pay' that legally entitled the bearer to present the note at the issuing institution and receive the face value in specie" (*Nation of Counterfeiters* 9). Yet people accepted the fact that in disseminating bills, banks made promises that they would not be able to keep if push came to shove. The reason they could still muster "ironic credulity" was that they also knew that as long as no one lost confidence in the banks and, even more importantly, as long as no one lost confidence in the confidence of others, the known lack of specie in the bank vaults would not matter at all.

I have already discussed at length where risk and security overlap and where they differ. At this point it is enough to repeat that security processes the uncertainty of the future by creating scenarios of threat and counter-scenarios of response. The resulting interplay of competing future courses brings forth a kind of agency that regards the uncertain future as shapeable, but only under the condition that it can never be fully brought under control. Security is thus a cultural practice that operates with scenarios of the future that can be described as fictions in the modern sense. Even if the scenario of insecurity poses a threat that necessitates action, it is a scenario that (to recall Gallagher) one is dissuaded from taking as literal truth. Only the awareness that the threat is a mere possibility – an uncertainty – makes it possible to find a response to it, i.e., to appropriate the uncertainty of threat and turn it to one's own advantage. In other words, just like in other instances of modern fictionality, security presupposes a stance toward future scenarios that enables one to "admire [their] likelihood and extend enough credit to buy into the game" ("Rise" 346).

There are at least two ways, then, in which literature is related to security. On one level, it is a frequent theme of modern fiction, particularly of that written in post-rank societies. On another level, reading literature must be regarded as a cultural practice that is related to security because both are based on the mental disposition necessary for the modern type of fictionality in which likely, probable, and plausible representations of reality can be credited (and acted upon) without being identified with the truth. If security is fictional in this modern sense, it is a practice that creates an arrangement with uncertainty.

Fictional literature differs in a crucial respect from expedient fictionality, i.e., from the practice of engaging uncertainty in such practical contexts as security or risk. What matters about everyday confrontations of uncertainty are practical results; a reader of novels, on the other hand, can take up a stance of ironic credulity toward the represented world without worrying about real-life consequences. Pragmatically freed, literature provides a pure form of fictionality that can serve as a kind of training simulator for trying out the flexible mental states required of the modern subject. Gallagher describes the cognitive training function of literature in these terms: "[A]lmost all of the developments we associate with modernity – from greater religious toleration to scientific discovery – required the kind of cognitive provisionality one practices in reading fiction, a competence in investing contingent and temporary credit" (347). This suggests that fictional literature has played a key role in the rise of the Age of Security. Fictional literature has helped moderns learn how to make use of uncertainty in turning the scenario of insecurity into an enabling condition.[22]

The question to address now is whether a logical link can be reconstructed between the cultural practice of fictionality and the ways in which American literature typically stages the concern with security. As I hope to have shown, linking literature and security via fictionality can explain the relevance of reading novels in a world that requires subjects to act under conditions of uncertainty. But fictionality itself leaves open what kind of stories literature tells about security. If we want to theorize the link between the literary and nonliterary dimensions of security, we therefore need to complement the above reflections about fictionality with an account of the characteristics and uses of fictional engagements with security.

1.5 Security and Narrative

In order to understand how and why American literature tells particular stories about security and what the implications of these specific fictions might be for the world beyond literature, we need to shift our analysis from fictionality to narrative. Both dimensions presuppose each other, for whenever we immerse ourselves in the fictionality of literature, we do so (at least partially) through the medium of plot. Charles Brockden Brown suggests as much when he describes how fictional literature satisfies curiosity: it allows the reader to speculate on the past and the future of facts which otherwise appear "in their disconnected state in natural order." Plot is the chief way in which past, present, and future are organized in fiction: it aligns events with each other, and in doing so it pushes them ahead. Stories come into being when events are tied together with a temporal trajectory. "Reading for the plot," as Peter Brooks has memorably phrased it, we anticipate and continually revise the future course of events and the development of characters. Following these temporal trajectories is what allows us to become invested in the unfolding fictional world.

To avoid confusion at this point, we must keep in mind that narrative and plot are not per se matters of fictionality. Building narratives seems to be a basic human activity necessary for such fundamental problems as the creation of a sense of who we are.[23] But we can only adopt the specific attitude of modern fictionality toward the kind of invented world that is equipped with the temporal trajectory of narrative. (Indeed, it strikes me as impossible to imagine a non-narrative fiction.)

Most plots have certain structural characteristics that pre-form how the reader becomes engaged in a narrative. Numerous narrative theorists have pointed out that in order for a plot to thrive, we need a particular kind of conflict. Such a conflict is not simply located between two characters, but between a formal or informal order (a law or normative frame) and an agent or force that violates this order. Hayden White, for instance, has found this hypothesis confirmed in historiographical writing. He approvingly paraphrases Hegel's remark in the *Lectures on the Philosophy of History* that "[t]he reality that lends itself to narrative representation is the conflict between desire and the law. Where there is no rule of law, there can be neither a subject nor the kind of event that lends itself to narrative representation" ("Value" 12–13). Plots chain together a series of events which disturb a given order, imposed by law, and thus break open the regular course of things in unforeseen ways. The momentum of narrative is in this sense transgressive, and though there are established patterns of transgression, each narrative produces individual events with individual openings. As Paul Ricoeur remarks, "There is no story if our attention is not moved by a thousand contingencies" ("Narrative Time" 174).[24]

I want to briefly consider the narrative theory of Yuri Lotman, the Estonian theorist of cultural semiotics, since his observations are particularly pertinent for the problem of security. As I will make clear, his theory of the literary text throws light on the ambiguity between threat and opportunity central to the works analyzed in the upcoming chapters. In his late works, particularly in *The Universe of the Mind* (1990) (a key chapter of which – "The Origin of Plot in the Light of Typology" – was published in *Poetics Today* in 1979), Lotman approaches culture semiotically as the dynamic exchange between different kinds of texts, each of which comprises a particular worldview. As one moves from a culture's center to its periphery, its degree of organization decreases: at its center, a culture is tightly structured and homogenous. Semiotically speaking, it consists of a single type of text. This text reconstructs "a completely regulated world" ("Origin" 173). By contrast, at the periphery, where a culture comes into contact with other cultures, it loses much of its coherence and becomes a heterogeneous hybrid: "Inasmuch as the plot elements of the texts which comprise this group will be excesses and anomalies, the general world-picture will appear extremely disorganized" (173).

The text of the center and that of the periphery create a contrast between two different kinds of plot. On the one hand, the center produces a narrative that moves from an initial moment of order and stasis to a phase of disorder and temporal changes and finally finds its way back to stasis and timeless order. This narrative carries the trace of myth: in its earliest instantiations, it expressed a unified cosmology and was organized cyclically, without beginning and end, akin to the cycle of the seasons and that of life and death. With its translation into linear form, it takes on the characteristics of eschatology, in which a drawn-out moment of crisis is resolved when the temporal order becomes displaced by eternity. By contrast, at the periphery of a given culture, we encounter a plot that is the exact inversion of that of the center: here chaos and chances events dominate; when order and stasis appear, they do so magically, as a wholly unexpected resolution of conflict, but only to soon give way to renewed chaos. The dynamic of cultures consists in the struggle for dominance between center and periphery and thus between these two groups of texts and plots. To put it into oversimplified terms, cultures carry out a violent conflict – a struggle over power – between the poles of order and chance. It should be noted here that Lotman's theory allows us to think of cultures on multiple scales. While he traces mythological cultures to ancient unified communities, we need not therefore assume that modern cultures, in Lotman's sense, coincide with national cultures and the territory of the nation-state (this distinguishes his concept of the border from that of borderland theory in American studies).

Lotman's semiotic perspective provides an account of the relation between the makeup of a culture and its negotiation in literary texts that is helpful for the present discussion. While cultures are constantly involved in dynamic and cross-feeding antagonisms – "each of these groups [of texts] affects its contracting party" (174) – the exchange between them has also brought forth artistic texts. In these literary texts, however, the antagonistic elements cease to be opposed to each other and instead enter into a dialogical relation. This becomes possible because literary plot-narratives draw on both cultural narratives. However, rather than harmonize them, literary texts bring them together in a manner that is radically ambiguous.

Literary texts, Lotman argues, create their narrative worlds on the basis of a topology that divides characters into two groups: those that are immobile and become a spatial function of order, and those that are mobile and manage to cross into the contact zone of the periphery (for illustrative examples, we only need to think of the *picaro* tradition or of the even broader tradition of adventure tales). These mobile characters can be seen as translators between cultures and become instrumental for cultural exchange.

Moreover, these mobile characters are the means by which both types of cultural text are brought into an ambiguous relation. On the one hand, they are the agents of contact, hybridity, and change. They experience order as obstacles that need to be overcome; they encounter "immobile enemy-characters fixed at particular points in the plot-space" (167). But on the other hand, the valuation of transgression and order can quickly turn upside down. Disorder and transgression, we need to remember, are also a part of the narrative of the center, as disturbing elements of crisis that must be resolved into order. In the course of the literary narrative, the mobile character may imperceptibly change tracks and move from the peripheral narrative to that of the center. Such a change is not a betrayal, but in fact part of the mobile character's task as a cultural translator. As a result of such changes of track, the enemy changes as well: the adversary no longer is the immobile character, but the force of chaos responsible for the crisis. In short, mobile characters negotiate between the texts of the periphery and the center, and by doing so they gain the capacity to change their perspective. It is these changes in viewpoint that are responsible for the fictional text's ambiguity regarding order and transgression.

This ambiguity provides another angle from which to consider the fact that literature tends to create zones of indistinction in which threat and the response to threat become a matter of perspective. In *The Professor's House*, for instance, Tom Outland practically carries the peripheral sphere of the mobile character in his name. He is a liberating force that resists the stasis of an increasingly materialist culture. Yet while he is in many ways an irresistible Romantic hero, Cather's text ultimately grants authority to the narrative of the cultural center and unsparingly reevaluates Outland as no more than "a glittering idea," as one character calls him (*Professor's House* 164). And considering that by emulating Tom, the Professor nearly loses his ability to take over any social role, so much so that his social apathy nearly tempts him into suicide, it does not go too far to suggest that it is Tom who becomes the most dangerous threat. As the narratives of periphery and center enter into dialogical exchange, security turns into insecurity, insecurity into security, and both become condensed in a single character.

I have proposed so far that fictional literature helps the modern subject become adept at taking the attitude of expedient fictionality, which has been made necessary by the pervasiveness of uncertainty characteristic of modernity. Modern literature is thus a cultural practice that is related to security in that both rely on fictionality. I have further argued that it is no coincidence that the stories literature tells about security highlight the ambiguity between security and insecurity. Literary fictionality is principally of a narrative character, and literary narratives gain their momentum from putting into dialogue the cultural forces of order and disorder. To a certain degree it is thus a structural given that literary narratives render ambiguous the distinction between order and disorder, threat and the response to threat. This does not mean that this principal disposition is actualized in all literary texts and traditions in the same manner; hence the greater urgency of the concern with security in literatures that evolve from a fluid social structure. What it does mean is that the formal link between literature and security (established via the cultural practice of fictionality), and the rendition of the problem of security as a conflict that creates opportunities for characters, is more than a sheer coincidence. Both dimensions constitute each other because modern literature joins fictionality to narrative. This in turn means that only through an analysis of narrative do we gain an understanding of why in literary fictions insecurity has little to do with incapacitating fear.

But why, we need to ask, do we seek out the confrontation with threat and the articulation of responses to it in the realm of narrative fiction at all? I have enlisted Catherine Gallagher's point that literary fictionality helps the modern subject rehearse for the expedient fictionality increasingly demanded by everyday life. However, the fact that literature helps us learn to deal with the uncertainties of modern life does not provide a satisfactory explanation for the appeal of security fictions. It would only do so if one could argue that the encounter with insecurity in literature allows for a degree of mastery not available in real life. But imaginative mastery is precisely not what the writers of my study offer. If, in other words, fiction provides training in managing (rather than wishfully undoing) uncertainty, this is less a reason why we seek fiction than a side effect of reading. Thus the question remains: What is the appeal for the reader in seeking out literary encounters with threat?

1.6 The Uses of Uncertainty

For Gallagher, the answer to this question lies precisely in literature's ability to make accessible the experience of fictionality in a worry-free (not to say "secure") environment. The pleasure of modern literature, on her account, "partly arise[s] from the ability to choose a state – suspended disbelief – that could then be experienced in a passive mode without risk." This "permits a more intense engagement with the fiction" (348). The fictionality of the novel allows for an intense experience because in reading fiction we can allow ourselves to give in to the likeliness of a world that we know to be invented, without having to worry about any real-life consequences. In effect, Gallagher argues that literary fiction is appealing because the cognitive stance of suspended disbelief (or ironic credulity) exposes us to uncertainty, but since this exposure is confined to the imagination, we come to feel all the more secure, free of worry. Fiction, in this explanation, creates the reassurance we know from awaking from a nightmare: thank God it was all just a dream![25]

This account, however, begs the question: Why should it be pleasurable to abandon ourselves intensely to fiction, and why is it necessary to counterbalance this intensity with the relief that it is all as unreal as a dream? I wish to suggest an alternative account that is capable of giving an explanation for why the uncertainty encountered in fiction is pleasurable, and that furthermore avoids explaining the pleasure of fiction by pointing to the relief that fiction is only fiction. The first necessary step in this regard is to leave behind Gallagher's view that the readerly abandon to fiction is enabled by an engagement with a character. In Gallagher's view, fictionality allows us to feel intensely for a person precisely because we know he or she does not exist (see 351–352). If we replace character with the shifting valuations of transgression and order that unfold in narrative, we can regard fictionality and narrativity as two elements that reinforce each other in making the fictional narrative pleasurable.

From this perspective, the activity of the reader can be described, as Winfried Fluck has theorized it in the tradition of the Constance School, as an "imaginary transfer." The term transfer indicates that texts need to be brought to life by the reader. In order to do so, the reader must bring the text on the page into contact with his or her own imaginary repertoire, consisting of memories, fantasies, convictions, doubts, fears, etc. As Fluck explains in a recent essay, "Without any investment from our side, this invented world [of fiction] would not take on any degree of reality and would thus not make any sense" ("The Imaginary" 242).

The imaginary, as understood in this context, is not a repertoire in the usual sense, for it is essentially a process or an activity, rather than a container filled with the debris of the past. This helps us explain why narratives of transgression hold a particular appeal: in the experience of reading plots in which boundaries are crossed and contact-zones entered, the reader imaginarily replicates or actualizes the transgressive movement into the uncertain. The text will thus encourage the reader to articulate, in the imaginary, what has so far remained amorphous, without acknowledgment by the self.[26] The transgressive movement of the text, in a sense, becomes the reader's experience of transgression. The point is not that the reader *identifies* with a mobile character in imagining that he or she is crossing a border, breaking a law, or starting a romance; rather, what matters here is that the transgressive plot enhances the text's capacity to animate the imaginary's activity. This experience relates to the imaginary experience of the self, but it is not therefore self-centered; it rather "extends" (Fluck's term) the self beyond its prior confines, into a dimension made available by the text. It is this imaginary stretching of the self that accounts for the intensity of the reading experience. This idea has also been articulated by Paul Ricoeur: "It is not a question of imposing upon the text our finite capacity for understanding, but of exposing ourselves to the text and receiving from it an enlarged self ... In other words, if fiction is a fundamental dimension of the reference of the text, it is no less a fundamental dimension of the subjectivity of the reader. As reader, I find myself only by losing myself. Reading introduces me into the imaginative variations of the ego" ("Hermeneutical Function" 85).

There is no reason to assume, however, that only narrative transgressions of established conventions, laws, and borders get the engine of the imaginary going. To recall Lotman, the narrative of the periphery, which highlights mobility, transgression, change, and translation, is in dialogue with the narrative of the center, which promises the resolution of conflict and aspires to the reinstatement of balance and stasis (or timelessness). Within the interplay between these two narratives, the narrative of the center allows the reader to extend himself or herself in the text's orientation toward the quietness of order.

From the view of the center, mobility appears as crisis, and the crisis must be met in a struggle for order. This accounts for the observation with which I started out this chapter, namely that the fictional encounters with insecurity explored in this book don't primarily aim to undo uncertainty, but rather find new possibilities opening up in the face of threat. While the narrative of the periphery appropriates threat as a liberating and mobilizing energy, the narrative of the center generates possibilities out of threat by representing insecurity as a struggle that takes place against the horizon of a future of order, peace, and the end of time.

The full measure of literature's dialogue between transgression (in the narrative of the periphery) and the struggle against transgression (in the narrative of the center) contributes to the intensification (and extensification) of the reader's sense of self in reading fictions of (in)security. In other words, rather than separate transgression and the horizon of stasis to two different actors, agencies, or texts at war with each other, narrative fiction allows the reader to imaginarily experience both poles in relation to each other. Both narratives deal with transgression, only from opposite sides.

As I have suggested, fiction in general relies on narrative structures that enable the reader's experience of self-extension. This raises the question whether fictional engagements with insecurity differ from other kinds of fiction. The answer I propose is that when a fictional narrative accentuates threat and the response to threat, the reader's imaginary becomes active concerning the conversion of threat into various kinds of agency, the spectrum of which is suggested in exemplary fashion by my choice of novels.

While the types of agency can differ drastically, what is common to all fiction that takes up the concern with security (as I have defined it) is the moment of conversion from vulnerability to budding possibility. As I have emphasized repeatedly, these two states remain closely tied to each other since they are both built on uncertainty. It is not the case, therefore, that vulnerability disappears into empowerment. Rather, we witness a "transvaluation" of security. In other words, narrative fictions concerned with threat convert the insecurity of a passively suffered disruption of order into the insecurity of an experience of self-activation. For an example, we only need to look to the classical quest story in which the hero must prove himself in the face of challenges that disrupt the established order. Crucially, the tests the hero needs to pass also constitute transgressions of that order. In fact, it is their very extraordinariness that qualifies them as suitable tests.[27]

The transvaluations of security provide an imaginary experience that can be enormously gratifying. Because the narrative of the center interacts with that of the periphery, the narrative response to threat can usher in an imaginary experience of agency that jumps tracks and associates itself with the mobile characters opposed to the fixity and timelessness of order. In other words, the conversion from weakness to power in the face of threat can produce an experience so liberating that the greatest imaginary appeal flows from peripheral figures that were initially associated with threat.

Rita Felski has called on literary critics to break with the dictates of historicism and the hermeneutics of suspicion, and to recover instead a perspective that can elucidate the "uses" literature has in store for the reader. As defined by Felski, "'Use' is not always strategic or purposeful, manipulative or grasping; it does not have to involve the sway of instrumental rationality or a willful blindness to complex form. I venture that aesthetic value is inseparable from use, but also that our engagements with texts are extraordinarily varied, complex, and often unpredictable in kind" (*Uses* 7–8). Felski discusses four clusters of such uses, or "modes of textual engagement" (14), by employing the categories "recognition," "enchantment," "knowledge," and "shock." The "use" of literature I have been working toward in these pages overlaps with some of these, but it is different enough to warrant its own rubric. Let's call it "empowerment" because it emerges from the engagement with a narrative conversion of the passivity of insecurity into the active encounter with uncertainty. ("Empowerment," however, ought not to be taken to mean that the empowered subject might have mastered and vanquished uncertainty.) In other words, "empowerment" lets the reader imaginarily take part in the conversion of threat into an uncertainty that can be actively engaged.

It is time at this point to tackle the argument I have been driving toward from the outset of this chapter. I propose that the literary analysis of security can contribute to our understanding of how security could become such a dominant concern in modern (and particularly contemporary) culture. My suggestion is that the pleasure, or use, of literary fictions of security (which consist of fictional engagements with insecurity) is also present in nonliterary security discourses. But whereas in literature, the pleasures of the particular kind of imaginary self-extension I call "empowerment" are made available in pure form, in the expediently fictional life of reality they become knotted into the threads that make up multi-scaled relations of power. In social and political discourse, security and insecurity involve concerns about practical outcome. They become inseparable from state institutions, economic circulation, media representations, and authority markets of expert knowledge. Nonetheless, the cultural appeal of security cannot be explained by the theories of security dominant today.[28] Saying that security is a technology of rule (as Foucauldians have it) or a speech act that withdraws issues from the realm of democratic deliberation (as the so-called Copenhagen School of International Relations contends) disregards the pleasure called forth by nonliterary security discourses.[29] (I speak of discourses here because I want to emphasize that we should not oppose literature to immediate encounters with vital threat, say, when we personally become the victims of crime. It makes much more sense to compare security in literature to media discourses about security because it is in and through the media that the *concept* of security gains its traction among the public.)

My claim, I am aware, may sound unsettling. If the pervasiveness of security is to be explained by the uses that the concept holds out for the imagination, then the implication seems to be that we like to be threatened, or that we enjoy identifying with violent criminals. Indeed, I argue that despite all pragmatic constraints, real-world security discourses enable an ambiguous imaginary experience in which we oscillate between transgression and counter-transgression. To be sure, the affective response to a real-world security crisis differs from that produced by narrative fiction. Most obviously, we experience a different level of fear. But as I argued at the outset, fear itself is oriented toward the uncertain future, and the activation of the public by threat demonstrates that fear mixes with a whole range of other emotions, including excitement and thrill.

Even the most cursory glance at recent security crises that shook the American public begins to reveal how enticing the narratives of real-life security are. After the Boston Marathon bombing in April 2013, the extraordinary measures of security politics (including a lockdown of Boston) were accompanied by the staging of a ritual that effected the imaginary conversion of vulnerability into heroic agency. TV coverage and amateur footage suggest that Bostonians celebrated the capture of Dzhokar Tsarnaev as if a national sports team had won a major championship. If there was a divide between actors (police) and audience (onlookers), the enthusiastic crowd in Watertown, Massachusetts (the scene of an extended shootout between the Tsnarnaev brothers and the police, the ensuing search for Dzokhar, who had survived the confrontation and managed to flee, and finally Dzokhar's arrest) seemed to applaud the police as much as itself. Cell phone videos capture the crowd chanting "USA! USA!"[30] Previously, immediately following the explosions during the Marathon, countless citizens had excitedly participated in the search for suspects by posting suggestions, guesses, and suspicions – witch-hunt style – on social media platforms such as Reddit and Twitter.[31] Here the initial transgression became imaginarily actualized in a version of Lotman's narrative of the center: people imaginarily engaged in a struggle for stasis by way of active retribution and thus converted the uncertainty of threat into their own empowerment.

In light of the fact that insecurity often refers to actual physical violence and death, my argument may smack of levity or even appear as the scandalous mockery of the victims of violence. But in response to such objections, it will suffice to turn the tables and insist that we will remain enthralled by the pathos of security, with all of its violent consequences, as long as we don't begin to face what's in it for us. Only if we understand what draws us to security can we begin to detect, isolate, and reject those kinds of politicizations of security which curtail democratic deliberation and sanction the state's arrogation of the right to suspend rights.

CHAPTER 2

The Virtue of Uncertainty
Securing the Republic in Arthur Mervyn

Weaving together a republican conception of threat with a liberal openness to uncertainty, Charles Brockden Brown's novel *Arthur Mervyn* (part I published in 1799, part II in 1800) offers an early case study of the uses of threat and insecurity articulated in and as fiction. Topically, Brown's negotiation of security and uncertainty arises out of the early republic's fear of corruption believed to result most immediately from the transformation of an agricultural society into a market one. For Brown and his contemporaries, the economic order we have come to refer to as market capitalism induces the spread of self-interest, which is feared for precipitating the downfall of the republic. In *Arthur Mervyn*, the logic of security refers to the attempt to contain and undo this threat. Yet this attempt brings about a narrative dynamic that calls into question the very identification of security and order. For on the formal level, Brown's engagement with security is made possible by his experiments with the novel's fictional duplication of reality organized by probability and conjecture. Such duplication is driven by transgressive events that undermine security's alleged aspirations to order. This produces what appears to be a contradiction between the thematic commitment to securing the republic and the formal emphasis on conjecture, uncertainty, and transgression. Yet it is precisely Brown's program to try to resolve this contradiction. Brown ties together the topical and the formal in the concern for the virtuous republic; he tests, within the realm of fiction, whether uncertainty can be understood as the substance of security. Doing so, he creates the imagination of a "republican individualism" in which the pursuit of the republic's security comes to set free the individual without reducing the republic to anomie.

2.1   Republican Security

In the last four decades, historians and literary critics have debated whether the Revolutionary era and early republic are best described as belonging to an intellectual tradition of classical republicanism or to the flowering of liberal thought.[1] I argue in this chapter that Charles Brockden Brown's *Arthur Mervyn* shows the author to inhabit a transitional position in the specific sense that it evinces an allegiance to classical republicanism while revising republicanism's central concept of virtue in such a manner that it begins to adapt to, and ultimately espouses, features that we today recognize as belonging to laissez-faire capitalism, all the while denying the legitimacy of market forces.

Scholars have given us a number of accounts of how virtue was transformed in the early republic in order to accommodate the new realities emerging from the market revolution.[2] Most crucially, critics have pointed out how controlled commerce (mercantilist rather than market-capitalist) came to be seen as virtuous thanks to its alleged capability of promoting refinement, and how debt became understood as the foundation of a social bond.[3] The redefinition of virtue in *Arthur Mervyn*, however, takes place on a different level. Because free trade was associated mostly with self-interest and corruption, Brown could connect virtue to activities that today are marked as capitalist but during Brown's time were more ambiguous, since they appeared as not immediately compatible with self-interest. Principally, these are activities that recognize, accept, and try to turn to advantage the conditions of contingency and unpredictability. This turn to uncertainty did not merely mark activities we associate with early market capitalism. As we will see, it also informs the emergence of probability and the development of fiction as a domain that begins to exceed moral, practical, and didactic utility.

What I develop in this chapter, then, is not an exercise in symptomatic reading that would present Brown as an ideologist of liberal capitalism disguised by a republican front, but rather an attempt to reconstruct an intellectual composite structure of security emerging in the early years of the republic that combines elements from republicanism and liberalism within a republican framework. Furthermore, my aim is to show that this composite structure of security must be understood in relation to its form; indeed, I argue that it is Charles Brockden Brown's temporary turn to the novel, during the second half of the 1790s, that allowed him to articulate his novel conception of security.[4] In my reading, the significance of a novel such as *Arthur Mervyn* lies in bringing forth, in part via its form, an understanding of security that subscribes to uncertainty, chance, and adventure rather than certainty, control, and defense against uncertainty and chance.

In order to sketch the republican notion of threat and insecurity against which Brown developed his own, it is useful to briefly visit the republican political discourse of his time. Threat and insecurity were the cornerstones of the early republic's political worldview and gained their urgency from the logical position accorded to them in a system derived from classical republican thought.

In the most famous of the Federalist Papers, *Federalist* No. 10, James Madison addressed "the mortal diseases under which popular governments have every where perished" (40). Madison's rhetoric suggests a classic case of insecurity-as-emergency modeled on the individual body and extended to the body politic. The medical emergency will consign the young republic to death if relief measures are not taken at once. The symptom Madison is most concerned with is what he calls "faction" – a splitting up of a disinterested public into a plurality of particular interests that violently compete for dominance without respecting either the public good or the very pluralism from which they sprang. Like classical republicans, Madison diagnoses deeper causes operating underneath this symptom: The fault, ultimately, lies with "the nature of man" (41), i.e., with human passions, the most dangerous of which is "self-love" (41). Since they are ingrained in human nature, the causes of the disease "cannot be removed, and … relief is only to be sought in the means of controlling its *effects*" (43, emphasis in original). But while human nature ineluctably endangers the virtuous and autonomous polis, Federalists, like classical republicans, held that the only solution, the only path to security, lies in the polis itself. Thus, "according to the different circumstances of civil society" (41), these passions either reign supreme and usher in tyranny or are controlled by reason and thus enable men to become or remain citizens.

However, for Madison, only a modernized type of republicanism could keep the United States from suffering the same fate as the historical model republics. In order to effectively control the detrimental effects of faction, a modern republic needed to combine popular sovereignty with the principle of representation. Popular sovereignty alone, Madison feared, would lead to a tyranny of the majority. But in combination with a system of representation, "it may well happen that the public voice pronounced by the representatives of the people, will be more consonant to the public good, than if pronounced by the people themselves convened for the purpose" (44).

In devising a strategy for how "to secure the public good and private rights against the danger of such a faction, and at the same time to preserve the spirit and the form of popular government" (43), Madison arrived at a modern conception of pluralism that would allow for "a republican remedy for the diseases most incident to republican government" (46). In

Madison's proposal, the representatives should consist of an enlightened elite capable, intellectually and economically, of moving above the messiness of interest and to act as a "disinterested and dispassionate umpire in disputes between different passions and interests in the State" (Madison to Edmund Randolph, April 8, 1787, qtd. in Wood, "Interests and Disinterestedness" 92). Madison acknowledged that the causes of faction could not be suppressed. The solution was to create a pluralist structure that would keep them from tearing down the entire scaffolding of the republic.[5]

Madison's contributions to *The Federalist* effectively modernized the republican theory of government, but the Federalist fascination with threat, fear, and insecurity nonetheless is deeply embedded in the republican tradition. Consider the following gloss on Machiavelli's *Discourses* by Quentin Skinner regarding the difficulties in maintaining liberty and *virtù*. It should be noted that in the republican tradition, *virtù* denotes the aggressive and imperial qualities, understood as "manly force" (*vir* means man), necessary for defending the autonomy of the republic. *Virtù*, aggressively directed outside, differs from the cooperative, inward-directed civic virtue of the active citizen. Yet both are related and overlap in their purpose because they are traditionally conceptualized as opposing the reign of *Fortuna*.

> While we can expect to find a surpassing degree of *virtù* among the founding fathers of cities, we cannot expect to find the same quality occurring naturally among ordinary citizens. On the contrary, most men 'are more prone to evil than to good' and in consequence tend to ignore the interests of their community in order to act 'according to the wickedness of their spirits whenever they have free scope' (201, 215). There is thus a tendency for all cities to fall away from the pristine *virtù* of their founders and 'descend towards a worse condition' – a process Machiavelli summarizes by saying that even the finest communities are liable to become corrupt (322). (Skinner, *Machiavelli* 62)[6]

As in Madison's text, the republican community is conceptualized as a body politic, and while for Madison it is disease that is threatening the republic, Machiavelli's republic is endangered by the loss of force that comes with age. In both scenarios, the threat arises from the weakness and wickedness of human nature and is therefore "most incident to republican government," which relies on the commitment of citizens to the *res publica*. Self-interest undermines disinterestedness. And in both cases, threat must be mastered by reinforcing virtue in a way that keeps human frailty in check. In the republican tradition, virtue is always insecure, but security is gained and maintained only by means of virtue.[7]

In the republican framework, the threat to virtue is mediated by *Fortuna,* and, as I argue, this idea plays an important role in structuring Charles Brockden Brown's novels. Beginning with republican thought in antiquity, *Fortuna* is the force of contingency, understood both as sheer chance resulting in misfortune and good luck. Virtue – more specifically, *virtú* – is the force and character trait that allows for the subduing of *Fortuna* in its negative characteristics and for the attraction, or commanding, of *Fortuna* in its dimension of success. Thus, the disease of interest and corruption, which threatens the survival of the republic, will bring on the supremacy of *Fortuna* as sheer chance. The triumph of virtue, on the other hand, will tame *Fortuna* and produce felicitous results.

In *Arthur Mervyn*, Brown takes up the republican conceptualization of insecurity and threat emerging from the decline of disinterestedness during the dawn of market capitalism. As in *Ormond* and an installment of his essay series "The Man At Home," in *Arthur Mervyn* Brown turns to the yellow fever epidemic of 1793 in order to literalize the disease plaguing the republic. He moreover stays within the republican paradigm by devising a security strategy *for* and *through* virtue. As a first approximation of the argument that is to follow, we may say that Brown's innovation lies in teasing out the ambiguity of *Fortuna*, its capacity to stand for ill luck *and* felicity. If the virtuous actor manages to command the felicitous side of *Fortuna*, the result differs from the certainty and security envisioned by the Federalists. This is because virtue retains the ultimately contingent character that characterizes *Fortuna* in both of its forms.

The form in which this virtue of uncertainty becomes imaginable is narrative fiction (more precisely, the novel), since the fictional reality of the novel comes to life through action, through its plot. And plot, as I have argued in my introduction with reference to narrative theorist Yuri Lotman, is the interplay of order and transgression, of stasis and events. Put differently, plot is the interplay of things happening to characters and characters reacting to what happened to them, thereby making more things happen. On this fundamental level, fictional plots may be described as the interplay between fortune and virtue, or chance and the attempts of self-controlled action.

Before turning to *Arthur Mervyn*, I would like to note that in his theoretical writings Brown lays bare this interplay as the moral and epistemological core of fiction. Recent criticism of Brown has paid little attention to the fact that these writings are concerned with chance, accident, and uncertainty. Instead, his most influential readers of recent years, invested in placing him in a context of the radical Enlightenment, have mostly focused on the didactic dimension of his fictional theory. In this view, didacticism presupposes certainty about how to achieve a moral result that is desirable with equal certainty.[8] This interpretation rests on the evidence allegedly provided by Brown's essay "Walstein's School of History," published in August–September 1799, about three months after the first part of *Arthur Mervyn*.[9] The essay presents Brown's theory of progressive literature in the guise of a review of the writings of one fictive Professor Walstein and his students, who form a circle of enlightened minds at the university of Jena and who treat history and fiction interchangeably because both can be used for progressive ends. In this article, fiction initially appears to act as a guidebook to virtuous action:

> Among the incidents which invention will set before us, those are to be culled out which afford most scope to wisdom and virtue, which are most analogous to facts, which most forcibly suggest to the reader the parallel between his state and that described, and most strongly excite his desire to act as the feigned personages act. These incidents must be so arranged as to inspire, at once, curiosity and belief, to fasten the attention, and thrill the heart. ("Walstein's School" 338)

As described in this passage, Brown's fictional project contains two dimensions. First, the reader should recognize the plot of the novel as a model to be emulated in real life. Second, for the reader to put the model into practice, more is needed than a volitional act. By making use of its aesthetic dimension, the novel must force itself on the reader, must "excite his desire to act as the feigned personages act." A reader whose attention is fastened and whose heart is thrilled, in this theory, will be moved to a kind of sympathetic action, except that sympathy here amounts to acting like, rather than feeling with or for, a character.

The didacticism of this passage becomes less strictly directed at a particular action (where the reader would behave exactly like the hero, or adopt a particular set of precepts for action) when taking into consideration what Brown understands as behavior worthy of imitation. For it is precisely the confrontation between passiveness and activity, accident (fortune) and virtue, powerlessness and power, that Brown's ideal literary text replicates from real life.

> Men hold external goods, the pleasures of the senses, of health, liberty, reputation, competence, friendship, and life, partly by virtue of their own wisdom and activity. This, however, is not the only source of their possession. It is likewise dependent on physical accidents, which human foresight cannot anticipate, or human power prevent. It is also influenced by the conduct and opinions of others.... The perfection of our character is evinced by

the transient or slight influence which privations and evils have upon our happiness, on the skillfulness of those exertions which we make to avoid or repair disasters, on the diligence and success with which we improve those instruments of pleasure to ourselves and to others which fortune has left in our possession. (338–39)

Virtue, in other words, consists of the ability to confront accidents that cannot be foreseen or prevented. To the degree that disasters cannot be avoided (to some extent they apparently can), virtue allows us to repair them, and even in calamity (the negative side of fortune), we must build on powers that, too, originate with fortune. If this is the situation humans face in the world, then fiction recreates that world by showing us how exemplary characters steer through the tangled mess of accidents, disasters, wisdom, and activity.

The proper strategy here is not stoical endurance and passive suffering, but coming to terms with uncertainties and possibilities. In his essay "The Difference between History and Romance" (published in 1800, about six months prior to part II of *Arthur Mervyn*),[10] Brown builds on Aristotle's differentiation between history and poetry by setting apart history from romance: while the historian describes unconnected facts, the romancer creates a narrative construction of cause and effect.[11] "Curiosity is not satisfied with viewing facts in their disconnected state in natural order, it is prone to arrange them anew, and to deviate from present and sensible objects, into speculations on the past or future; it is eager to infer from the present state of things, their former and future condition" ("Difference" 341). While history is no more than a catalog of given objects, the romancer, who deals with cause and effect, past and future, must speculate: "He is a dealer, not in certainties, but probabilities" (341).[12] What sets the writer of fiction apart is fiction's particular object of probability: motives behind actions. Motives "cannot be subjected to the senses" and therefore "cannot be certainly known. They are merely topics of conjecture. Conjecture is the weighing of probabilities" (342). For Brown, then, fiction is a medium in which the motives operating behind human actions become open to exploration by means of conjecture. More precisely, conjecture, as I want to show in my analysis of *Arthur Mervyn*, is not merely applied to actions that have already taken place in order to retrospectively gauge the motives that have operated behind them; conjecture becomes an essential element of action. It is what allows the virtuous character to make his way through a world consisting of chance and action. Conjecture, the weighing of probabilities, is itself an endeavor located ambiguously between chance and action because it helps make sense of what has happened to us (speculation on the past) and it allows for getting a sense of the possible consequences of our actions (the speculation on the future). Moreover, conjecture involves characters in a complex network of social contingency (we might call it, with Talcott Parsons, "double contingency") since the accidents that happen to them are in part the result of the "conduct and opinions of others" (as Brown phrased it in "Walstein's School of History"), whose motives require speculation, but who for their part also speculate on others' motives.

In this light, the didactic tone of "Walstein's School of History" begins to frame the function of literature as instilling a particular outlook on the world, rather than prescribing actions that derive from a set of moral precepts. The emulation of the hero which readers are asked to perform in their own lives chiefly concerns an *ars conjectandi*, a skillful dealing in probabilities that entertains no illusions about the possibility of turning probability into certainty. All we can hope for is what Jacob Bernoulli (1654–1705), the author of *Ars Conjectandi* and innovator of a posteriori probability theory, influentially called "moral certainty": certainty that is good enough for practical matters, even if it cannot become absolute certainty.[13] For Brown, the weighing of probabilities will allow us to do no more than act under the conditions of uncertainty.[14]

By turning fiction into an *ars conjectandi*, Brown charts and effects an implicit transformation of the function of fiction. Officially he remains beholden to the Enlightenment goal of using fiction as a model for virtuous action. In this paradigm, fiction is legitimate only if it points beyond itself, to real life. The imaginary engagement in the fictional world, on the other hand, must not become an end in itself. If it does, fiction is to be seen as a force of corruption that exploits the reader's passions and fancy and keeps him or her from civic engagement. Reading (and writing) is here positioned in opposition to the *vita activa* of the republican citizen and must ultimately give way to the latter. This goes to the core of the much-discussed aversion to fiction in the early republic.[15]

But as we have begun to see just now, Brown's version of using fiction as a model for action begins to tear down the clear distinction between the two worlds.[16] For if novels train the reader in the art of conjecture, then what the reader carries over from reading to the real world is not a solid set of guidelines for virtuous behavior but rather a skill in reading the world conjecturally. Means and ends begin to blur. More problematic still, the model of the world offered by fiction cannot be transported back in adequate fullness to the real world. For only in the fictional double of reality do we perceive and feel the complexity of reality's social dimension. So, while means and ends become difficult to tell apart, the fictional world at the same time becomes a world *sui generis* that resists its reduction to real-world conduct and instead insists on its capacity to provide a richer world for the reader.[17]

As I will proceed to show in a detailed reading of *Arthur Mervyn*, this ramification of the literary *ars conjectandi* ensnared Brown in a serious contradiction: How could the republican demand that literature reinforce a virtuous republic be negotiated with the shift in the function of literature toward modeling as an end in itself?

2.2 The Productivity of Threat

Arthur Mervyn is the report of the protagonist's account of his life told under the pressure to secure his reputation and dispel accusations of deep entanglements in criminal plots. For this reason, the text is a performance of virtue in a twofold sense: the protagonist tells the story of his life according to which he let virtue be his guide in acquiring property, friends, and knowledge; and the telling of the story is a performance that must instill in its listeners and readers confidence in Arthur's virtue.

I will explore the problems of Arthur's production of confidence later on. Because it establishes the problems of threat and security as central to the book, I want to begin by considering Brown's decision to place Arthur's story inside a frame narrative which renders the young man suspicious of being a carrier of the disease threatening the republic in ways both literal and metaphorical.

The frame narrative begins with Dr. Stevens, an enlightened physician from Philadelphia, who finds Arthur crouched on his porch, stricken with yellow fever. Arthur's sudden appearance burdens Stevens and his wife with having to take a risky decision. Consulting with his wife whether to take care of Arthur or send him to the hospital, Stevens alerts her to "the danger which was to be dreaded from such an inmate" (6). Arthur himself reaffirms his being a physical threat: "Do you not know … what my disease is? Why should you risk your safety for the sake of one whom your kindness cannot benefit, and who has nothing to give in return?" (7).

During this first encounter, the physical threat emanating from the disease is sharply distinguished from moral threats faced by the virtuous republic. Stevens and his wife take in the sick stranger because moral duty overrules calculations of risk. "I have no fear about me," Stevens's wife proclaims, "in a case where the injunctions of duty are so obvious. Let us take the poor unfortunate wretch into our protection and care, and leave the consequences to Heaven" (6). Mrs. Stevens's behavior demonstrates virtuous fortitude by rejecting a mindset that would take into consideration consequences of her decision possibly harmful to herself. Arthur, on the other hand, displays virtue by highlighting precisely those consequences. Though they may seem to contradict each other, both confirm the republican notion of virtue by making the case against their respective self-interest. For Mrs. Stevens, possible consequences to herself must not take precedence over the needs of a "wretch" whom *Fortuna* has abandoned and given over to the plague. For Arthur, the opportunity to get help must be subordinated to ensuring the health of those who offer their benevolence. This initial meeting also indicates the novel's correlation between *Fortuna* and virtue as it pertains to threat and security: from the encounter of a malign force emerges the possibility of rising to virtue. Threat is thus an enabling as much as a destructive force. However, what is enabled by threat is *virtù*, which in the republican tradition must be beneficent to the public good. This criterion is assessed negatively, as *not* furthering the actor's self-interest. This constitutes what I call a republican "agency dilemma", security requires acting (virtuously) despite the fact that (self-interested) action is the cause for the crisis of security. It is this agency dilemma which provides the narrative raison d'être of Brown's novel. The story of Arthur's life to be unfolded in the main narrative explores precisely this injunction: What are the different ways in which action can be virtuous, and can such action be securely marked as the antithesis to self-interest?

This fictional thought experiment cannot begin, however, until the physical threat of yellow fever becomes a potential moral threat. Hence the accusation, brought forth by Stevens's friend Wortley, that Arthur Mervyn stands in some relation to Thomas Welbeck, the novel's villain. Whether Arthur is Welbeck's accomplice or disciple, Wortley is certain that Arthur is complicit in a fraudulent scheme of which he himself was the victim. With Wortley's accusation, Arthur becomes the potential embodiment of the physical *and* moral threat to the republic.

Stevens and his wife are strongly inclined to side with Arthur's claims of innocence on the basis of his performance. While Stevens recollects "the uniform complacency and rectitude of his deportment for the period during which we had witnessed it," his wife goes so far as to attest that she would "vouch … before any tribunal, for his innocence" (12). Nonetheless (and somewhat contradictory), the couple agrees to allow Arthur "the continuance of [their] friendship on no other condition than that of a disclosure of the truth" (12). So far, disclosure is what Arthur has been reluctant to provide. While he admits to knowing Welbeck, he also professes to have promised the latter to keep any information about the nature of their acquaintance secret. It is only when he is faced with the choice of either breaking that promise or being dispelled from the polis that he decides to tell them his "simple tale" (13).

"Disclosing the truth" serves a set of functions for Arthur and his listeners. Arthur must reaffirm his esteem with his new friends, and his friends must reaffirm their initial judgment of Arthur and thus their capability of judgment. The problem, however, is that Arthur telling his life story is a poor way of converting initial intuitive judgment into certainty. What Arthur's account provides is no more than an occasion for conjecture. But the condition of uncertainty, which makes conjecture necessary and possible, pertains not just to Arthur's audience and, by implication, to the readers of the novel. Uncertainty also characterizes Arthur's experiences in the world, that is, the content of his story. And this is not only because the world as Arthur gets to know it in the city of commerce and yellow fever is fundamentally uncertain (though that certainly is an apt description), but also, and more crucially in the context of the present discussion, because uncertainty allows Arthur to portray his attempts to make a living in the city as compatible with the injunction to act in ways that are untainted by self-interest.

Indeed, Brown uses Arthur's life story as a fictional test case in order to explore options for dealing with the republican agency dilemma. To this end, he differentiates between three different kinds of action. In the first mode, Arthur appears less as an actor than a reactor to accidents. We may think of this as "passive action." Uncertainty here pertains to the sheer opacity of the world, forcing Arthur to act blindly and witness his surroundings secretively. Second, once he finds himself in the midst of the yellow fever epidemic, Arthur is compelled to help others. He now appears as a more active protagonist, but rather than acting willfully and deliberately, he is *forced* to take action by the emergency logic of impending death. We may call this "compelled action." In this mode, uncertainty revolves around unintended consequences and becomes elevated to the principle of life. Finally, beginning toward the end of the novel's first part and extending through the second, we increasingly witness Arthur trying to shape the future by making plans and carrying them out, often at hazardous risk, to himself as much as to others. Importantly, these actions are carried out on behalf of others, turning Arthur less into an agent than an agency. He acts as if on a mission, but the mission is really someone else's. Let's call this "commissioned action." Uncertainty, in this mode, appears as the implementation of an anti-consequentialist moral stance. Picking up on a problem explored in the mode of compelled action, it makes the case for the inevitability of unintended consequences and interprets it as an opportunity for conjecture. In effect, the anti-consequentialist moral stance makes it possible to absolve the republican actor from the responsibility for his actions.

Throughout the course of the novel, Arthur details his experiences in order to dispel the suspicion that he himself may be morally endangering the republic; his actions must therefore be recognizably virtuous. Yet in becoming an actor, he increasingly gains control of his doings: his need to prove himself effectively sets free his capacity to engage in the world. The security crisis thus leads to what may be called a form of republican individualism. But the idea of a republican individualism is a most precarious construct: it moves the individual into the spotlight by burdening that individual with the requirement to constantly reaffirm his or her virtuous public-mindedness. This leads to the circuitous character of what I call the agency dilemma: to prove his virtue, Arthur must act. But acting only exacerbates the need to prove his virtue.

2.3   Passive Action

Arthur Mervyn is an overly convoluted novel that differs perhaps most markedly from later nineteenth-century novels in that it crams together manifold events and background stories without taking the time to unfold individual scenes that create the space for exploring the interiority of individual characters. One prime exception to this may be the entrapment scenes in the novel's first part, which take place in the homes of Thetford and Welbeck. Here, Arthur is caught alone inside dark rooms. It is in these situations that narrative time approaches narrated time. Because entrapment also stops the flow of events, we get a glimpse of Arthur's mind in action as it processes information – available only to an insufficient degree – in order to arrive at a sense of what's going on.

The first of the entrapment scenes is a telling example of how Brown crafts a Gothic poetics in order to stage Arthur's passive action. During his initial trip to the city, Arthur seeks help from a rich acquaintance. That person is out of town, but a young man named Wallace offers Arthur his help. He buys him dinner and puts him up in his family home nearby. He leads Arthur into what he claims to be his bedchamber and, having by chance extinguished the only candle, claims to go fetch another light. From this errand, however, he never returns, leaving Arthur behind, alone in the dark. To his consternation, Arthur must soon realize that the room is not Wallace's: he has unknowingly stepped into the bedroom that belongs to a merchant named Thetford and his wife. As the couple enters the room and goes to sleep, Arthur is hiding undetected in the closet; now he must find a way to leave the room without being noticed.

In this scene, passive action consists of conjecture, which springs from entrapment and darkness as the two factors that determine Arthur's situation. Entrapment stifles action: Arthur can neither leave the room (the door, as he finds out before the couple enters, is locked) nor interact with the couple. Darkness limits his range of sense impressions and forces him to use his imagination and probabilistic speculation to make up for the lack of information from the senses. His reliance on the imagination also heightens his affective susceptibility to "fear," "panick," and "terror" (29), much like Edmund Burke had theorized sublime terror to arise from obscurity.[18]

From the first, Arthur's abandonment by Wallace gives his mind a push start. Still alone in the room and just having found the door locked, he begins to speculate about the probable consequences that would flow from his detection. "Should my conductor have disappeared, by design or by accident, and some one of the family should find me here, what would be the consequence? Should I not be arrested as a thief and conveyed to prison? My transition from the streets to this chamber would not be more rapid than my passage hence to a gaol" (29). His imagination of a disastrous future leads to the curious outcome that he must prolong the entrapment and thus continue to engage in guesswork. Speculation breeds more speculation.

Taking up a *topos* more fully explored in *Ormond; Or, the Secret Witness* (1799), Arthur, by hiding in the closet, unwittingly becomes a "secret witness."[19] First he overhears Thetford soothing a baby in the bedroom, which apparently is not his wife's; then he overhears Thetford's plan to defraud Welbeck (whom Arthur has not yet met). Both occurrences give reason for further inner deliberation and terror.

Secret and unwitting witnessing brings about the conversion of action into passiveness. The action in question is curiosity. In Enlightenment writings, curiosity most often appears in a benign form, as the inquisitive spirit leading to rationally acquired knowledge, a Kantian *sapere aude*. Franklin's *Autobiography* is the obvious case in point. But especially in the Godwinian novel, curiosity turns into something more problematic: either a snooping around in other people's affairs for dubious reasons and with disastrous effects, as in Godwin's *Caleb Williams*, where Caleb – often noted to be the most immediate model for Arthur Mervyn – cannot resist spying on his employer Mr. Falkland and thereby creates for both himself and Falkland a "theater of calamity" (*Caleb Williams* 59); or a Promethean penetration of a sacred realm that should have remained taboo, as in Shelley's *Frankenstein*, where Victor cannot withstand the temptation, made possible by science, to match God's power of creation, leading to the ruin of creator and creature.

It is the Godwinian type of curiosity to which *Arthur Mervyn* responds by presenting secret witnessing as an act of curious inquiry in the passive mode, made possible by entrapment. Again, enclosure and obscurity play together to fuse the passive with the active: because he receives information as a witness (rather than seeking it out himself), Arthur has to work with what little his senses pick up. And this, in effect, necessitates an activation of the imagination, forcing him to actively create and incessantly revise in his mind what has happened. These constant revisions, made necessary by the persistence of uncertainty, assuage Mervyn's doubts about the rightfulness of making conjectures about other people's affairs and of thus becoming actively involved in his social scene. Since he continuously suspends and undoes his speculations, they can appear to not have taken place at all – a handy way of dealing with the agency dilemma.

But passive action in the entrapment scenes is by no means limited to provisional mental constructs. Groping in the dark is what Mervyn does literally, whether in Thetford's bedroom or in Welbeck's cellar. Stumbling about without any sense of orientation, Arthur neither knows where he is, nor does he seem to have a clear idea of where he is going. But in the end, curiously enough, he finds a way out. In Thetford's room, the anticipation of being caught – "the bare possibility of being ranked with thieves" (35) – frightens him again and again, though rather than being paralyzed by his fear, it inspires his "ingenuity in the search of the means of escape" (35) and leads him to conduct an "experiment": since his sense impressions are contradictory – he has overheard Thetford say to his wife that the door is locked, but he has not heard Thetford lock it – might he not risk opening it? Sure enough, the door opens, but not before Mervyn can emphasize again that "it was my fears, rather than my hopes" that made him search for the exit.

In a later entrapment scene in Welbeck's cellar, Mervyn's passivity in the act of fleeing is even more pronounced. His first attempt to leave the cellar fails. An excruciatingly long scene of groping in the dark results in no more than a head wound; having ascended the wrong staircase, Arthur ends up at a closed door, turns around, and heads back into the cellar. After helping Welbeck bury Watson, a man whose sister Welbeck has seduced and whom

Welbeck has just shot in a duel, Arthur eventually leaves with Welbeck and ascribes all agency to him: "I was driven, by a sort of mechanical impulse, in his footsteps. I followed him because it was agreeable to him and because I knew not whither else to direct my steps" (88).

As if it were an incidental side product of entrapment, these scenes also give him an education in the ways of the world, "a crash course in deception and wickedness," as Norman Grabo phrased it (*Coincidental Art* 94). Yet if meddling in circles of vice might suggest Arthur's complicity (familiarity with the milieu of crime needs to be actively sought out), entrapment is geared at dissolving this suspicion. Arthur's stories resemble captivity narratives that drag the victim into the hellish world of the heathen. Thanks to the passivity of his own actions, he seems to be able to stay unpolluted and fend off the contagion of fraud and deceit.

2.4 Compelled Action

In the mode of passive action, Arthur witnesses economic dealings that break with the controlled form of mercantilism ("control" here refers to the power of the state to steer and delimit commercial interactions). Welbeck, Thetford, Watson, Wortley – all of these men are involved in the uncontrolled (laissez-faire) exchange of the transnational merchant trade of early capitalism. Their schemes of fraud are portrayed not as the corruption of trade, but rather as the epitome of trade itself, which is characterized by self-interested striving for riches coupled with the willful ruining of competitors.

In the novel's central storyline of white-collar crime, Thetford and Welbeck have teamed up, at the suggestion of Thetford, to purchase a ship, stock it with goods, send it to the West Indies, and reap immense profits from the cargo's sale. Welbeck agrees to provide the capital, but, as it turns out, he is not the *nouveau riche* his public self-presentation suggests: the only funds he has available is the fortune stolen from Lodi, a young man who at his untimely death entrusted his family endowment to Welbeck in order to deliver it to his sister. As Arthur casually mentions, Lodi's fortune, in turn, was amassed on a Guadeloupian slaveholding estate and is thus the deathly treasure of stolen lives. Thetford, who despises Welbeck as an undeserving startup – a "Nabob," as he calls him – has developed a mischievous and intricate plan for exploiting the Caribbean trade restrictions of the time in order to get his hands on the money Welbeck has invested: Though the ship is fully insured, the insurance will not cover any losses if the voyage breaks the political neutrality between England

and France demanded of American ships. Thetford therefore engineers a violation of neutrality by having two mulattos plant contraband articles on the ship. When the ship is searched, its cargo is forfeited in its entirety. Welbeck, not covered by the insurance, loses his investment. Meanwhile Thetford's plan can take effect: Knowing that in the case of forfeiture, the ship's supercargo (a merchant manager who oversees the operations on board) will be offered the forfeited goods for purchase at a fraction of the original price, he has arranged for his younger brother Thomas to be the ship's supercargo. This way, Thomas gains what Welbeck has lost – a very complicated, but ultimately successful, scheme of stealing from Welbeck. The purpose of the crime, however, is not simply to sit on the money, but to establish Thetford's brother as a merchant. Thus, as both Thetford's and Welbeck's cases are designed to attest, commerce is built on the foundation of fraud; trade and theft become difficult to distinguish.[20]

The scheme of deception hinges on the particular social constellation associated, in this novel, with trade. This constellation may be thought of as a paranoid network that comes to light by bits and pieces, surprisingly revealing ever new "intricate relations."[21] Thus, Thetford can only profit from Welbeck's loss because his brother acts in the privileged position of supercargo. Acting as a node between his younger brother and Welbeck, Thetford manages to position himself at once on the side of loss and gain.

Such networks also structure the makeup of the novel itself and contribute to its extraordinarily convoluted plot. Individual characters appear and reappear, often many chapters apart and in the context of different relations. Relations, in fact, should be thought of as related stories so that we end up in a network of stories, which, to add to the confusion, often mirror each other. Arthur's tale thus consists of a multiplicity of stories that are tangled into an open-ended profusion of other people's multiple stories.[22] The more people he meets, the more he re-encounters in different relations, which come to life in the telling of yet another story.[23]

One such example is Wallace, the young man who tricked Arthur into entering Thetford's bedroom. Wallace works as an assistant to Thetford and is therefore part of the shady world of fraud. Unexpectedly, Wallace crosses Arthur's path again after Arthur has left the city and temporarily settled down on the farm of the Hadwin family. Arthur, infatuated with Hadwin's younger daughter Eliza, is also concerned for Susan, the elder daughter. Susan worries about her fiancé, who is missing somewhere in the plague-ridden city. This young man turns out to be Wallace.

In the mode of passive action, Arthur would have registered this coincidence and played out competing explanations in his mind. He would have entertained alternative positions that would have considered Wallace either an imposter and seducer, or, his reputation having been affirmed by the love of Hadwin's daughter, a more or less virtuous young man innocently drawn into Thetford's schemes. But Arthur's position vis-à-vis this network of coincidence, which links Wallace to Thetford and the Hadwins, is no longer limited to passive observation. Arthur now tries out what he has learned from schemers like Welbeck and Thetford: he intervenes into the trade-like network and attempts to manipulate events so that they will unfold according to his design. He forges a plan to sneak away from Hadwin's farm, find Wallace in the city, and bring him home safely to Susan – a hazardous endeavor that requires him to re-enter the by now fever-ridden city, but one that is nonetheless morally sanctioned, at least in his own eyes: he intends to relieve Susan of her worries about Wallace, and, moreover, he wants to save Wallace, for whom he has suddenly discovered sympathy; surely, he convinces himself now, Wallace's earlier offense was nothing but a youthful prank.

How is it possible for Arthur to begin to actively reconfigure the relation between Hadwin, his daughter Susan, Wallace, and Thetford, with himself in the position of the central node? How does Arthur manage to manipulate a network without aligning himself with the criminal schemers of the city?

Arthur's actions become legitimated as emergency measures in the mortal ravages of the yellow fever. In most readings of the novel, the yellow fever is interpreted as a metaphor of the havoc commercial capitalism wreaks on the republic.[24] While this reading has its merits, it is incomplete: building on the point I made earlier – that threat is an enabling condition for pursuing security measures; that *Fortuna* creates the possibility to rise to virtue – we can regard the yellow fever as an unexpected turn in the wheel of fortune that allows Arthur to act in ways not wholly different from a schemer in the free market, yet to do so in a selfless manner.

This opening for action is not merely a result of the plague's rendering Arthur's initiatives necessary. The disease also produces an effect of Arthur's acts that distinguishes them from the fraudulent plots of commerce. Whereas a character like Thetford designs his scheme in order to arrive at an advantageous result, the result of Arthur's scheme stands in the service of life. But working for life is not quite what one might expect it to be. *Arthur Mervyn* does not define it as an action of benevolence that will materially help others by securing their survival (a stabilization of life against physical and mental threats). Rather, working in the service of life becomes a service to uncertainty, which, I will show, the disease has elevated to the primary principle of life. From this valorization of life emerges a relation between the imagination and disease/survival that turns around how Brown scholarship has generally interpreted that relation. Rather than underlining the Enlightenment position that an unruly imagination goes hand in hand with bodily decomposition,[25] the imagination's fundamental incongruity with fact becomes the only defense of life.

Arthur initially experiences the epidemic as an imaginary construct fed by rumors. Traveling to the city, he encounters refugees who report to him tales of terror that outdo even the worst stories he had previously heard at the Hadwins'. "From every mouth the tale of sorrow was repeated with new aggravations. Pictures of their own distress, or that of their neighbours, were exhibited in all the hues which imagination can annex to pestilency and poverty" (107). Ultimately, however, his imagination of the dreadful scenes and dangers awaiting him in the city proves more attractive than repelling and compels him to proceed into the city. His imagination of disaster captivates him and drives him to an encounter with death.

Arthur blurs the line between the psychic and the physical by fearing that he has contracted the disease.[26] Panicked by the observation that the city's streets are deserted, he imaginarily relates his surroundings to himself: "Death seemed to hover over this scene, and I dreaded that the floating pestilence had already lighted on my frame" (108). Rather than incapacitating him, Arthur's reflection on his state of health pushes him forward: "This incident, instead of appalling me, tended rather to invigorate my courage. The danger which I feared had come. I might enter with indifference, on this theater of pestilence" (111). The conviction of disease – a fact of the imagination more than a physical fact – puts him in yet another state of mind, one of resolved despair: he has nothing to lose. At the same time, "nothing" is not quite absolute yet, for it will "be left to the decision of the future" whether he should "recover or perish" (111). His future now fully in the hands of *Fortuna* (the "future" deciding over the future), he can act freely, absolved from the responsibility for his fate. His imagination may have pushed him into physical disease, but the perception of physical symptoms makes accessible new avenues of action that are freed, thanks to the imagination, from the impediments of future fear.

Arthur, however, is not the only character who is fully resolved to act. His first interaction with others, upon entering Philadelphia, is with the agents of the city who act under martial law (see Gould, "Race, Commerce" 160) and whose ostensible task it is to provide order and relief. These are what we would call today security forces, and it is indeed instructive to compare the concept of security they represent with that represented by

Arthur. During the fever scenes, we meet with hearse drivers, undertakers, and the attendants at Bush-Hill hospital. The hearse drivers and undertakers are particularly revealing for the way in which the novel opposes death to life. They become figures of horror not because their presence acts as a sign of nearby victims of the fever, but because they habitually precipitate the death of those who are still suffering or who suffer from different causes.

"'It wasn't right to put him in his coffin before the breath was fairly gone,'" one undertaker says to another about a man they have just consigned to death in his coffin, only to get this chilling response: "'Pshaw! He could not live. The sooner dead the better for him; as well as for us'" (109). The recurring Gothic nightmare image of being buried alive is the result of the undertakers' assumption of the power to resolve the contingency adhering in the crisis situation of disease. Such crises – understood in the medical sense as the moment that will decide whether a patient will live or die – are moments of uncertainty and can logically be undone only by deciding in favor of death. It is crucial to specify the decision the security volunteers make. It is, strictly speaking, not between life and death, but between disease and death. Disease is a liminal moment, which may or may not result in death and which, in its undecidedness, comes to stand for the uncertainty of life itself. The agents of death – acting in a mode one might call thanatopolitical – do not look to create security by saving and promoting lives, but by looking for disease, which they push into the deathspace of the coffin and whose contingency they extinguish.[27] To evade these forces of death, disease must therefore be kept a secret and made to look like – indeed, must be redefined as – life.

This point is underlined by Arthur's own experience. When he himself is knocked unconscious while looking for Wallace in a stranger's house, he awakes inside a coffin, the last nail ready to be hammered in. He is rescued just in time by an enlightened neighbor and will do his very best to convince this man that his head wound did not result from the fever. Arthur is so absorbed in making his case that he seems to completely forget that he has not long before declared himself to have fallen victim to the fever. Arthur pleads to be left alone rather than be prematurely killed by being sent to Bush-Hill, the emergency hospital, which is presented in the novel as a huge coffin that will put to death any patient. Pressed by the enlightened neighbor, "If thou art [sick], though must consent to receive the best treatment which the times will afford … [at] the hospital at Bush-Hill" (114), he recollects, "The mention of that contagious and abhorred receptacle, inspired me with some degree of energy. No, said I, I am not sick, a violent blow reduced me to this situation" (115). His imagination is holding on to the fundamental instability of his body's future, making disease become the essence of (healthy) life.

In *Arthur Mervyn*'s thanatopolitical logic of the yellow fever, life and death become intelligible through disease. For those willing to live, disease becomes equated with life so that life is essentially contingent. For those officially tasked with the security of the living, disease is to be turned into the fait accompli of death.

The undoing of disease by the state's security agents serves as a backdrop and contrast for Arthur's own actions. Though he is initially shocked that the epidemic has shut down the regular transactions in the city – he can purchase neither lodging nor food – he soon finds that the fever is a transgressive force that can be appropriated in a way that is morally much more benign than the transgressions of commerce could ever be. Looking for Wallace, Arthur enters strangers' houses without permission, a behavior that, in times of the plague, seems well accepted: Thetford's neighbor Medlicote, for instance, freely reports having entered his neighbor's house several times. Moreover, thanks to the fever, Arthur meets people from different parts of the world (Maravegli, a merchant from Venice, who has retired to die in the very room where Arthur expected to find Wallace) and from a variety of classes and races (ranging from enlightened citizens like Eastwick and Medlicote to the lower-class, racially mixed group of hearse drivers). Given the context of benevolence that facilitates these social and physical transgressions of boundaries, this wide variety of characters must consist of people both healthy and sick: another crossing of boundaries, exemplified by Arthur, who, as we have just seen, moves quickly from one side of the divide to the other and back again. The yellow fever epidemic, in other words, allows Arthur to enter into a social circulation marked by chance meetings made possible by the emergency suspension of regulated boundaries.

Now that the plague allows him to engage in the complex social networks of the city without being polluted by the corruption of commerce, Arthur realizes that his plans are difficult to carry out therein. The principle impediment lies in the impossibility to foresee the consequences of one's actions. Brown condenses this problem around the fate of Wallace. What ensues is a dizzying sequence of unintended consequences, many of which turn out fatal. First, Arthur feels remorse for not having told Mr. Hadwin about his plan to search for Wallace in the plague-ridden city. Though he had his reasons for doing so, the unforeseen consequence is that Hadwin, not knowing about Arthur's trip, also comes to the city to search for Wallace, thus exposing himself to the risk of catching the disease. To minimize this risk, Arthur sends back Mr. Hadwin as soon as he arrives, though not without sharing the news he just received from a neighbor: Wallace has died from the fever after having been brought to Bush-Hill hospital. Later, it will turn out that Arthur's secrecy was indeed disastrous: on his superfluous trip to the city, Mr. Hadwin contracts the disease and dies before he reaches his daughters. Anticipating this worst-case outcome during his meeting with Hadwin, Arthur pledges to henceforth abstain from any secrecy. But ironically, this does not at all help him from unintentionally putting others in serious danger. Immediately after Hadwin's departure, it turns out that the information of Wallace's death was wrong: Wallace has survived Bush-Hill and returns to Thetford's house in the city, where he runs into Arthur. Now Arthur must worry that Hadwin's daughter will die from grief arising from a mistaken belief in the death of her fiancé. He therefore sends Wallace to the Hadwins'. But because he does not accompany him, he has no way of finding out whether Wallace ever makes it there. It turns out that Wallace does not. But when Arthur arrives at the Hadwins' some time later, Susan, believing her fiancé to be returning, dies from grief upon seeing that it really is Arthur.

In the mode of compelled action, the chance outcomes of transgressive deeds undertaken with good intentions are part and parcel of a politics of life that aims to sustain life as contingency.[28] Indeed, Arthur articulates a notion of virtue that is no longer a defense against disease, but that allows for the feverish embodiment of uncertainty and defines it as the antithesis of the unambiguousness of death. Arthur's disease – his contraction of it, as well as the suspicion that he might be a morally contagious force of disorder (a suspicion which he set out to disprove with his narrative) – has by now come to look less like a threat than an expression of the contingency of crisis that defines and sustains life.

2.5 Commissioned Action

In the mode of compelled action, Arthur is driven to act by the emergency of the plague, but action, it turns out, is less a purposive, linear pursuit of a particular goal than an entry into a complex circulation where input and output, cause and effect, intention and outcome are difficult to correlate in advance. In other words, while the yellow fever episode presents a version of Arthur who surpasses the passive action of entrapment and groping in the dark, the newly active Arthur is distinguished from commercial schemers pursuing goals of self-interest by the fact that action appears as participation, compelled and enabled by the medical emergency, in the circles of chance.

But the role of compelled agent is merely a transitional phase in Arthur's story, and it gives way to a mode of acting in which Brown presents Arthur as significantly more in charge. In the novel's second part, written after the publication of part 1 and published in 1800, Arthur increasingly appears as the master of his actions. It is only in the mode of action extensively tried out in this part of the novel that Brown fully takes on the challenge of imaginatively devising a solution to the republican agency dilemma. Arthur's empowerment is tied to the ways in which Brown revises the notions of "revolution" and "adventure," thus creating an explicit contrast to the earlier mode of passive action. While in the book's early chapters, revolution had been understood as a turn of the wheel of fortune to which the individual is passively exposed, Arthur now reflects "on a revolution in my mind" (221) brought about during his second visit of the city. No longer just "the chosen seats of misery and vice," cities now appear to him also as "the soil of all the laudable and strenuous productions of mind" (221). This is a world to which it is desirable to belong, and this in turn requires "direct inspection" of "the influence of manners, professions and social institutions" (221).

What here sounds like a wish to merely observe soon becomes a desire for intervening in others' lives and thereby mastering events through action: Hastening to save Clemenza Lodi, a victim of Welbeck's for whom Arthur feels responsible, he reports a "total revolution [that] had occurred in the course of a few seconds": henceforth, "my muscles trembled with eagerness, and I bounded forward with impetuosity" (236). Rushing after the "object of [his] pursuit" (236), he intrudes into the house of one Mrs. Villars, boasting, "My design will not be opposed. I have only to mount the stair, and go from one room to another, till I find what I seek" (238). This version of Arthur, revolutionized from passive to active, is justly called, by Stevens, an "adventurous youth" (170), and indeed, Arthur, in looking back on his life, now ascribes to himself an "adventurous spirit" (248). Adventure here takes a decidedly more active cast than in the early stages of his account, where it was a matter not of the spirit, but of events "meeting" Arthur in a fate-like *adventura*.[29]

In line with the moral injunction of the agency dilemma, his newly found empowerment hinges on Arthur not acting for his own advancement. He decides to make the fates of others his own, to act as if he were commissioned by duty to work in the interest of others. In most cases – especially Clemenza Lodi's – this leads him to patronize his intended beneficiaries as if they were unable to look after themselves. But this patronizing attitude can also be seen as the flip side of the rational optimism that only benevolence makes morally acceptable to embrace. This optimism promises to bring the future at least partially within the reach of his powers and is therefore at odds with his acceptance of chance in the modes of action discussed so far. Musing about what Clemenza has suffered, he concludes that "[t]he past was without remedy; but the future was, in some degree, within our power to create and to fashion" (202).

"Creating and fashioning" the future, however, poses similar problems as those he encountered in his engagement during the yellow fever. Goals are to be pursued in complex social networks. Unintended consequences are bound to thwart all rational planning. The beneficiaries of his actions, moreover, may not define their interest in the same way Arthur does. Finally, since he cannot pursue his plans all by himself, he needs to convince others to collaborate with him. His doings no longer sanctioned by the logic of emergency, he constantly comes up against the problem of authority. As a result, we observe him persuading others and thus engage in what his entire account is intended to do with his listeners and, by extension, us, the reader: to present a convincing case of his righteousness. Arthur becomes truly adept in the art of persuasion and even shares his stage tricks, as when he details how he tries to win over Eliza Hadwin's infuriated uncle:

> There was but one mode for me to pursue; all forcible opposition to a man of his strength was absurd. It was my province to make his anger confine itself to words, and patiently to wait till the paroxysm should end or subside of itself. To effect this purpose, I kept my seat, and carefully excluded from my countenance every indication of timidity and panic on the one hand, and of scorn and defiance on the other. (229)

Remarkably, Arthur's strategy of persuasion depends on gestures and facial expressions much more than on the content of his words. But the rehearsed physicality of his performance – what we may call his face value – is regarded by his listeners as the unfalsifiable expression of sincerity. Just as Stevens initially trusts Arthur on account of "the uniform complacency and rectitude of his deportment" (12), he later, upon hearing new accusations against Arthur, renews his trust in Arthur's performance: "As long as the impression, made by his tones, gestures and looks, remained in my memory ... suspicion was impossible ... the face of Mervyn is the index of an honest mind" (175). Indeed, Stevens hinges his entire capacity of judgment on the trustworthiness of Arthur's face: "If Mervyn has deceived me, there is an end to my confidence in human nature. All limits to dissimulation, and all distinctness between vice and virtue will be effaced" (190).

Arthur, on the other hand, is acutely realistic about the fact that "looks and professions ... may be dissembled" (245), and he displays a cheerful self-confidence about his persuasive powers of performance. When Welbeck, repenting on his deathbed, entrusts to Arthur the family fortune of the Maurice family, which Welbeck himself has stolen from a girdle attached to Watson's buried corpse, Arthur decides to deliver the money to Mrs. Maurice. He is convinced in the righteousness of this plan, which consummates the "commission [that was] punctually performed" by Watson, but then stopped short by his death in a duel with Welbeck (185). Though Stevens expresses doubts whether Arthur's adopting Watson's commission will not confront him with new accusations of criminal complicity, Arthur's calm cannot be ruffled: "These are evils, but I see not how an ingenuous and open conduct is adapted to increase these evils. If they come, I must endure them" (262).

Arthur is caught up here in the paradox of the idea of ingenuous and artless conduct. On the one hand, artlessness is precisely the ideal of virtuous behavior. But because such behavior is defined as disinterested, claims to artlessness expose themselves to the suspicion of artfulness, of behavior that is in truth studied and therefore self-interested.[30] This problem is compounded for Arthur because in laying open his strategies of persuasion, his artlessness goes so far as to openly admit the artfulness of artlessness.

Before the onset of the recent historico-political turn that has insisted on Arthur's straight-faced credibility[31] – a model to be emulated by the reader – critics often pointed out how difficult it is made by contradictions and paradoxes like these to tell Arthur Mervyn apart from a confidence man and sharper.[32] This earlier line of readings continues to be valuable in my eyes, provided that the point of such discussions does not lie in coming to a decision on whether Arthur is worthy or unworthy of trust.[33] Arthur's case is rather instructive about the search for solutions to the early republic's moral problem of having to find ways of engaging in an increasingly commercialized world in ways that are recognizably disinterested – which, in *Arthur Mervyn*, creates the sequence of propositions leading from passive action to compelled action and finally to commissioned action.

Seen from a different perspective, however, the problematic requirement made of Arthur to act disinterestedly creates the opportunity for his listeners and readers to engage in conjecture about motives and thus permit romance as conceptualized by Brown to fulfill its purpose. Conjecture about Arthur's motives presupposes that motives are not transparently deducible from visible actions. If conjecture about Arthur's motives becomes increasingly pressing the more active he becomes, then observing him must entail an acute sensibility of the problem of unintended consequences, that is, of the incongruence between invisible motive and visible outcome.

As far as the immediate story goes, the problem of unintended consequences seems designed to underline Arthur's innocence by attributing his deeds to coincidence. "How slender are these [my] powers!" (248), Arthur laments about his failure to carry out his plans, thereby conveniently abnegating responsibility for his actions. Unintended consequences, however, must not only explain the danger to which Arthur exposes others while trying to do them good (as when Mrs. Watson collapses upon learning that Arthur has come to unexpectedly restore a large sum of money to her), but also to the surprising benefits accruing to Arthur. This happens both on the level of details and broad developments of plot. Arthur unexpectedly gains a comfortable reward of one thousand dollars from delivering the money to the Maurice family (not without having to fight for it in court, however), and he finds a wealthy and educated wife, Achsa Fielding, who affords him to spend his life in the disinterested leisure of study and enlightened conversation, or, put more morosely, in idle luxury.

In his *Enquiry Concerning Political Justice*, William Godwin had articulated a consequentialist conception of virtue that insists that "intention no doubt is of the essence of virtue. But it will not do alone. . . . Intention is of no further value than as it leads to utility: it is the means, and not the end (*Enquiry* 74). Throughout *Arthur Mervyn*, this consequentialist stance is rejected. Rather than opposing intentions to outcomes as means and ends, intentions in the novel appear as projections of outcomes, and means are the measures adopted to fashion the future according to the intention. The choice of suitable means, however, remains a matter of educated guesswork. This becomes particularly clear by Arthur's reflection on his search for Wallace during the fever, at a point when he has just sent Wallace, freshly returned from Bush-Hill hospital, to the Hadwins' farm and then lost track of him.

> My purpose was just, and the means which I selected, were the best my limited knowledge supplied. My happiness should be drawn from reflecting on the equity of my intentions. That these intentions were frustrated by the ignorance of others, or my own, was the consequence of human frailty. Honest purposes, though they may not bestow happiness on others, will, at least, secure it to him who fosters them. (205)

There are good reasons for taking Arthur's words at face value here, not the least of which being that his argument receives the approbation of his enlightened companions as the novel proceeds towards its strangely happy ending. Arthur recognizes human ignorance, or frailty, as part of the human condition, not as a transitional shortcoming that can be improved and surmounted with the accumulation of experience. For this reason, the arrival at desired outcomes simply cannot be guaranteed.

In a move as radical as it is disconcerting, Arthur absolves himself from the responsibility for the outcomes of his actions to such a degree that outcomes seems to cease to matter altogether. Not knowing whether Wallace has survived the trip to the Hadwins' farm on which Arthur has sent him, Arthur reports: "I prepared to rejoice alike, whether Wallace should be found to have escaped or to have perished" (205). If this sounds like the opposite of sympathy, it is not meant to be: Arthur's – and Brown's – position simply insists that sympathy, too, cannot extend beyond intention. The novel, it should be noted, bears out Arthur's stance in a way that is easily overlooked but all the more chilling upon close reading: After Arthur's decision not to care about Wallace's fate any longer, Wallace simply disappears from the novel, save for a casual mention of "the death of Wallace" a few pages later (209). He has ceased to be a matter of concern – and therefore ceases to be – because his fate from here on is mere outcome and no longer a matter of intention.

It would be possible, of course, to argue that Arthur's extreme anti-consequentialism is the surest sign that we are in fact dealing with a confidence man. Indeed, throughout his best-selling 1798 *Memoirs*, Stephen Burroughs, the most infamous confidence man of Brown's time, resorts to the same argument in order to justify his long list of crimes, ranging from forgery and fraud to jailbreak and sexual harassment (possibly rape). All these crimes, he claims, are the unfortunate outcomes of good intentions, a utilitarian catastrophe of happiness thwarted by the unhappy interventions of chance.

> Those very means which we make use of to answer our purposes of promotion and exaltation are often the direct and only causes of our calamity. We all wish to be happy, and all use such means to obtain happiness as our judgment points out. From daily experience we learn how incompetent we are, to form right estimates of the various effects which will follow the measures we pursue. (Burroughs, *Memoirs* 268)

Rather than take the obvious parallels between Mervyn's and Burroughs's anti-consequentialism as a sign that Mervyn is yet another confidence man (possibly even modeled on Burroughs), I suggest that Burroughs's recourse to this strategy of defense indicates its potential acceptability and plausibility at the time. Brown's novel is in dialogue with Burroughs's memoir by transferring the anti-consequentialist apologia to the domain of fiction, thereby suspending judgment of his character and turning it into an occasion for conjecture and estimation that is ultimately as insecure as Mervyn's/Burroughs's judgment in choosing the means to achieve happiness. In other words, while Burroughs bemoans how chance ruins the attempt at virtuous behavior, Brown goes a decisive step further and elevates the acceptance of chance to the foundation of virtue.

The three modes of action Arthur Mervyn tries out throughout the novel are all supposed to highlight his disinterestedness. Since the failure to control outcomes of actions is regarded as a proof of disinterestedness, the novel's moral universe all but rules out that the commercial strife for profit might be related to action under the conditions of uncertainty. The failure to move from good intentions to desired result becomes the antithesis to commercial activities, because the novel defines the latter as schemes in which agents successfully and methodically pursue their own interests, starting with an egotistical intention and ending with the desired outcome of profit.

Indeed, at least among the novel's voices of rational enlightenment, there is no awareness of the fact that the principle uncertainty regarding future outcomes may have anything to do with market behavior. Only Wortley, who throughout the novel loses much of his standing with the enlightened Dr. Stevens as his involvement in finance capitalism comes to light, expresses an awareness of the dependence of capitalist markets on chance: "Happily you are a stranger to mercantile anxieties and revolutions," he tells Stevens. "Your fortune does not rest on a basis which an untoward blast may sweep away, or four strokes of a pen may demolish" (174).

Wortley's anxieties, however, have their source less in the vagaries of finance capitalism than in finance capitalists' vulnerability to fraud carried out by individual rogues. A case in point, Wortley's anxieties specifically refer to Welbeck's forging checks by changing the amount stated on them from 800 to 1,800. The anxiety caused by paper money rests on the fact that the assigned value of a note may be manipulated. It does not involve an awareness that values in a credit economy of paper money are necessarily unstable even if no one willfully manipulates checks; that, indeed, instability does not arise from the falsification of an otherwise stable relation between a piece of paper and the real value it represents, but rather from money's nonrepresentational and self-referential nature.

The novel thus misrecognizes the way in which its promotion of the virtue of uncertainty makes virtue compatible with market principles. The reason for this misrecognition seems to lie in Brown's moral stance regarding the theories of markets available at the time. As conceptualized by a line of thought extending from Bernard Mandeville to Adam Smith, the market contains a mechanism for balancing out individually pursued interests – Smith's famous "invisible hand," which leads the self-interested actor to "promote an end which was no part of his intention" (Smith, *Wealth of Nations* I: 421).[34] Thus, if the individual market actor, in caring only for his own interest, is blind to the interests of the common good, this appears not as a problem but rather as an advantage, because the market's balancing capacities are sure to create an equilibrium that weds self-interested endeavor with the disinterested demands of the public good, or common wealth. It is a solution that seems tailor-made for Brown's non-consequentialist position: it approves of unintended consequences by invoking a mechanism (the invisible hand) that guarantees such unintended consequences to be in the interest of the public and thus disinterested.

But Brown, perhaps out of deep-seated republican convictions, rejects the doctrine of the emerging economic liberalism. *Arthur Mervyn* presents the schemes of transnationally operating merchants like Thetford and Welbeck as self-interested, and in the moral universe of *Arthur Mervyn*, self-interest remains associated with vice. But precisely because it insists on the equation of commerce with self-interest, Brown's novel is able to promote a notion of disinterested virtue (which he locates strictly outside economic transactions) that is steeped in uncertainty and seems surprisingly compatible with the principles of market capitalism as they appear today. From today's perspective, capitalism is a high-risk system in which future developments are fundamentally uncertain. Though over the last decades the capitalist system has been directed toward drastically increasing economic inequality (in that sense, it is foreseeable: the rich become richer), on the level of the individual transaction and larger development of the markets, the illusions of efficiency and of the possibility to effectively hedge bets have been crushed. Market capitalism once again appears as a domain of luck much more than as the arena in which self-interested intentions can be steered with certainty to their desired outcomes.

In *Arthur Mervyn*, by contrast, the economic and the social dimension seem to be characterized by entirely different principles: markets are arenas of self-interest and thus full of vice, but in noneconomic social interactions uncertainty abounds, the systematic pursuit of self-interest is rendered impossible, and virtue has a real chance. It is on the basis of this differentiation that Brown comes to regard uncertainty as the portal to disinterestedness. To put it in yet another way, only because in *Arthur Mervyn* uncertainty does not appear as the foundation of capitalism, can it become the principle of a new kind of virtue.

2.6 Romance Undoing Romance

Arthur Mervyn ends on a note unusually happy compared with Brown's other novels. As Arthur is united with the Jewish immigrant heiress Achsa Fielding, all threats seem to be resolved and order is solidly reinstated. The yellow fever is long past; Arthur's reputation is firmly established; his financial insecurities, which drove him to the city in the first place, are resolved by Achsa's wealth. Though Achsa's father originally gained his fortune from trade, it now allows for a life of leisure at a safe distance from the vulgar considerations of profit. The project of security has found its fulfillment in the *sine cura* of romance.

On the way to this end, the novel takes a metafictional turn, with the effect of putting into question the sustainability of the virtue of uncertainty as well as of the literary text. While the largest part of the novel is presented as Dr. Stevens's oral rendition of the report Arthur has given of himself, the fictional author of the final section of part 2 is Arthur himself. The existence of the text we are reading is now explained as commissioned by Mrs. Wentworth, one of the characters who initially suspected Arthur of criminal complicity in Welbeck's affairs but who in the course of Arthur's performance has been won over as a friend. Mrs. Wentworth asks Arthur for a "written narrative" of his life. This will complete the written version of the report which Stevens originally gave orally and in the meantime has written down.

Adopting the narrative logic of the epistolary novel, Arthur, acting as the author and protagonist of his story, must end the account of his life as the events catch up with the present moment of writing. The novel's ending thus becomes a leave-taking of the protagonist from the pen with which he has been creating, autopoietically as it were, his fictional world:

> But why am I indulging this pen-prattle? The hour [Achsa] fixed for my return to her is come, and now take thyself away, quill. Lie there, snug in thy leathern case, till I call for thee, and that will not be very soon. I believe I will abjure thy company till all is settled with my love. Yes; I will abjure

thee; so let this be thy last office, till Mervyn has been made the happiest of men.

In these final lines, Arthur is in the middle of a strange encounter with his pen. More is at stake than the official reasoning that there is no more time to write or read, now that his wedding nears and his future with Achsa is about to begin. A pen that needs to be put to rest until Arthur "has been made the happiest of men" stands in a troublesome relation to happiness. It is as if happiness needed to be secured before Arthur can risk releasing the pen from its box.

Considering Arthur's story, the pen's role as antagonist of happiness makes perfect sense. It was the pen that initially got him into trouble: writing, or rather copying, was his only marketable skill and allowed him to become Welbeck's amanuensis. Indeed, copying and other falsifications of the pen lay at the core of Welbeck's business, whether it concerned his plan to plagiarize a potentially profitable manuscript left by the deceased Lodi, or the forgery of bills and checks.

But writing is not only hostile to happiness on the level of plot. As the union of author and protagonist indicates, the plot and the text fictionally become one and the same. The pen is not just the tool that has rendered Arthur's life suspicious; it is also the instrument that has created the text at hand, a text that exists in order to relate a network of stories. As the pen copies bills and checks, it also creates stories of forged bills and checks. And these stories stand in an antagonistic relation to *happiness*, to the worry-free state of security: they relate things that have *happened*, upsetting order, giving cause to worry and care. In other words, stories can be told only when things happen that contradict the state of happiness. The reverse is also true: as Arthur begins to experience the security of happiness, he becomes drawn into the domain of the unnarratable and must stop telling stories. Indeed, he seems to lose the ability to do so.[35] He can no longer relate how time has passed, what has happened. Here is his account of uneventful happiness in the circle of his friends Fanny Maurice and Mrs. Watson:

> This intercourse was strangely fascinating. My heart was buoyed up by a kind of intoxication. I now found myself exalted to my genial element, and began to taste the delights of existence. In the intercourse of ingenuous and sympathetic minds, I found a pleasure which I had not previously conceived.
>
> The time flew swiftly away, and a fortnight passed almost before I was aware that a day had gone by. I did not forget the friends whom I had left behind, but maintained a punctual correspondence with Stevens, to whom I imparted all occurrences. (289)

It is not just that these two weeks chanced to be uneventful. And it is not that communication among the circle of friends has stopped. The conversations are "strangely fascinating," and they are regularly extended to Stevens by letter. But things are taking their course in an orderly manner. The time with his friends has produced no suspicions, no deviations from expectation, no questions of motives, no conjecture – in other words, no romance. And this end of romance is exactly what the romance of the happy ending must bear out. In putting away his pen, Arthur is preparing to enjoy his nuptial happiness by moving beyond what Brown takes to be the essence of romance: the conjectural constructions, steeped in the ultimate uncertainty of probability, of the connections between cause and effect, past and future, motive and action, and intention and consequence.

In unwriting the world's fictional double, *Arthur Mervyn* seeks to reinstate a concept of security of perfect order and harmony: a world without events and hence without stories. It is a desperate attempt to undo the unleashing of the imagination that came with the doubling of the world in fiction. In this sense, the end of the novel anticipates Brown's decision, made just one year after the completion of *Arthur Mervyn*'s second part, to abandon the genre of the novel altogether.

Brown, however, could not erase his novel, and if Arthur's victory over his pen completes the trajectory of a *Bildungsroman*, his education nonetheless consists in a virtuous *ars conjectandi*. Against its final wishes, security in *Arthur Mervyn* does not begin with the end of romance (and the consummation of love), but with the challenge to develop a world made up of stories that are merely probable. If not for long, Brown dared to imagine that republican security begins and ends in uncertainty. In this vision, security cannot afford any epistemological certainty, but may form the basis of a moral order and thus secure the virtuous republic in a way that is attuned to the centrifugal dynamics of the modern world.

CHAPTER 3

Harriet Jacobs's Imagined Community of Insecurity

After Linda Brent, the pseudonymous protagonist of Harriet Jacobs's *Incidents in the Life of a Slave Girl* (1861), has successfully escaped from slavery, what awaits her in the North contradicts the expectations set up by the narrative thrust of her story. "I called myself free, and sometimes felt so; but I knew I was insecure" (912). Insecurity instead of freedom: this, Jacobs's slave narrative makes clear, is the essence of the fugitive's experience. In *Incidents*, insecurity grows out of the legal status of the fugitive slave, who finds herself in limbo between enslavement and freedom: no longer under the direct power of a master, the fugitive in the antebellum United States, particularly after the passage of the Fugitive Slave Law of 1850, is nonetheless without protection by the law. But as I will show in this chapter, insecurity actually encompasses several dimensions of being: legal, ontological, and affective.

In fleshing out this multidimensionality of insecurity, Jacobs does more than *represent* the paradigmatic condition of female fugitive slaves. Insecurity rather becomes the ground on which Jacobs's narrating voice assumes an authority that topples the hierarchical order of sympathy sanctioned by sentimental abolitionism, a hierarchy in which sympathetic whites feel for blacks while retaining their sense of superiority. As I will show, at some critical moments Jacobs extends the referent of her representativeness as a fugitive beyond "her class" and thus instantiates a transracial collective united in its antagonism and subjection to "the slave power." Jacobs's text reinforces an argument I aim to establish throughout my readings, namely that in American literature rhetorical invocations of security gain compelling force by staging scenes of insecurity. While this is first and foremost an aesthetic argument, Jacobs's slave narrative stands apart from the other texts in this study precisely because she not only exploits the aesthetic and philosophical potentials of insecurity but actively politicizes the state of being threatened by calling into being an imagined community of insecurity.

In my introductory chapter, I argued that security is marked by an "expedient fictionality," which allows people to credulously commit to the attainment of future security in the face of threat, despite knowing that security is a receding horizon that will never be realized. This "ironic credulity," I further suggested, is accentuated by the reading experience of narrative fiction, where the investment in counterfactuals is pragmatically freed from considerations of real-life consequences. Logically tying security to fictionality in this manner raises the question whether a nonfictional genre, such as the slave narrative, similarly allows the reader to bracket the real-life consequences of the imaginary encounter with threat.

In the antebellum period, fiction and nonfiction were not differentiated to the same extent they would be later: an openly fictional novel like Harriet Beecher Stowe's *Uncle Tom's Cabin* could be meaningfully accused of misrepresenting slavery, as if it were a documentary text – and Stowe, in turn, deemed it necessary to reconfirm the truthfulness of her fiction by backing it up with a volume of documentary evidence: *A Key to Uncle Tom's Cabin*, published in 1853. The rise of fictionality in its full modern meaning had yet to occur. And no matter whether literature was fictional or not, it was conceptualized as an intervention in the public sphere.[1]

In terms of insecurity, this meant that threats and dangers represented in the text had to be read as having a basis in the shared present of the readers, even if a given literary text was fictional. If reform literature was meant to reform the world represented in that literature, then the threats staged in slave narratives had to be understood as real. One hundred and fifty years after the abolition of slavery, we of course still can imaginarily experience the insecurity faced by fugitive slaves, even if there are no longer fugitives who fear recapture by southern slaveholders. But it is also the case that today these texts carry the trace of their erstwhile embeddedness in their public. For this reason, I approach Jacobs's text as a set of rhetorical maneuvers geared at specific effects in the antebellum public sphere of the United States.

3.1 Slave Subjectivity, Part I: The Slave's Chances

The remarkable fact that Jacobs describes her condition in terms of insecurity only once she reaches the North (as does Frederick Douglass in his 1845 *Narrative*) would seem to invite the application to the slave of an argument I have developed in the introduction: security and insecurity emerge as problems for the subject of modernity; they are concepts that rely on a certain degree of agency, even autonomy, to shape one's life, surroundings, and future. Security only becomes a problem once there is no longer a social, political, and divine order whose authority must be taken for granted. In this sense, security and insecurity would seem to be logically excluded from the life of the slave: while the slave is in the hands of the master and thus constantly in danger of being injured, raped, and killed, she has no access to the future of her life.

However, this somewhat axiomatic tenet becomes complicated in slave narratives, since it is one of the genre's main points to emphasize that slavery failed at total subjection. This is borne out by the simple fact that slaves resolved to escape. How do we square the fact that insecurity becomes a topos for slave narrators only once they have turned into fugitives, with the observation that slave narrators must have already conceived of the future as shapeable in order to flee in the first place? To address this question, I begin by looking at Jacobs's representation of enslaved subjectivity and subsequently turn to Jacobs's staging of insecurity as the fugitive's condition.

Most of the critical attention generated by Jacobs's narrative has focused on her sexual history: the continuous abuse and threats of rape by her owner, Dr. Flint (in real life, Dr. James Norcom), and her decision to "give" herself to another white man, Mr. Sands (Samuel Tredwell Sawyer), a lawyer, politician, and social superior to Flint, and the father of her children. Indeed, the scene in which Jacobs relates her decision to enter a sexual relationship with Sawyer (the reader never finds out whether the relationship could be called romantic, or whether Jacobs desired Sawyer) is central to the entire narrative, since it structures Jacobs's appeals to her readers throughout the text. Because of her sexual relationship with Sawyer, Jacobs speaks as a woman who had to be considered a sinner and a fallen woman by the dominant moral standards of her time. Jacobs acknowledges and affirms the sexual morality of her middle-class readers – and demands their sympathy on the grounds that slavery has barred her from virtuous womanhood: "It is deemed a crime in her to wish to be virtuous" (776).[2]

Explaining her decision to enter a union with Sawyer, Jacobs can sound outright contradictory. On the one hand, she emphasizes repeatedly that she acted voluntarily: "I knew what I did, and I did it with *deliberate calculation*" (800, my emphasis). On the other hand, she insists that her sufferings under Flint severely curtailed her agency. From this perspective, Jacobs appears as completely subject to another, abandoned by anyone who might come to her help. She acts out of despair and is hardly in control of her doing: "You never knew what it is to be a slave; to be entirely unprotected by law or custom; to have the laws reduce you to the condition of a chattel, *entirely subject to the will of another*" (801).

To some degree, the contradiction between her professed rational deliberation and powerlessness can indeed be resolved: what slavery takes away from her is the capacity to act morally, not because she is deficient in morality, but because in emergency situations such as those experienced by slaves, survival takes precedence over morality. Facing the gravest threats, the slave cannot but make use of goal-oriented rationality. Jacobs has her uncle, named Benjamin in the narrative, make this very point. Having fled, Benjamin gets caught, returned to his master, and imprisoned. During a visit of his mother, he responds to her query whether he thought of God during his flight: "'No, I did not think of him. When a man is hunted like a wild beast he forgets there is a God, a heaven. He forgets every thing in his struggle to get beyond the reach of the bloodhounds'" (768).

Jacobs's narrative exemplifies the fact that whereas the *fugitive* is preoccupied with the problem of insecurity, the *slave*'s life is determined by problems of agency that are rendered in the language of risk. Maurice S. Lee has elaborated on the fact that slave narrators routinely capture the decision-making process that leads to flight by employing the idiom of risk and the calculation of chance:

> From "Box" Brown's "calculating the chances of danger," to the Crafts, who (misquoting Shakespeare) remind their readers to "judge of probabilities," to the Georgia fugitive John Brown, who makes a "calculation to run away" and "turn[s] over in [his] mind the chances," slave narrators seldom depend utterly on providence or see the world as so random as to be beyond human manipulation. Instead they make the most of their limited knowledge and agency and run the risks of escape. That they must highlight their ability to judge and manage chance testifies to a racist ideology that denied them such capacities, and that their highlighting must be highlighted today suggests that probabilistic thinking is something modern readers take for granted in human beings. (97)[3]

Faced with a power regime legally endorsed to control all aspects of the slave's life, the slave is forced into risky calculations aimed at the self's removal from the master. While the fugitive – who has already succeeded in the risky venture of flight – finds herself in a state that is thoroughly pervaded by insecurity, the slave, positioned under the master's purview, engages in a risky wager that puts life and death in the balance.

Risk is a meaningful idiom for the subjectivity of the slave because it emphasizes the binary structure of either/or. From the slave's perspective, life presents itself as either enslaved or free; correspondingly, risk depends on a calculation of the future that will result in either gain or loss. For the fugitive, on the other hand, the binary distinction between life and death, freedom and slavery, turns out to have been a misconception. The category of risk (centered on an event perceived as imminent and decisive) therefore becomes replaced by insecurity, which describes a state (rather than an event) that is pervasive and seemingly endless.

One should note, however, that while the dominant variant of risk calculation is economic – based on future gains or losses – the stakes of the slave narrators' risk discourse are life and death. If assessing possible gains and losses resulting from one's calculation of the future concern life and death, the calculation itself begins to change. Risk calculations depend on a future that is open (only the uncertain future can yield gains); for the slave, however, the future's openness is itself the object of the calculation. More precisely, it is the open future that must be regained from a power constellation built on the foreclosure of the slave's future. In his 1845 *Narrative*, Frederick Douglass recalls his master admonishing him that "I must lay out no plans for the future. He said, if I behaved myself properly, he would take care of me. Indeed, he advised me to complete thoughtlessness of the future, and taught me to depend solely upon him for happiness" (*Narrative* 352). Yet, thoughtlessness of the future is precisely what Douglass rejects in continuing "to think, and to think about the injustice of my enslavement, and the means of escape" (352).

Tim Armstrong has recently argued that foreclosure is a temporal logic that grows out of slavery and extends into twentieth-century African-American literature. Modeled on the slave whom slave law considered either an article of total possession or a human being who owed his labor to the master,[4] the black subject, in Armstrong's reading, is always already conceived as indebted and in canceling that debt will live up to and repeat socially set expectations that keep the future from opening up:

> If, in its traditional attachment to the rise of the bourgeoisie, narrative in the novel depends, in economic terms, on a hermeneutic equivalent of investment and hope (on 'Great Expectations' fulfilled; on that personal 'growth' of the bildungsroman), then foreclosure is a denial of the possibilities of a forward investment in the self. The subject can only hope to pay its debts, or see them called in, enacting an already prepared narrative enclosure. (*Logic* 52–53)

Clearly, however, the slave narrative *does* make use of the *Bildungsroman* template. But we might say that the forward investment of the slave's self must be won against the forces of foreclosure operative in chattel slavery, forces that aim to deprive the slave of the future. If risk calculations are a sign of a modern attitude toward the future that is remarkably tolerant of – and even dependent on – uncertainty, Jacobs, before her flight, encounters the uncertainty of risk against the backdrop of a lethal threat. The precise nature of this threat is important here: it is not so much that in the risky endeavor of escape the prospect of (re-)enslavement appears as lethal because it necessarily leads to physical destruction, though that fate is by no means unlikely. Rather, the future of a life in chains is perceived as fatal because it disallows any hope for change, transformation, and uncertainty. In other words, a life in slavery is a life divested of futurity. The slave's risk calculation aims to gain access to a life that is open to the risky forward investment in the self. Put differently, the risky decision to flee confronts the slave with an uncertain outcome. If things go wrong, the uncertainty of risk-taking will be resolved by the absolute loss of uncertainty. As the slave recognizes uncertainty to constitute the essence of life, the possibility of losing the uncertainty of the future becomes a matter of life and death. Risk, for the slave, can thus be thought of as *meta-risk*: flight amounts to the assumption of risk. In the case of failure, the price will be the foreclosure of further risk-taking. The slave risks access to risk.

But the stakes are high in the slave's risk calculation not only because the potential loss results in the foreclosure of futurity but also because by the mid-nineteenth century freedom itself had come to be conceptualized increasingly in terms of risk. As Jonathan Levy has shown with admirable lucidity, the legal debates surrounding insurance law had defined personhood as the ability to assume one's risk (see *Freaks of Fortune*, chapter 2). Whether in maritime law or workers' compensation cases, agency and subjectivity appeared as the ability to foresee the future, calculate uncertainties, commodify them as risk, and, if so desired, sell them to third parties. By the same token, famous legal cases involving slave ships established that the slave was defined as an entity whose risk could only be borne by another person. Freedom was being articulated "in a commercial vernacular, which implied that to be unfree was for another man to own your risk, while to be free was to own that risk yourself" (49).

This opened the door to the argument that if the slave exercised the same foresight as the free person and fled from a plantation or started an insurrection, she in effect assumed the risk of her person. The conclusion was legally scandalous because it revealed the contradiction inherent in what Aristotle called "thinking property": property could transform itself into free persons. In the most famous of the nineteenth-century maritime insurance cases involving slave cargo – the lawsuit following the insurrection on board the *Creole*, in 1841 – both the legal counsel of the insurance company, Judah P. Benjamin, and Justice Henry Adams Bullard, who presided over the case at the Louisiana Supreme Court, argued that the slaves who had started the insurrection were not covered by the insurance policy because they had acted as free men. As Levy summarizes Benjamin's argument, "By foreseeing a probable chance, acting upon it, and becoming responsible for the event afterward, the *Creole* slaves simply did what free men do" (51). Assuming their risk, they had taken it from their masters. Hence it could no longer be insured by the masters. Justice Bullard (like Benjamin anything but an antislavery proponent) essentially followed this line of argument. As he saw it, the rebelling slaves acted with the foresight characteristic of risk owners: the insurrection was "brought about so suddenly, and yet with such evident readiness of preparation at the first signal, as to leave no doubt that the arms used were already loaded, and the plot formed" (qtd. in Levy, *Freaks* 56). Having come about by actions of risk-taking subjects, the loss suffered during the insurrection was therefore not covered by the insurance policy. The *Creole* case demonstrates the non-metaphorical ramifications of risk-taking for the slave: the risky decision to resist enslavement could under certain circumstances bring about legally recognized freedom because capitalist society had begun to legally define freedom precisely as the ability to take risks. But the political power realities made such recognition highly unlikely. With a high degree of probability, the slave's risk-taking ended up re-enslaving the resisting slave in ways (for instance by putting house slaves on tightly controlled plantations) that made future risk-taking significantly more difficult. The prospective gain of freedom was counterbalanced by the prospective loss of uncertainty. For these reasons, taking risks for the slave was of existential import.

We find this existential register throughout Jacobs's ruminations on risk. After having fled from the Flints' plantation, she exchanges messages with her family from her first place of hiding (which she does not identify in the text, most likely in order to protect her benefactors, who have become burdened with sharing her risk). To her family's pleas to return to Flint "and let him make an example of me," she responds by stating her resolve, made "upon [starting] this hazardous undertaking," "that there should be no turning back" (844). Bolstering her determination by quoting Patrick Henry – "'Give me liberty, or give me death,' was my motto" (844) – she not only appropriates the symbolic capital of aligning her struggle with that of the Founding Fathers but also points to the difference between the hyperbolic poetics of Revolutionary discourse and its allegedly literal meaning for the slave.[5]

In a related manner, risk is invoked when Linda's brother William (John Jacobs) decides to flee from Mr. Sands, who has in the meantime purchased him from Flint. Sands presents himself as a benevolent master who promises to set William free after a certain number of years. Nonetheless, during a trip to the North William escapes. As William later explains to Linda, trusting Sands would have meant putting himself at the mercy of incalculable contingencies that might well have returned him to a plantation existence. As Linda reports, "I knew that his master had promised to give him his freedom, but no time had been specified. Would William trust to a slave's chances?" (877). "A slave's chances" does not just refer to any kind of future uncertainty; they arise from the uncertainties of being alienable property. Neither do the slave master's promises have any binding effect, nor can the master's good intentions help the slave in the event of his unexpected death (in which case his slaves are passed down to his heirs[6]) or in case he becomes indebted and is forced to sell his slaves. Linda lays out this rationale in a telling image:

> *He looked at his hands, and remembered that they were once in irons.* What security had he that they would not be so again? Mr. Sands was kind to him; but he might indefinitely postpone the promise he had made to give him his freedom. He might come under pecuniary embarrassments, and his property be seized by creditors; or he might die, without making any arrangements in his favor. He had too often known such accidents to happen to slaves who had kind masters, and he wisely resolved to make sure of the present opportunity to own himself. (880, my emphasis)

A slave's chances constitute a type of contingency that comes with the status of alienable property and that can at any moment cancel out the contingency attached to futurity. There is no security here for the slave as long as he or she is in the hands of the master: even if treated well for the time being, the slave faces a future with his or her hands in irons. The shackled bondsman – an icon widely distributed in abolitionist material culture[7] – here takes on a particular significance: the slave whose tied hands condemn him to passivity becomes tied to the logic of foreclosure. But if a future of passivity is one whose futurity has been foreclosed, then the contingency of the future presupposes a position endowed with a modicum of agency. This is remarkable, since contingency might be understood as an expression of a position of passivity: we are helplessly subject to what might happen. But in Jacobs's text, a future endowed with contingency depends on having one's hands free: a particular freedom that has less to do with the *homo faber* (the traditional connotation of power over one's hands) than with being able to literally manage or manipulate (though by definition not control) what the future might bring. Without having one's hands in it, what will happen in the future cannot be said to constitute a future proper.

On a philological note, it is interesting that Jacobs here uses the term "security" (understood as a guarantee, and thus in line with the term's financial usage predominant at her time), but not "insecurity." As I have said before, she reserves "insecurity" for the experience in the North; the term describes a type of uncertainty the slave experiences *after* having taken the risk of flight from bondage, i.e., after having reached what should, according to the logic underlying the calculation of risk, amount to freedom. But as long as the slave has not reached that anticlimactic state, he or she is in the hands of the master as property barred from access to the future. If this type of existential precariousness is encapsulated in "trusting a slave's chances," the way out can only be by taking the chance of flight, "mak[ing] sure of the ... opportunity to own [one]self." To put it differently, in view of the slave's chances, taking a risk is always a gamble with the futurity that sets apart life from the living death of slavery – which is set in the timelessness of foreclosed futures – but not taking such risk is no less dangerous than taking it.[8]

3.2 Slave Subjectivity, Part II: The War of Her Life

Slavery, however, by no means reduces Linda's being in the world to an emergency logic that merely attends to the immediate needs of staying alive, inside of temporality. Jacobs's presentation of slave life in North Carolina is in fact marked by determination and willpower, which attests to the slaves' unwillingness to accept the status of being property. Jacobs may appeal to her readers by asking them to imagine what it is like to be completely subject to the will of another, but this kind of subjection does not in fact capture the defiance cultivated – both as an attitude and mode of action – by the female and male members of Jacobs's circle in Edenton, North Carolina.

Throughout her time in the South, Linda makes legible that the paradox of "thinking property" resides in the fact that it will not think of itself as property, but instead identify thinking with will and exercise that will by resisting the very designation of property. "The war of my life had begun," Linda explains at one point, "and though one of God's most powerless creatures, I resolved never to be conquered" (764). Her master's power, indeed, utterly fails to subdue her. On the contrary, it strengthens her own willpower by providing her with something to grow by. After a confrontation with Flint she writes, "My master had power and law on his side; I had a determined will. There is might in each" (831). Being property, therefore, appears as an alterable and potentially temporary position, not an identity.

It is remarkable that in Jacobs's Edenton community, virtually all of those closest to her are in the process of moving out of slavery, even if that requires strategically playing along with the system of ownership in the person. Martha, Linda's grandmother (Molly in real life), first effectively buys herself by providing a benevolent white woman with the funds to purchase her and then set her free. And once a free woman, Martha undertakes to free some of her children by purchasing them. Thus, the former slave woman buys her own son, Phillip, and liberates him through a financial transaction. Enslavement, the family members tell each other, can be undone by willpower, and remaining a slave is a willful decision, too: "The happy mother and son sat together by the old hearthstone that night, telling how proud they were of each other, and how they would prove to the world that they could take care of themselves, as they had long taken care of others. We all concluded by saying, 'He that is *willing* to be a slave, let him be a slave'" (773). The sentence takes to its radical conclusion the ascription of agency to the slave: ultimately, the slave is complicit in his or her own enslavement. The point here is not to blame the victims, but to insist that the system of chattel slavery cannot strip the subject of the intelligence and will to shape one's fate. Indeed, in a logic recalling Hegel's theorization of the master's dependence on the slave, enslavement even equips the slave with the necessities of self-reliance (conceived communally, set within a circle of freed blacks): having taken care of others as slaves, their capacity to take care of themselves and each other exceeds that of the slaveholders.

The place accorded to the will puts the defiant slave into a complicated relation to the law. On the one hand, will diminishes the scope of legal definitions of subjecthood and citizenship. Because slave subjectivity is asserted despite the law and located in a source – will – that becomes understood to be not accessible by law, the resistance against slavery is not merely resistance against a particular unjust law, but against law as such. This argument is familiar from the much-discussed higher law discourse, a strategy of argumentation that gained tremendously in influence during the 1850s and was based on the assumption, traced back to the Somerset decision of 1772, that slavery was incompatible with natural law and could thus only be legitimated by positive law.[9] On the other hand, the slave's purchase of herself and her children presupposes a compliance with law and contract and presupposes a self-understanding as an economic agent (see Armstrong, *Logic* 47–49). Accordingly, the slave's willful alteration of his or her position becomes possible only by becoming a contractual subject endowed with the right to ownership. As I will argue in regard to Linda's position in the North, a version of this ambiguity toward the law will live on in her treatment of insecurity.

I have emphasized Linda's grandmother as a model of defiance because scholarship tends to characterize her as a stern proponent of Christian morality who chides Linda for her sexual transgression and counsels against escape. The upshot of this reading is the establishment of a gender difference, according to which the family's men are construed as heroic rebels whereas the women act as quietist conformists who shirk from open confrontation and instead try to find a niche of survival inside slave society.[10] But the women of the family experience their subjectivity through the medium of defiance no less than the men do. Besides Linda's grandmother, who makes Dr. Flint fearful of her public reproaches, these models of female resistance include Aunt Nancy (Martha's only remaining daughter), who manages Dr. Flint's household and encourages Linda to flee from the hiding place in Martha's house, since (as Linda restates the argument) "even if I perished in doing it, that was better than to leave [my children] to groan under the same persecutions that had blighted my own life" (889). It also includes marginal characters like Rose, who makes only a short appearance in the text yet seems to be on familiar terms with Linda and Martha. Having been sold by Flint to a trader, Rose is granted permission to spend the time until her deportation to the slave market with Linda's grandmother. At Martha's house, Rose meets Flint, and though still a slave, she fearlessly defies his authority: "He ordered Rose out of the house; but he was no longer her master, and she took no notice of him. For once the crushed Rose was the conqueror" (827).

I have barely begun to discuss Linda's own strategies of insolence, and I only mention her "competition in cunning" (872) with Flint, during which she has friends mail him her letters from the North, though she writes them from her hiding place in her grandmother's garret. Outsmarting the master, Linda makes clear, is part of the slave's war, and it also provides a source of the greatest satisfaction: "Thus far I had outwitted him, and I triumphed over it. Who can blame slaves for being cunning? They are constantly compelled to resort to it. It is the only weapon of the weak and oppressed against the strength of their tyrants" (846–847).

Jacobs's narrative, then, presents slave subjectivity from two angles: first, slaves intervene in the course of events, but they do so from a position of the gravest peril. Facing the threats of violent death and loss of temporality, they take on risks whose negative outcomes could be lethal. Second, Jacobs stages slave subjectivity as marked by willpower, resolve, and the capacity to both enjoy victory and suffer from defeat in the incessant warfare with the master. This kind of consciousness, developed in communal interaction with free blacks, fugitives, and fellow slaves, takes shape against the foil of the powers of domination. In Jacobs's world, the slaveholders' idea that slaves can be broken in – and psychically broken down – is told the lie.[11] Even someone like Rose, maltreated and "crushed" by Flint, will use her first chance to "conquer."[12]

Slave subjectivity, in other words, is marked by a psychological and bodily struggle against an identifiable opponent who puts the slave in constant danger. And yet, it is a situation that Jacobs does not describe as "insecurity." For her situation to become "insecure," the slave must gain a degree of freedom – which is not least a freedom of movement and the physical distance from the master entailed therein – that he or she stands to lose by being recaptured. To be insecure, the slave must become a fugitive.

3.3 The Insecurity of the Fugitive

After their arrival in Philadelphia, Linda Brent and Fanny, a young woman who was hiding in the immediate vicinity of Martha's home and ends up fleeing North on the same vessel, face the world from a wholly new perspective. "We had escaped from slavery, and we supposed ourselves to be safe from the hunters. But we were alone in the world, and we had left dear ties behind us; ties cruelly sundered by the demon Slavery" (904).

Besides the fact of being torn away from her family, this experience is attributable to her peculiar situation as a fugitive. At first sight, it may seem that her sensations of the city are not so different from, say, Arthur Mervyn's upon first entering that same metropolis. Both exemplify the overwhelming effect that suddenly entering modernity has on the young person from the provinces.[13] "The noise of the great city confused me ... I had never seen so large a city, or been in contact with so many people in the streets" (905). But instantly, Linda specifies what makes her experience so disorienting. It is not merely the busyness of the city but the task of having to disappear in its anonymity. Stepping off the vessel, Fanny and Linda are so sunburned that they attract undesirable attention: "It seemed as if those who passed looked at us with an expression of curiosity. My face was so blistered and peeled, by sitting on deck, in wind and sunshine, that I thought they could not easily decide to what nation I belonged" (905). The first thing she accomplishes on shore further exemplifies the challenge of blending in: she purchases black veils for herself and Fanny. But even such a simple act as purchasing an article nearly gives her away: though she has money, she lacks the practical knowledge necessary for the transaction: "I found the shops, and bought some double veils and gloves for Fanny and myself. The shopman told me they were so many levies. I had never heard the word before, but I did not tell him so. I thought if he knew I was a stranger he might ask me where I came from. I gave him a gold piece, and when he returned the change, I counted it, and found out how much a levy was" (905). While the exchange of money integrates her into a community of economic agents and complements the protection of the veil, not knowing the currency almost reveals her to be the non-contractual subject as which the peculiar institution defines her.

We see, then, a first outline of Linda's insecurity in the North: she feels alone and disoriented, she is subject to detection and recapture, but she also gains the opportunity of maneuvering in a community of free persons, and she instantly begins to engage in economic transactions. Linda faces a set of dangers that arise from the fugitive slave's newly gained liberties. I will argue in the remainder of this chapter that Jacobs adopts insecurity as a topos because it allows her to pursue the rhetorical aim of making her reader imagine a community of insecurity. In order to be able to capture the dynamics of this rhetorical strategy, I want to differentiate between three orders of insecurity – ontological, legal, and affective – prevalent in the narrative's final chapters.

On the ontological level, the slave's insecurity expresses her unstable position between property and person. If, as I have argued about the main sections of Jacobs's narrative, the very act of escape is undertaken on the basis of the slave's conviction – articulated in willful defiance – that she is not property but a human being, Tim Armstrong is nonetheless right in arguing that "the property rights invested in the slave remain central to the narrative" (41). That crossing of property and personhood becomes audible in the way Jacobs's usage of insecurity differs from, and yet resonates with, the ways insecurity was habitually linked to fugitives: fugitives were regarded insecure in the sense that "runaway property" or "fugitive property" was insecure. It is noteworthy that we find references to the slave as insecure property both in the southern and the abolitionist press (abolitionist writers generally adopted the phrase "insecure property" with the bitter sarcasm characteristic of the movement's recitation of legal language supportive of slavery). To name just a few examples roughly from the decade preceding the Civil War: in 1849, the *National Era* (the abolitionist publication that would soon serialize *Uncle Tom's Cabin*) took up the debate about fugitives by remarking that "perhaps one or two thousand more, parents and children, may be scattered in the free States. The majority of them have escaped by their own unaided exertions. Insecurity is an essential characteristic of this kind of 'property,' for the simple reason that it has intelligence, locomotive powers, and a disposition to improve its condition" ("Our Readers").[14]

The ramifications of the conceptualization of "insecure property" become quite explicit in several articles that followed over the next years, as the problem of runaway slaves mingled with the fear of slave uprisings: quoting the Virginia correspondent of the *New York Times* on the general hysteria that followed John Brown's Raid on Harpers Ferry, the *National Era* wrote in 1859 that "a feeling of insecurity in respect of life and property has narrowed down the sphere of patriotic labor to a concern about one's own peculiar or individual interests" ("Reign of Terror in Virginia"). The same argument, only looked at with a sense of vindication, had been proffered by the same paper three years earlier: "we venture to assert that ... more slaves have been induced to escape from their masters, more desperate resolutions have been put into their heads, and more general insecurity entailed upon that species of property, within the past year, than during any five years preceding" ("Slave Insurrection Movements"). Along the same lines, *Frederick Douglass' Paper* wrote in 1853 that "the insecure condition of property in slaves in Missouri is the best illustrated in the general alarm which pervades counties in which this description of property is most numerous" ("Abolition in Missouri"). In all these cases, the insecurity of property – and of life – refers to the owners. Property here is not only insecure in the sense of being liable to disappear but also of displaying a particular fugitive *character*, a force that spreads "general insecurity" and "alarm," as if – in the punning phrase of the *National Era* – this effect were insecure property's inalienable entail.

What I am arguing here is that the slave narrators' discourse, which emphasizes the insecurity of formerly enslaved humans, is not quite adequately described as the antithesis to the official discourse, which conceives of the insecurity of fugitive property as a function of the slave owner's "insecurity in respect of life and property" (a logic which holds that property can only be insecure with reference to its owner). It is true of course that Jacobs's whole point is to reveal the human suffering that insecurity imposes on the fugitive, something that the legal discourse of insecure property cannot begin to conceptualize. But even the official discourse, in highlighting the precariousness of the slaveholder, cannot but concede the power of the fugitive slave to render fearful the entire South. And by the same token, in Jacobs's text the fugitive's insecurity arises from its continuing status as property. After all, this is precisely what makes Linda flee repeatedly from her new home with the Bruce family (real life: Willis) in New York City: she knows that she, as well as her daughter Ellen (who lives with relatives of Mr. Sands in Brooklyn in a state of semi-enslavement, working as a maid), might be successfully claimed by Flint. She thus continues to be, for all practical purposes, property. Thus, whether insecurity has its primary referent in the humanity of the fugitive or in the fugitive's objecthood, insecurity ties both ends into an insoluble knot.

What I call the ontological level of the fugitive's insecurity is of course inseparable from the legal dimension, since it is the law that defines humans as property. But I separate the two for the analytic purpose of highlighting the contested and ambiguous character of the law as it applies to Linda and her children. Linda arrives in the North in June 1842, a few months after the Supreme Court decision (on March 1st) on *Brigg v. Pennsylvania*. The Taney Court had to decide whether state liberty laws that prohibited the removal of blacks with the purpose of enslaving them violated Article IV, Section 2 of the Constitution (the "Fugitive Slave Clause") and the Fugitive Slave Law of 1793.

In his opinion, Justice Joseph Story – known for his antislavery sympathies since his opinion in the 1841 *Amistad* case, which set free a group of black captives from Africa – made clear that federal law superseded state law, which made Pennsylvania's liberty laws unconstitutional. While this seemed to indicate that northern states could no longer impose the impediment of legal process on the recapture of slaves, the court also ruled that the enforcement of the Fugitive Slave Clause and Act of 1793 were the sole responsibility of the federal government, thus absolving state officials from enforcing them. Legal protections for free blacks dwindled (runaways did not have them to begin with), but enforcement remained a different matter.

The situation for fugitives and free blacks became much more severe, however, after the passing of the Fugitive Slave Law of 1850. As has been extensively detailed in the scholarship of the antebellum period, the new law contributed to the radicalization of sectional tensions, in part because it amounted to a blank check for the kidnapping of free blacks, and in part because all Northerners were legally required to participate in the recapturing of slaves and were thus outraged by the sense that they had become subjects to a federal government taken over by what was referred to as "the slave power." Jacobs participates in the outrage at the Fugitive Slave Law at several points in her narrative, and she is particularly scandalized at the North's willingness to go along with it (I will come back to this momentarily), but the point to make here is that a good deal of her narrative covers the period between 1842 and 1850, a time in which the legal position of fugitives – and particularly the enforcement of the laws – is less clear.

From the moment of her arrival, New York is a decidedly dangerous place for Linda. Her work as a nurse requires her to take her employer's baby outside, but doing so exposes her to the Southerners "swarming" the city, "some of whom might recognize me. Hot weather brings out snakes and slaveholders, and I like one class of the venomous creatures as little as I do the other" (918). New York City, in these moments, is not so different from hiding in the Snaky Swamp outside of Edenton, North Carolina. For Linda, the situation in New York is aggravated by the fact that her daughter Ellen's legal status is open to interpretation. Flint contests the sale of Ellen and her brother Benny to Sands on the basis that Linda was never his slave (and therefore neither were her children) but his daughter's. Sands, for his part, has not kept his promise to set free the children but simply explains that he considers them free. Moreover, while he has provided the funds for their purchase, it is Linda's grandmother whose name was put down as the new owner on the bill of sale: "At the south," the narrating voice explains, "a gentleman may have a shoal of colored children without any disgrace; but if he is known to purchase them, with the view of setting them free, the example is thought to be dangerous to their 'peculiar institution,' and he becomes unpopular" (917).

When deciding to take Ellen with her to Boston, Linda eventually resorts to the fact that it is her grandmother who legally owns Ellen, but Linda cannot legally claim her while still in New York. Not only is it unimaginable that her grandmother could prevail in a legal confrontation with Sands, but Linda also knows that she must "keep on the right side of" Sands's Brooklyn relatives, since "their knowledge of my precarious situation [as a fugitive] placed me in their power" (913). But if New York allows her to carry on a daily life only by running the chance of recapture, life in Boston and Rochester is significantly different, though the legal situation differs primarily in its pragmatics. Arriving in Boston, "I felt as if I was beyond the reach of the bloodhounds; and, for the first time during many years, I had both my children together with me" (925–926). The law is one thing; its enforcement – and the comfort, or discomfort, that grows out of it – another.

While being insecure in the ontological dimension places the fugitive between person (the fugitive's insecurity) and thing (insecurity as a quality of runaway property), legal insecurity refers to the ambiguity of the law, which chiefly results, particularly before 1850, from the heterogeneity of state law and the politicized ruptures between federal and state law, but which also includes the discontinuity between legislation and its enforcement.

How, then, does insecurity emerge as an affective state in *Incidents*? It is helpful to look at Jacobs's precise wording, particularly in light of the sudden towering presence of the term "insecurity" in the final chapters and its absence in the earlier sections. Here are three of the occurrences in the text:

> [Mrs. Bruce] noticed that I was often sad, and kindly inquired the cause. I spoke of being separated from my children, and from relatives who were dear to me; but I did not mention the constant feeling of insecurity which oppressed my spirits. (913)
>
> The old feeling of insecurity, especially with regard to my children, often threw its dark shadow across my sunshine. Mrs. Bruce offered me a home for Ellen; but pleasant as it would have been, I did not dare to accept it, for fear of offending the Hobbs family. (913)
>
> But when summer came, the old feeling of insecurity haunted me. It was necessary for me to take little Mary out daily, for exercise and fresh air, and the city was swarming with Southerners. (918)

Three elements are particularly striking in these passages: first, Linda experiences insecurity not as a momentary feeling but as something that is constant, that pervades her existence as a fugitive. Indeed, insecurity can be understood quite simply as the affective dimension of being a fugitive. In this context, it is also remarkable that she refers twice to the "old" feeling of insecurity. Why "old?" Clearly, it is a feeling utterly familiar. But, moreover, insecurity is registered self-reflexively (as if Linda were saying, "Here it is again, that old feeling") because its presence chafes against the expectation of what life after the escape from slavery should be like.

Out of this self-reflexivity – insecurity as "the old feeling" – grows the second remarkable aspect of Jacobs's treatment of insecurity as an affective state. For Linda, insecurity is a feeling associated with "sadness" and the oppression of spirits. Sounding more like depression than fear, insecurity "threw a dark shadow across my sunshine." Part of what makes insecurity so depressing is its endless continuation: "I had been chased during half my life, and it seemed as if the chase was never to end" (941). If her narrative of enslaved life in the South had been characterized by willpower and defiance, life in the North nearly depletes those energies. The aftermath of the flight – which in the slave narrative is supposed to mark the beginning of a new life in freedom – leaves the fugitive weakened and nearly demoralized. Needless to say, insecurity is also connected with fear: it is the anxiety about the very real possibility of recapture that is "greatly increased by the passage of the Fugitive Slave Law" (933). Thus forced to preoccupy herself with future threat, Linda has "to keep close watch of the newspapers for arrivals" of Southerners in New York (939). And the one instance she fails to do so nearly turns out to be fatal, thus driving up her fear to new levels of intensity that Linda describes as an "acute sensation of suffering at my heart" (939). The affective substance of insecurity, then, combines sadness and exhaustion with constant fear. Significantly (as I will elaborate more fully), this mélange allows for a reaction by her readers that combines sympathy with an imaginary participation in fear.

Finally, a third dimension of insecurity concerns Linda's inability to protect her children. Insecurity as experienced by Linda in not a mere matter of individual survival, but has a social dimension in the responsibility to nurture and protect. Significantly, the reference to her children in several of the above passages puts insecurity in a mirror relation to security as spelled out by Linda throughout the text. Linda stays beholden to the ideal set by her grandmother in identifying security with the protections that come with the ownership of a home. For Linda, the physical walls of the home – which after all provided her with a hiding place for seven years, uncomfortable though it was – enable the vision of a protectively walled-in community centered on the nuclear family, a vision charged with particular resonance for the slave whose status as alienable property routinely meant the denial and violent severance of family ties.

We first encounter the aspiration to domestic security when Linda mentions her grandmother's house: "By perseverance and unwearied industry, she was now mistress of a snug little home, surrounded with the necessaries of life. She would have been happy could her children have shared them with her" (763). It further resonates in her misgivings about having to leave the Bruce family, that "friendly home where I had hoped to find security and rest" (925). The protective walls of the family home that keep the family together furthermore distinguish the condition of the poor in England from that of the American slave: "Their homes were very humble; but they were protected by law. No insolent patrols could come, in the dead of night, and flog them at their pleasure. The father, when he closed his cottage door, felt safe with his family around him. No master or overseer could come and take from him his wife, or his daughter" (927). Finally, in the penultimate paragraph, Linda describes her vision of security as the "dream of my life," which has not yet been realized: "I do not sit with my children in a home of my own, I still long for a hearthstone of my own, however humble. I wish it for my children's sake far more than for my own" (945). Far from aspiring to a bourgeois ideal, Linda's dream must be seen in the context of the insecurity – ontological, legal, and affective – that pervades the life of the fugitive.

3.4 Sympathy and Critique

I have so far traced a development in Jacobs's narrative from slave subjectivity to fugitive subjectivity in order to explain why insecurity appears as a condition peculiar to the fugitive. But in so doing, I have necessarily treated the text as a *representation* of the fugitive slave's experience. In fact, of course, slave narratives were rhetorical speech acts aimed at political effects that were to be generated by means of involving the reader in an experience of feeling. To comprehend the achievement of *Incidents*, it thus becomes necessary to change the perspective and reconsider the text as a performative contribution to what Robert Fanuzzi has called "abolition's public sphere."[15]

The point I aim to establish is that throughout *Incidents*, the narrator's involvement of the reader begins to change. Initially Jacobs, the narrator-author, addresses her readers by alternating between appeals to sympathy and critiques of northern complacency and complicity. But toward the end of the text, an additional mode of address begins to become audible: the reader becomes – for the most part implicitly – redefined as sharing the fugitive's predicament.

We find the text's best-known appeal to sympathy during Linda's confession of her deliberate decision to enter a sexual relationship with Sands. Since Linda would have qualified as a fallen sinner, the narrating self intervenes in order to protect her from her readers' judgment. She does so by calling on the reader to judge enslaved women and free women by different standards, and she formulates this demand by drawing on a rhetorical strategy found in virtually all slave narratives, a strategy I want to describe as an altered version of the "topos of the inexpressible." In its established variant, the deployment of the topos of the inexpressible has the function of inciting the reader's sympathetic imagination while also maintaining a divide between heroine and reader. Taking the form, "what I experienced at moment x is impossible to express," it turns the overwhelming experience that leaves the narrator speechless into a moment of authorial empowerment, since it attests to an increase in the intensity of the experience, while simultaneously explaining it to be unavailable to the reader. The narrator in effect claims a monopoly over the experience described. Yet this distancing of the subject of experience from the reader is ultimately undertaken precisely with the aim of making the reader feel more strongly as well. The topos of the inexpressible, in other words, aspires to induce sympathetic feeling in the reader *on the speaking subject's terms*.[16]

In slave narratives, the topos of the inexpressible is frequently altered so that it is not the failure of language per se that is expressed, but the incommensurability of the slave's and the free person's experience, an incommensurability language cannot bridge. The rift between experience and expression thus becomes crossed with the social (or political) rift between freedom and enslavement. I term this altered version "topos of incommensurability." Jacobs, while confessing her sexual transgression, uses this topos to appeal to the reader to apply a moral double standard. Her use of the topos of incommensurability makes the point that the reader never knew – and will never know – the experience of a slave woman: "Pity me, and pardon me, O virtuous reader! You never knew what it is to be a slave" (801). The topos of incommensurability makes explicit its dual function of shielding Linda from the moral censure of the reader and at the same time reigniting, even deepening, the reader's sympathetic identification. This is accurately captured in her two demands, "Pity me, and pardon me."

While Jacobs's text addresses both women and men, black and white, her direct modes of address make clear that it is white readers (predominantly women) who are the official addressees. (The official address by no means excludes other forms of address, for instance those directed specifically at blacks; I'll come back to that point). This form of official address replicates the power structure within the abolitionist movement,[17] but it also allows Jacobs to turn the tables on her white readers by mixing her appeals of sympathy with sharp critiques directed at the North for becoming subservient to the South. In these passages, it is Jacobs's point to resist a differentiation between antislavery or abolitionist and proslavery Northerners and instead bemoan a general complicity among "you at the north" (774).

How, one might wonder, could Jacobs muster the audacity to criticize her white readers, especially since she writes from a morally precarious position? Her voice of critique, I suggest, is only taking to its conclusion the moment of distancing already present in the topos of incommensurability. This becomes clear if we look at an early instance in the text in which the narrator addresses the stark differences between the norms of motherhood and the fate of the slave mother.

> O, you happy free women, contrast your New Year's day with that of the poor bond-woman! With you it is a pleasant season, and the light of the day is blessed. … Children bring their little offerings, and raise their rosy lips for a caress. They are your own, and no hand but that of death can take them from you.
>
> But to the slave mother New Year's day comes laden with peculiar sorrows. She sits on her cold cabin floor, watching the children who may all be torn from her the next morning; and often does she wish that she and they might die before the day dawns. … she has a mother's instincts, and is capable of feeling a mother's agonies. (761)

While motherhood becomes naturalized and thus universalized ("mother's instincts") so that it can act as the bridge between Jacobs and her readers, the fact that the difference between these two types of motherhood is so tremendous, and that white mothers need to be made aware of the difference, anticipates what in later passages will be sharpened into outright critique of her white readers' political quiescence. Connecting the account of the narrated self's abuses by Flint to an intervention by the narrating self about the Fugitive Slave Act, Jacobs completes the step from the appeal to sympathy – phrased once again by using the topos of incommensurability – to critique:

> The degradation, the wrongs, the vices, that grow out of slavery, are more than I can describe. They are greater than you would willingly believe. Surely, if you credited one half the truths that are told you concerning the helpless millions suffering in this cruel bondage, you at the north would not help to tighten the yoke. You surely would refuse to do for the master, on your own soil, the mean and cruel work which trained bloodhounds and the lowest class of whites do for him at the south. (773–774)

The passage starts out with the familiar topos ("more than I can describe") and seems to extend its logic to the reader: it is impossible, she seems to suggest, to even imagine the sublime horror that befalls slave girls who become the victim of their predatory master. Yet after this sentimental beginning, the passage takes a tongue-in-cheek turn of direction: Jacobs effectively tells her readers that the problem does not lie in the impossibility to imagine; rather, her readers must be *unwilling* to believe what she is telling them or else they would not do the work of bloodhounds and white trash slave catchers. Using the pronoun "you" repeatedly, she could hardly make her attack any sharper.

The force of the attack, while certainly audacious, will turn out to be instrumental for extending the plight of the fugitive to her readers. As the narrative continues, Jacobs subtly hints at differentiations among Northerners. Not only does she have high praise for her benefactresses, particularly for the first and second Mrs. Bruce and for her Rochester abolitionist friend Amy Post (who was instrumental in getting the book published), she also pays tribute, if in condensed form, to the political strife among Northerners that unfolds following the Compromise of 1850. Addressing the security she felt in Massachusetts at a prior point in time, she comments that "the Fugitive Slave Law had not then passed. The judges of Massachusetts had not then stooped under chains to enter her courts of justice, so called" (930).

Jacobs's contemporary readers would have recognized the reference: several times during the early 1850s, Boston became the scene of unrest over the capture of fugitives. While Shadrach Minkins was liberated from the Boston Courthouse in 1851 by African American abolitionists, Thomas Sims, in 1851, and Anthony Burns, in 1854, were both turned over to the slave states despite violent protest. In both cases, chains surrounded the courthouse, watched over by militia men (see DeLombard 59–60).

Now pointing to the judges of Massachusetts rather than "you at the north," Jacobs registers the public's division over the Fugitive Slave Law and thus lays the foundation for imagining a community united in opposition to the "bloodhounds." It is not only blacks who oppose a legal system brought under proslavery control, the chains under which the judges symbolically stoop attest to the public unrest in Boston, which, the despair over the Fugitive Slave Act notwithstanding, provides a sign of hope.

3.5 Imagining a Community of Insecurity

As her narrative progresses, Jacobs turns insecurity into a means of identification for her northern readers and thus displaces the coordinates of sympathy. In order to trace this movement, a bit of contextualization is helpful. This will show that her decision to follow this path, while unusual for a slave narrative, and particularly for one written by a female fugitive, was embedded in a public discourse of intensified sectional confrontation, which was quickly gaining ground and came to a climax between Lincoln's election to the presidency and the Confederate shelling of Fort Sumter in April 1861 – at the very moment, in other words, when *Incidents* appeared.

For decades, Northerners had detected an existential threat stemming from what they called "the slave power." Crucial to the slave power thesis was the idea that the proponents of slavery did not merely want to spread slavery over the whole continent but that slavery undermined the foundations of civilization. In effect, slavery's threat consisted in its power to enslave whites as well as blacks. Strong evidence for this thesis was found in a wave of lynchings and shootings of white abolitionists in the 1830s, the most famous one being that of Elijah Lovejoy at Alton, Illinois, in 1837. As historian Rachel Hope Cleves has recently shown, abolitionists adopted and politically turned around what she calls an "uncivilizing discourse" inherited from Federalist anti-Jacobins – a discourse that originally served conservative ends by warning of the imminent danger to the social order through a revolutionary (French-Jacobin) reign of terror in America (see Cleves, "Savage" and *Reign*). In the hands of abolitionists, this conservative discourse was put to progressive ends, identifying the slave power as the agent that would bring on a reign of terror destructive of civilization.

After John Brown's Raid on Harpers Ferry in 1859, North and South entered what we might call an insecurity contest. The northern perception of a reign of terror instigated by the South intersected with the southern perception of a reign of terror instigated by the North. And it is not merely that both sides felt threatened: echoing what International Relations scholarship calls a "security dilemma," their sense of threat grew by the observation of how the other side responded to feeling threatened.[18] After John Brown's Raid, the northern press, and particularly abolitionist publications, closely observed the South's extralegal security measures in response to Southerners' sense of insecurity. This in turn resulted in a heightened sense of insecurity – increasingly coupled with fantasies of violent retaliation – among Northerners. A good example of this dynamic is William Lloyd Garrison's 1860 pamphlet *The New "Reign of Terror" in the Slaveholding States*, which collected reports from a local postmaster of Virginia who had been barred from delivering northern papers and which further assembled newspaper clippings about the expulsion of citizens from Kentucky who were accused of being abolitionists. Garrison's pamphlet, written shortly before the publication of Jacobs's narrative, captures the interlocking perceptions of insecurity of both North and South at their most hysterical.

Garrison quotes the resolution of a public meeting of a Kentucky small town that justified the removal of citizens deemed "abolitionists." The community members resolved that it was "necessary and justifiable by a proper regard for the protection of their [the community members'] property, and the safety and security of their families" to expel the abolitionists – if necessary by force: "Duty, safety, and the interest of the community compelling us, in the event of non-compliance, to resort to means alike painful to us and hazardous to him" (18). Carried out in the name of security, these actions were interpreted as proof, in the words of the Virginia Postmaster (apparently from the North) also quoted by Garrison, that "we are in the midst of a Reign of Terror here. ... All men of Northern birth now here are under *surveillance* by the so-called Vigilance Committee; and any one suspected of thinking slavery less than divine is placed under care" (10). Garrison, who had by this time left behind is long-honed non-violence stance, used his preface to cite a *New York Tribune* report on the "the risk of personal indignity, and danger even to life and limb" (iii) suffered by every Northerner in the South, and then proceeded to unfold his own violent revenge fantasy authorized by references to the American Revolution:

> Let us suppose the tables to be turned; suppose there existed here a little of the spirit '76, such as our fathers manifested in their treatment of the tories at that time, and we should catch, and tar and feather, every slaveholder coming into the North, by way of retaliation, and to show our jealous appreciation of the sacred cause of freedom – how long would 'our glorious Union' hold together? How many victims would be subjected to Northern Lynch law, before the South would bring this matter to a head? And yet, there are scores of Northern men so treated at the South, – not one of them an Abolitionist, or in sympathy with their movement, – and the intelligence excites no popular indignation among us, and scarcely elicits a comment from the press. (iv)[19]

This feedback loop of insecurity and retaliation demonstrates how difficult the perception of insecurity – of being drawn into a reign of terror – was to square with a commitment to the rule of law. While the law would seem to be the antidote to terror, the law appeared less and less as a promising source of protection. What we encounter here is the principal philosophical conflict between the normativity of the law – which must apply to everyone and requires the transfer of the right to violence to the state – and the normativity of security, which argues from the basis of case-specific necessity and thus shuns the generalized rule on which law is based.

Recently, scholars working in the law and literature movement have intensely debated the complex status of the law during the antebellum period. While Gregg Crane, in *Race, Citizenship, and Law in American Literature* (2002), has described how the appeal to a higher law (popularized by the Transcendentalists and, in political discourse, by William Seward) helped undermine the authority of positive law which upheld slavery, Deak Nabers, in *Victory of Law: The Fourteenth Amendment, the Civil War, and American Literature, 1852–1867* (2006), has offered a corrective view according to which the appeal to higher law was in fact reconcilable with positive law so that the tumultuous 1850s could ultimately culminate in the Fourteenth Amendment. But by focusing on the relation between higher law and man-made, positive law, this debate has failed to take into consideration the ways in which the increasingly hostile sectional conflict turned on the image of the reign of terror and the corresponding sense of insecurity. This discourse provided an alternative approach to the ambivalence of the law, one that did not confront positive law with higher law, but instead opposed the rule of law to the logic of necessity.

In theory, the two debates can be kept apart by specifying what precisely was perceived as problematic about the law. Alarm about the reign of terror tended to presume that the rule of law had been suspended, whereas the proponents of the higher law fought against positive law perceived as unjust. In practice, however, both discourses tended to melt into each other. Jacobs's narrative is a case in point. On the one hand, she rejects the law on the basis of its unjustness. "I knew the law would decide that I was his property, and would probably still give his daughter a claim to my children; but I regarded such laws as the regulations of robbers, who had no rights that I was bound to respect" (930). In instances such as this one, she rejects "such laws" rather than the law per se. The same goes for rights: if slaveholders possess rights which she does not feel bound to respect, this is not to say that there are no rights at all – natural rights, for instance – which do warrant respect. Her critique of the injustice of positive law – and here Nabers is surely right – is not at all incompatible with a commitment to the ideals of the rule of law. In fact, she makes explicit this commitment whenever she bemoans the slave's lack of legal protection.

But on the other hand, Jacobs also participates in the discourse of "the reign of terror." She even uses the phrase in a chapter on the Fugitive Slave Law of 1850, which she describes being "of disastrous import to the colored people" (933). In this context, her purpose is not merely to show how black people suffer but also to make clear that the indifference of whites, who prefer escaping into cultural pursuits over caring about their marginalized fellow citizens, is a sign of a civilization in decline: "while fashionables were listening to the thrilling voice of Jenny Lind in Metropolitan Hall, the thrilling voices of poor hunted colored people went up, in an agony of supplication, to the Lord, from Zion's church" (933). This connects with a whole series of indictments of the pernicious effects of slavery on civilization. Whether she describes the contagious effect of cruelty in slave society (792), the systemic sexual corruption of female slaves in the South (797), the "spectacle … for a civilized country" that is the "rabble, staggering under intoxication, assuming to be the administrators of justice!" after Nat Turner's revolt (813), or whether she recommends sending missionaries to the South to convert slaveholders (820): the systematic corruption of civilization by slavery undermines the entire moral, political, and legal infrastructure that could uphold the rule of law. Though she is less explicit here than, say, *Frederick Douglass' Paper*,[20] the question she in effect poses is whether in such a decivilized state, the law provides an avenue to protection at all.

If slavery really undermines civilization, then everyone – black and white – is affected. This idea forms the basis for Jacobs's move to extend insecurity beyond the lot of the fugitive slave and to render it as the condition of Northerners more generally. With New York "no longer being *free* soil" (935, emphasis in original), the fear of insecurity is experienced not specifically by fugitive slaves, women or blacks, but by, what she calls, "inhabitants, guiltless of offence, and seeking to perform their duties conscientiously" (934).[21] The description of herself as a "slave in New York" (*Incidents* 936) gains critical edge because the fugitive's insecurity is a condition that she now defines in broader terms than before: no longer referring only to the fugitive's liability to be recaptured into slavery, the fugitive's enslavement in New York points to a general subjection to the slave power, a subjection suffered by blacks as well as by whites.[22]

In a particularly striking example of this dynamic, Linda explicitly claims fugitive status for the second Mrs. Bruce's baby at a critical stage during her northern experience: finding out that her old tormentor has been informed about her location in New York, she makes preparations to flee from the city. As no substitute nurse can be found at short notice, Linda takes the baby with her. This has the added advantage of providing Linda with a kind of surety: if Linda were traveling by herself, she might simply disappear in the hands of kidnappers; with the white baby by her side, whoever might claim Linda as property would have to bring the baby back to Mrs. Bruce, which would enable her to save Linda. While this plan hinges on the distinction between the free, white girl[23] and the fugitive slave, Linda claims the child as sharing her fate so that the distinction behind the rationale is erased:

> It was a comfort to me to have the child with me ... But how few mothers would have consented to have one of their own babes become a fugitive, for the sake of a poor hunted nurse, on whom the legislators of the country had let loose the bloodhounds! (937)

Linda, unwilling to accept the notion that she is someone else's property, does not refer to herself as a slave, but as a hunted nurse. Being hunted potentially extends to all subjects of the country's legislators, and it includes the white baby. More than that, the baby has explicitly become a fugitive. The significance of this ascription becomes clear perhaps only when considering that, for Jacobs, "fugitive" constituted an important political identity with which she publicly identified even after having been freed by her employer: she signed one of her first publications – a letter written to the *New York Tribune* in 1853 – simply as: "A Fugitive" (Yellin, *Family Papers*, Vol.1, 202).[24]

The fact that the present danger emerging from the Fugitive Slave Law has ramifications for whites is also made clear by the baby's mother (real-life Cornelia Willis). Asked if she was aware of the penalty for harboring a fugitive, Jacobs cites her willingness to break the law: "'I am very well aware of it. It is imprisonment and one thousand dollars fine. Shame on my country that it *is* so! I am ready to incur the penalty. I will go to the state's prison, rather than have any poor victim torn from my house, to be carried back to slavery'" (937). Mrs. Bruce's resolve to disobey the law hovers between a sentimental discourse in which whites nobly stand up for the defense of blacks and the self-interested motivation to protect her own domestic sovereignty. She is ready to go to prison both for the sake of the "poor victim" and for the purpose of ensuring the sanctity of her home. If her sentimentalism is conventional, her concern for the security guaranteed by her home registers the degree to which the fugitive's insecurity has become her own. Though remnants of the sentimental discourse are still audible here, white sympathy with the slave is becoming supplemented by a logic of identification that puts black and white in principally the same place – much in resonance with the transracial alliance needed to win the Civil War.

Even in this passage, to be sure, Jacobs seems to cling to the master meaning of insecurity as the *fugitive slave's* virtual bondage. In the final chapter, when discovering in a newspaper that Flint's daughter and her husband (Mr. and Mrs. Dodge) have arrived in New York to claim her, she resorts one last time to the topos of incommensurability: "Reader, if you have never been a slave, you cannot imagine the acute sensation of suffering at my heart, when I read the names of Mr. and Mrs. Dodge" (939). But by now, the founding condition of the topos has become uncertain. Though Jacobs would not go quite so far as to claim that her target audience had ever been slaves, her readers emerge in her text as incapable of representing a free counterpart to the plight of the fugitive. Jacobs has claimed her readers as part of a community of insecurity. And just as this community is being created, freedom itself is being redefined as a state measured by degree. In her final address to the reader, incommensurability makes way for the commonality of freedom reduced to relativity. Now that freedom is no longer a secure state but a mere improvement over the immediate subjection to the slaveholder, insecurity becomes the experience that unites what once was the free North:

> Reader, my story ends with freedom; not in the usual way, with marriage. I and my children are now free! We are as free from the power of slaveholders as are the white people at the north. And though that, according to my ideas, is not saying a great deal, it is a vast improvement in my condition. (944–945)

Insecurity – which here figures as the compromised freedom from the power of slaveholders – is an apt basis for a cross-racial imagined community, since what unites Northerners (whites, free blacks, and fugitives) against the slave power is less a substantively given commonality than the subjection to threat. Being collectively insecure is a remarkably low requirement of commonality. Indeed, Jacobs's rhetorical strategy of ascribing the conditionality of threat to both blacks and whites cannot be said to be inaccurate (especially against the backdrop of the Civil War), even if the likelihood and quality of the threat differ substantially for both groups.

However, if Jacobs's community of insecurity is imagined, this also means that it stands in contrast to what has been recognized as the real. Jacobs, I propose, opposes her imagined community of insecurity to the social formations sanctioned by entrenched power constellations. The transracial community of insecurity that her text instantiates is thus in deliberate tension with what she presents as the realities of Jim Crow segregation,[25] her accusations of northern whites (mentioned earlier) to be effectively complicit with the slave power, and her allusions to a black support community that remains secretive and becomes revealed in her text only in the vaguest outline. In all of these cases, the color line remains firmly in place. And whereas the transracial community of insecurity is built on the notion that slavery has created a reign of terror in which the law no longer provides protection, her insistence on black suffering (offset by white complacent privilege) is part of a struggle to guarantee civil and human rights for African Americans, whether free, fugitive, or enslaved, and thus remains deeply invested in the law.

I conclude by briefly pointing to two of the dimensions of the recalcitrant reality that sets the limits to the imagined community of insecurity: the dangers and injustice to which blacks – but decidedly not whites – are exposed and the black shadow community that forms partially in response to them. I have already discussed how Jacobs uses the topos of incommensurability to highlight the experiences that set apart the vulnerability of blacks from that of whites. To this I want to add the civil rights discourse against segregation that runs through Jacobs's text. Beginning with her arrival in Philadelphia, Linda is shocked by the Jim Crow system in the North: "This was the first chill to my enthusiasm about the Free States. Colored people were allowed to ride in a filthy box, behind white people, at the south, but there they were not required to pay for the privilege. It made me sad to find how the north aped the customs of slavery" (908). She increasingly defies the discriminatory practices of segregation. Her resistance comes to a climax during an extended stay at a fashionable hotel in Rockaway, New York, with Mr. Bruce (Nathanial Parker Willis) and his daughter Mary. The hotel management asks Linda not to sit down with Mary and to take her meals in the kitchen, but "finding I was resolved to stand up for my rights, they concluded to treat me well" (921). This is followed by an exhortation directed not toward her usual addressees – white women – but toward her black readership (rarely acknowledged in the text): "Let every colored man and woman do this, and eventually *we* shall cease to be trampled under foot by *our* oppressors" (921, emphasis added).

Her sudden turn to a black readership points to the lineaments of a black community that appears in the text as a series of gaps. Hidden behind the cast of characters to whom Jacobs leaves the main stage, there is a deeply textured social (and, indeed, personal) world that is almost entirely kept out of sight. It appears as if Linda's life is embedded in a black community about whose existence the reader receives no more than coded signals. Looking at her text from this perspective, the personnel of her narrative grows considerably: it includes a nameless "friend in New York ... in comfortable circumstances" who proves wrong all the southern lies about the alleged wish of fugitive slaves to return to their masters (789); anonymous friends who want to buy her from Flint (825); an unnamed benefactor who provides Linda with her initial hiding place in Edenton (842); her friend Peter, who helps her repeatedly in Edenton, and who is introduced merely as "young man" and apprentice to her late father's (857), whom Linda has known "for years" (later we also learn that he considers Linda's father his "best friend," 873); several friends from Edenton who reside in New York and Brooklyn (909, 910); a friend who takes her place as nurse in the Bruce family when Linda flees to Boston (917); a friend in Boston with whom she shares an apartment (926); members of vigilance committees (934); and the many abolitionist activists in Rochester, of whom she only mentions her brother (932).

It is safe to say that Linda's social self would appear quite different if Jacobs had allowed these characters the space which their roles in her life seem to warrant. The pragmatic reasons why they remain confined to a shadow existence are manifold.[26] What's remarkable here is the effect the hints at this off-stage world have on Jacobs's creation of the community of insecurity. By shielding her friends' and supporters' anonymity and confining them to the role of shadow characters, Jacobs implies how vulnerable they are to the consequences of publicity. But in the context of white paranoia about black resistance – I have already mentioned the hysterical reactions to John Brown's Raid on Harpers Ferry in the South and the repercussions in the North – it is also the case that the vague hints at a dense and well-organized network of blacks in New York are conducive to raise the specter of blacks secretly threatening white Northerners.[27] As Jacobs's text confronts the imagined transracial community of insecurity with the stubborn facts of racial injustice, she thus simultaneously creates a proliferation of insecurity-collectives. Not only are Northerners, white and black, threatened by the slave power, but additionally blacks appear as threatened by whites, and whites by blacks.

Recent critics have extensively commented on the fact that Jacobs initially wrote a concluding chapter on John Brown,[28] which her editor Lydia Maria Child urged her to cut. (It should be noted, however, that Child, a committed Garrisonian, was a public supporter of Brown, even if she criticized his use of violence.) That chapter, now lost, holds out the interpretive temptation to claim Jacobs as a political radical held in check by her white, middle-class editor.[29] Child wrote to Jacobs, "I think the last chapter, about John Brown, had better be omitted. It does not naturally come into your story, and the M.S. is already too long. Nothing can be so appropriate to end with, as the death of your grand mother" (Yellin, *Jacobs Family Papers*, Vol.1, 279). It is difficult to imagine that Child's primary worry really had to do with these formal concerns. But it is also less than clear that the inclusion of the Brown chapter would have radicalized *Incidents*. Even as it stands, the text projects a politics that is anything but timid. And this is precisely because Jacobs's presentation of a black community of resistance remains powerfully latent and thus allows her to construct a reversible figure that switches back and forth from endangered blacks to endangered whites and that, in addition, alternates with the imagination of the inclusive northern community of insecurity.

Jacobs, in effect, plays a kind of rhetorical *Fort-Da* game, in which the construction of the community of insecurity takes turns with her insistence on the differences between the predicaments faced by blacks and whites, respectively. It is as if she put the community of insecurity in sight of her readers only to make it disappear in the next moment. And as in the Freudian *Fort-Da* game, the alternations of appearance and disappearance give the speaker who rhetorically enacts them a degree of control. By creating and revoking the imagined community of insecurity, Jacobs assumes an authority that displaces the power hierarchies of sentimental abolitionism but nonetheless grows out of sentimentalism's investment in the weak and marginalized. Owning up to the position of the suffering fugitive and creating out of that position the prerogative to define who and what counts as truly insecure, Jacobs begins to wield control over the terms in which sentimental abolitionism can be transformed into a transracial collective united in its opposition to proslavery forces. And not only does she replace antislavery sentimentalism with the invocation of collective insecurity that demands of whites, rather than mere sympathy, the outright identification with blacks; whenever she deflates this collective imagination, she also supplements the portrayal of blacks as mistreated with the outlines of a black population in defiance, ready to create a world in which "we shall cease to be trampled under foot by our oppressors" (921).

What I hope to have demonstrated, then, is that the insecurity that structures the fugitive's subjectivity is deftly exploited by Jacobs for a performative maneuver that allows her to instantiate the imagination of an inclusive community of insecurity and that further puts her in the position to instantly undo that imagination by highlighting racially differentiated social realities. The result is a rapid alternation between different scenes of insecurity, generated by their interlocking appearance and disappearance. The moving force behind these flickering images is none other than Harriet Jacobs, who has succeeded in turning the incidents in the life of a slave girl into a source of authority over her audience.

CHAPTER 4

Willa Cather and the Security of Radical Contingency

Among Willa Cather's novels, *The Professor's House* (1925) stands out for its unique structure: In its main storyline, history professor Godfrey St. Peter battles a growing sense of alienation from his family and modern America; in the midst of it arises, rock-like, "Tom Outland's Story." Told in the first person in sparse prose, this inner story goes back in time some twenty to thirty years and relates the adventures of Tom Outland, the novel's mythical embodiment of youth, during his summer in the Cliff City of the Blue Mesa in New Mexico (Cather's fictionalized version of Mesa Verde in southwestern Colorado).[1] The mesa and "Tom Outland's Story" mirror each other in their respective place: The "naked blue rock set down alone in the plain" (211) captures how Tom's spirited narrative towers out of St. Peter's romance with fatigue.

The Blue Mesa belongs to the Catherian rock that also shapes the landscapes of *Death Comes for the Archbishop* (1927) and *Shadows on the Rock* (1931); it promises firm resistance against the malaise of modernity. Placing the rock at the symbolic and textual center of her novel, Cather thus builds *The Professor's House* around a concern with security that emerges in tandem with, and against, the cultural, social, and economic transformations of the early twentieth century. In *The Professor's House*, however, security plays a more specific and explicit role than in her other novels. The Blue Mesa is represented as having once been a haven of security for the Pueblo Indians who had built a small city of dwellings into the rock and thus gained both protection from external enemies and the ability to live a life dedicated to spiritual and artistic pursuits. The first thing to note, then, about the central place of security in *The Professor's House* is that it gains more substance in this novel than in any other text discussed in this study. For Arthur Mervyn (discussed in Chapter 2) and Linda Brent (discussed in Chapter 3), security is a future aspiration that sets into relief present insecurity; this creates spaces for action, whether individual or political, that otherwise would not have opened up. Cather, by contrast, creates a fictional site at which security was once a reality. Actual security, however, becomes narratively available only on the condition that it has already been lost. This is because, as I argue in the introductory chapter, narrative depends on a conflict between a formal or informal order (a law or normative frame) and an agent or force that violates that order. In other words, since narrative requires events that by definition upset the order of a literary world, narrative comes to rest once this order is secured. Narratively speaking, therefore, security can be part of a narrative only as a prospect or as a remembrance of the past. And only in the latter case can one claim that security has been actually obtained. Loss, then, is the precondition for rendering actual security as narrative, which is to say that security needs to be reconstructed with the help of memory. Cather, I will argue in this chapter, brings to life the memory of security in a nostalgic mode and thus carries into the modernist 1920s a tradition developed by regionalist writers of the late nineteenth century.

Nostalgia, of course, is generally the most pejorative of aesthetic terms[2] (as, to a lesser degree, is Cather's association with the regionalists); indeed, it served as a rhetorical weapon for Cather's fiercest critics, who, particularly in the 1930s, tended to dismiss her work as sentimental and irresponsive to real life. Granville Hicks, for instance, faulted Cather on the basis that "most of her books [are] elegiac, beguiling [their] readers with pictures of a life that has disappeared, and deliberately exploiting the remoteness of that life in order to cast a golden haze about it" ("Bright Incidents" viii). Similarly, Lionel Trilling attacked her on the grounds that "the 'spirituality' of Miss Cather's latest books consists chiefly of an irritated exclusion of those elements of modern life with which she will not cope" ("Willa Cather" 10–11). To these judgments, subsequent Cather scholarship has reacted by claiming her works to be anything but nostalgic.[3] By contrast, I am calling into question the critical reflex of dismissing nostalgia *tout court*. Doing justice to the aesthetic appeal of Cather's security fictions requires that we not deafen ourselves to her poetics of longing for what has been lost; moreover, rather than shying away from nostalgia, we need to have a better understanding of its Catherian variant. Upon a closer look, Cather's use of the rock as a metaphor for the state of security turns out to be highly ambiguous and tricky, and it helps us begin to articulate Cather's notion of nostalgic security: As dreamily grasped in *The Professor's House* and other novels, nostalgic security circumscribes a space of regularity and order belonging to a lost past, but this rock-like security cannot therefore be squared with the dualism of premodern stability and modernity's melting all that is solid into air. The reading I propose in this chapter holds that Cather identifies the lost state of security with a romantically inflected vision of radical contingency – a potentiality not yet narrowed down by choices necessarily made in the course of time. Such a state of contingency is less modernity's other than its radicalization, the laying open of its roots.

I take the prominence of security in Cather's novel – its rendition in a nostalgic mode that differs from the way we have come to recognize nostalgia – to be paradigmatic of the modernist self-positioning in the midst of a historical rupture. Though certainly not a straightforward high modernist, Cather represents a wider tendency, typical of modernism, to perceive security as situated in a bygone past, without therefore simply yearning to restore that past at the cost of confronting the new.[4] I have argued in the introduction and throughout my readings that American fiction makes use of security by exploiting – for the development of plot as much as for the experience of the reader – the imaginary potential opened up through security's conceptual twin, insecurity; the modernist nostalgia for security, then, is not an exception but rather a particular variant of this thesis: What is found in the secure past is a plentitude of possibility that the present doesn't offer. Despite nostalgia's inherent pessimism about the present, this concept of security is so deeply invested in the potentiality opened up by the nostalgic rendition of the past that this very same pessimism will not stand unchecked.

Making this claim, however, requires having a good grasp of Cather's relation to modernism, which has been a rather vexing problem in Cather scholarship.[5] On the one hand, modernists tended to define themselves against the literary values for which hardly anyone may have stood as pointedly as Cather: "Cather may seem to epitomize the kind of writing that literary modernism notoriously sought to displace. Her works were stylistically conventional, popular, nostalgic, and regional at a time when writers like Eliot and Pound were demanding that literature be difficult, up-to-date, and international," writes Michael North (*Reading 1922*, 173). On the other hand, Cather's works, and particularly *The Professor's House*, hardly live up to the antimodernism she outwardly embraced in her essay collection *Not Under Forty*, published in 1936. Not only was she a committed reader of writers like Virginia Woolf (who in turn described Cather as belonging to a small group of American writers that the British "should do well to examine carefully" [*The Moment* 174, qtd. in Poresky 69]), but in breaking apart Book Two from the rest of the novel she also experimented, if only with moderate zeal, with a modernist structure. Ultimately more important, however, is Cather's diagnosis of an epochal rupture marking her present moment, a gesture that lies at the root of modernism, no matter the exact nature of the response to the perceived *epoché*.

In the prefatory note to *Not Under Forty*, Cather famously proclaimed that "the world broke in two in 1922 or thereabouts" (812). It may seem as if this proclamation set her apart from the more experimental modernists. Indeed, in her essay on Annie Fields ("148 Charles Street"), she bemoans this break by linking the geopolitical explosion of "the Great War" to the demise of nineteenth-century literary culture personified by Fields and her companion Sarah Orne Jewett and thus presumably inherited by Cather. "When and where were the Arnolds overthrown and the Brownings devaluated? Was it at the Marne? At Versailles, when a new geography was being made on paper? Certainly the literary world which emerged from the war used a new coinage" (848). However, Cather cannot quite be taken at face value when she makes the case for her own foreignness to this "new coinage." The year 1922 marked the death of Marcel Proust, whom she claims, in "148 Charles Street," as a kindred spirit. She reports his statement that "when he came to die he would take all his great men with him: since his Beethoven and his Wagner could never be at all the same to anyone else, they would go with him like the captives who were slain at the funeral pyres of Eastern potentates" (848). But Proust, whose *À la recherche du temps perdu* was published between 1913 and 1927, is hardly the premodernist as whom Cather seems to define him in order to align herself, through her identification with him, with the premoderns. If she imagines her own death along with Proust's, her own demise may in fact resound deeply visions of decline that are part and parcel of modernism itself. Pound, Eliot, Hemingway, and Fitzgerald all saw in World War I a great catastrophe that turned civilization into a waste land, and all shared, moreover, a sense of the aesthetic and spiritual impoverishment of modern culture.

This isn't to say that modernism is appropriately characterized as nostalgia plain and simple. Rather, looking back to an unreachable past on the far side of the *epoché* becomes integral to the aspiration of making it new. In North's apt formulation, in modernism "the old and the new are not opposite but co-dependent" (29). From this perspective, Cather is not viewed as an antimodernist; rather, this highlights with particular clarity a component recognizable across a whole spectrum of modernist responses to the perceived rupture. Starting from the critique of modern life as having become spiritually and aesthetically impoverished, this spectrum ranges from T. S. Eliot's insistence that the poet learn to assert his ancestors' immortality in order to inhabit "what is not merely the present, but the present moment of the past" ("Tradition and Individual Talent" 42) to the avant-garde's desire to clear the ground for a fresh start with "an inexhaustible machine gun pointing at the army of the dead . . . whom we want to strip of their authority and subject to the bold and creative young," as F.T. Marinetti put it in a 1913 manifesto on futurism ("Open Letter" 105). Cather's position on this spectrum was closer to Eliot's than to Marinetti's in that she, too, was invested in the past. Rather than believe that the way to cope with the historical rupture was to preserve the past in a tradition-infused present, however, Cather recognized, as Tom Lutz puts it, "that what was being preserved was already past, that actual preservation was impossible" ("Cather and Regional Imagination" 448). Her stance, I suggest, can be described as a prospective nostalgia, a look back that creates a position in the past from which to imagine a future all the more radically contingent, while remaining fully conscious of having lost that past.

4.1 Security and Loss

At the heart of *The Professor's House* lies a plot of discovery in which old and new interpenetrate each other, providing a view of security strangely intact in a form of loss. After having come upon the Blue Mesa, Tom, his friend Roddy, and their housekeeper Henry establish themselves in the long-deserted Cliff City and soon begin their work as amateur archeologists, reconstructing, as methodically as they can, the pre-Columbian Pueblo civilization that carved its dwellings out of the cliffs. They seek the advice of Father Duchene, a Belgian missionary priest whose general education in all things ancient and medieval turns him into a mentor. Here is Duchene's anthropological assessment of the extinct Pueblo civilization:

> I am inclined to think that your tribe were a superior people. Perhaps they were not so when they first came upon this mesa, but in an orderly and secure life they developed considerably the arts of peace. There is evidence on every hand that they lived for something more than food and shelter. They had an appreciation of comfort, and went even further than that. Their life, compared to that of our roving Navajos, must have been quite complex. There is unquestionably a distinct feeling for design in what you call the Cliff City. Buildings are not grouped like that by pure accident, though convenience probably had much to do with it. Convenience often dictates very sound design....
>
> With grain in their storerooms, and mountain sheep and deer for their quarry, they rose gradually from the condition of savagery. With the proper variation of meat and vegetable diet, they developed physically and improved in the primitive arts. They had looms and mills, and experimented with

dyes. At the same time, they possibly declined in the arts of war, in brute strength and ferocity. (233)

As Duchene sees it, the remnants of the cliff-dweller population tell a story of captivating civilizational progress. Nestled in their dwellings, hidden from the mesa-top above and the plains below, the natives' lives demonstrate what the ever-elusive aspiration of security could ideally come down to: a life that is "orderly" and "peaceful," arranged with respect for the past and forethought alike, whether it concerns the architecture or the skillfully varied diet. Perfectly regulated, Pueblo life flourishes into a pastoral state of nature – less an original state than a civilizational achievement – from which all evil and conflict seem absent: "Wherever humanity has made that hardest of all starts and lifted itself out of mere brutality, is a sacred spot. Your people were cut off here without the influence of example or emulation, with no incentive but some natural yearning for order and security. They built themselves into this mesa and humanized it" (234).

Duchene seems to act as a mouthpiece for Cather's own views of the Pueblo culture. In a 1916 article on the "Mesa Verde" for the *Denver Times*, written a few months after her first visit, she emphasizes that the Pueblo dwellers' civilizational development is a result of their strict adherence to regularity, ritual, and tradition: "Everything in the cliff dweller villages points to a tempered, settled, ritualistic life, where generations went on gravely and reverently repeating the past, rather than battling for anything new. Their lives were so full of ritual and symbolism that all their common actions were ceremonial – planting, harvesting, hunting, feasting, fasting... Their strong habitations, their settled mode of living, their satisfying ritual, seem to have made this people conservative and aristocratic" ("Mesa Verde" 332).

Cather's fascination with security and order arising from the reverent repetition of the past intensified as she began to position herself as an outsider to modern culture and a member of the "backward," as she phrased it in the preface to *Not Under Forty* (812). In her enthusiastic essay on Thomas Mann's *Joseph and His Brothers*, included in that collection, she praises his literary means of portraying Joseph and his forebears for capturing the "rightness of the rhythm" and "dreamy indefiniteness" of a shepherd people who live at the pace "of grazing sheep." Mann's Old Testament herdsmen, like the Anasazi, live in a state so committed to the ways of tradition that any notion of progress is foreign to them. The life of security requires a dreamlike state of mind, a rhythm of life that is slow and steady, built around the ever-recurring repetitions of ritual. And yet it is this kind of life, so contrary to the principles of rationality and goal-oriented striving, that brings about a gradual rise, in Father Duchene's words, "from the condition of savagery" (233).

Cather's vision of security as emerging from a people's fidelity to order was by no means peculiar to her later works. Even in her prairie novels from the 1910s – roughly the time of her initial exposure to the Southwest – the remembrance of the regularity of the everyday allowed her to generate moments of intensely felt security. "Every Saturday night we popped corn or made taffy," Jim Burden remembers in a typical scene from *My Ántonia* (1918), "and Otto Fuchs used to sing, 'For I Am a Cowboy and Know I've Done Wrong,' or, 'Bury Me Not on the Lone Prairee.' He had a good baritone voice and always led the singing when we went to church services at the sod schoolhouse" (754–755). In closely reading a passage like this one, we may wonder, of course, how many times Fuchs actually sang these songs, how often he led the singing in the schoolhouse church services, how many Saturdays the corn was popped. Clearly a past is being invented here. But this is exactly the point: What matters in such scenes, so characteristic of Cather's style of longing, is the feeling of an uncountable "always," a memory of secure regularity that can be formed only against the fact that "always" has ended long ago. And precisely against this loss can such memories be conjured up as images frozen in time: "I can still see those two men sitting on the bench; ... I can see the sag of their tired shoulders against the whitewashed wall" (755).

But if Cather's nostalgic style is built on a vision of a past ruled by the order of tradition, this by no means captures the full extent of her poetics of security. "Tom Outland's Story" makes this amply clear. While Father Duchene's views of the dwellers are adopted by the other characters, there are moments in which the novel undercuts the idyll he describes. The most obvious irritation is caused by a dried-up female corpse that Tom, Roddy, and Henry find above the main group of dwellings. They call her "Mother Eve" – not least, one might speculate, because someone seems to have tried to violently take back her rib: "We thought she had been murdered," Tom relates. "There was a great wound in her side, the ribs stuck out through the dried flesh. Her mouth was open as if she were screaming, and her face, through all those years, had kept a look of terrible agony" (229). Duchene tries to explain the occurrence of lethal violence by surmising a merely "personal tragedy": "Mother Eve" must have been unfaithful, and "in primitive society," he explains, the husband was allowed to punish such a transgression by death (235). But while Duchene's anthropological language attempts to contain even murder in the lawfulness of tradition, he can hardly cancel out the obvious mythico-religious overtones of Eve's Fall.

(To drive home the point, Cather has Eve fall down a canyon later on in the novel as the dried-up "mummy" is being hauled off by the German dealer Fechtig; 248–249.) In this mythical register, violence is no longer a personal matter, but bespeaks the intrusion of evil into the garden.[6]

Cather's pastoral vision of the security idyll of the past itself has a kind of fall built into it. Here she plays on a deeply ingrained topos of *securitas*, which accounts for a good deal of the violence in her fiction. In Father Duchene's rendition of the cliff dwellers' progress of civilization, we find the seeds of security turning into its opposite: the "arts of peace" lead to a decline in the "arts of war," which will lead to the brutal demise of the best of men. Having begun to develop a taste for the finer aspects of life – food, pottery, astronomy – they neglect to care for their defense. As Duchene conjectures, the disappearance of the cliff dwellers can only be explained by their being wiped out by Navajos while staying in their summer camp on the plains outside the Blue Mesa. Cather here echoes the post-Augustan usage of *securitas*: as I noted in my introductory chapter, a wide range of writers from Quintilian and Seneca to Christian thinkers such as Augustine, Luther, and Calvin, conceptualized security both as the absence of harm and as "carelessness, that is, as the baneful negation of attentiveness or diligence," as John Hamilton puts it (61).

In her 1916 newspaper article, Cather herself adheres to this topos and gives it a naturalist slant: "The most plausible theory as to their extinction is that the dwellers on the Mesa Verde were routed and driven out by their vulgar, pushing neighbors of the plains, who were less comfortable, less satisfied, and consequently more energetic" ("Mesa Verde" 332). Cather here echoes a theory for the mysterious disappearance of the Anasazi that was popular during her time, though it had recently become contested. As anthropologist Catherine M. Cameron notes, "early scholars, such as the young Swede Gustav Nordenskiöld in 1891, argued that the residents of the Mesa Verda proper were driven off by 'their enemies.' Twenty years later, one of the most influential Southwestern archeologists of the early twentieth century, Jesse Walter Fewkes, suggested that Cliff Palace was abandoned because of a 'change in climate that caused the water supply to diminish and crops to fail'" ("Leaving Mesa Verde" 139). Anthropologists today have refined Fewkes's position: they see the causes for emigration from the area in the combined impact of drought, resource depletion, overpopulation, and the liabilities that came with Maize monoculture, and rather than attributing the archeological record of intensified violence during the thirteenth century to outside enemies, they believe that it was committed by Pueblo communities from the region (see Kuckelman 134–135).

The point here is not to show that Cather clung to an anthropological explanation challenged even during her own day, but rather to explain the use of Nordenskiöld's theory of invasion by nomadic tribes for Cather: it allowed her to integrate the history of Mesa Verde into an underlying narrative of life energy and its loss, a narrative that organizes, as we shall see, *The Professor's House*. Thus, Cather suggests to her readers that comfort and security sapped the Anasazi's toughness while the nomadic Navajos' mobility kept them aggressive and alert.[7] The age-old warning of the false sense of security that is paradoxically built into the striving for security reappears in Cather's words as a quasi-Darwinist culture clash, in which the fittest and most primitive crush those whom culture has effeminized. As we shall see momentarily, this naturalist orientation was indeed central to Cather's perspective on security, though more typically she would turn the equation of force around and imagine past security not as characterized by the softening effects of culture, but instead by the vital force of youth.

4.2 Cather and Regionalism

In *The Professor's House*, the ideal of the secure life of the past becomes equated with youthful vitality. As I want to show in this section, this interpretation of nostalgic security grows out of Cather's indebtedness to regionalism. But whereas regionalists tended to construct a past that pointed to a series of pasts removed ever further from the present, Cather's fiction redirects this open-endedness and converts it into the past's potential futures.

For the last few decades, scholarship has struggled to come to terms with regionalism's nostalgic mood. For the conventional approach (though referring to the British pastoral tradition) we might point to Raymond Williams, who, in *The Country and the City*, argued that nostalgic ruralism pitted portrayals of industrial urbanity, fraught with social conflict, against the peaceful country life available to "men with a considerable banking account," as Williams, quoting George Eliot, phrases it (180). Richard Brodhead and Amy Kaplan proposed influential Americanist variants of this argument. In *Cultures of Letters*, Brodhead argued that regionalist writing catered to a new upper class, which defined itself through its connoisseurship of high culture as well as through its "distinctive leisure practices ... particularly its arts of leisure travel" (125). Similarly, Amy Kaplan argued in her essay "Nation, Region, and Empire" that regionalism "performs a kind of literary tourism," simplifying rural life with the effect of serving "the national agenda of reunion," and simultaneously naturalizing empire (251).

More recently, however, critics have emphasized that American regionalists did not necessarily simplify life in the regions. Stephanie Foote develops this position most pointedly. Like Brodhead, she is interested in the uses of regionalism for the urban elite, and like Kaplan, she is intent on showing regionalism's role in consolidating national and imperial ideologies, but unlike both Brodhead and Kaplan, Foote is also convinced of regionalism's self-reflexive critique of idyllic conventions:

> It is no longer possible to regard regional writing as representing a common national past; rather, we must see it as helping construct a common past in the face of, and out of the raw material of, the increasing immigration and imperialism of the nineteenth century. This means that regional writing was responsive to the nationalizing demands of the era that produced it and that its depiction of regions showed them all to be heterogeneous, founded on the differences that regional writing was assumed to eradicate. (13)[8]

Recent correctives such as Foote's are helpful for drawing conclusions about regionalism's possible extraliterary functions while remaining acute to the internal complexities of regionalist texts; they tend, however, to misconstrue the relation between nostalgia and the complexity of rural representation as mutually exclusive. In fact, the nostalgia effect of much of American regionalist writing does not hinge on the reduction of the complexity of rural life to an idyll of orderly simplicity. Since, strictly speaking, the concept of nostalgia – the longing (*algia*) for home (*nostos*) – consists in the act of longing, not in its satisfaction, it ought not surprise us that to the extent that regional writing actually is nostalgic, it never quite yields the simplicity which the urban traveler to the rural scene (who is often also the narrator and protagonist) expects to find. By the same token, the fact that life in regional rurality, as represented by writers such as Jewett, Hamlin Garland, or Charles Chesnutt, yields surprising complexities does not mean that these texts are not nostalgic.

By briefly looking at Jewett and Garland, I want to suggest that regionalist nostalgia, which is often discussed in terms of "place-attachment,"[9] primarily depends on a temporal rather than spatial mechanism, though this mechanism can only work in a particular spatial setting. It begins as an expectation of a well-ordered, simple life, which remains unfulfilled and becomes refueled at the very moment disillusionment sets in. Narratively speaking, this dynamic requires that the consciousness engaged in longing changes with each new round, for each time the expectation of simplicity is renewed, nostalgia becomes located in an anterior past one step further removed from the present than before. And since the past is a mental construction in relation to a particular viewpoint, the viewpoint must change with each replacement of one past by another. This – potentially infinite – regress to anterior pasts can be achieved by assigning the different viewpoints to different characters, or the change of perspective can happen to a single character, in which case the substitution of one instance of nostalgic longing for another results in a broadened consciousness.

The Country of the Pointed Firs (1896) may seem to pose the greatest obstacles to establish this point, considering that the mindset of Jewett's protagonist upon her arrival in the fictional Maine coastal town of Dunnet Landing really does seem to reflect, as Richard Brodhead claims, the desire of wealthy city-dwellers for rejuvenating countryside vacations. But while the well-off visitor/narrator (a female writer who aims to finish a book during her stay and thus seeks isolation) initially seems to find her expected repose in the quiet coastal life, Jewett redoubles the structure of longing for a lost past when she sends a second visitor, a friend of the narrator's hostess by the name of Susan Fosdick, to the scene. Mrs. Fosdick's arrival marks an actual instance of homecoming and threatens to disrupt the narrator's idyll. She tells stories that reach far into the past of the local seafaring culture, which since has declined almost entirely. Doing so, she reinserts Dunnet Landing into history and moreover creates an anterior past to long for, a secondary longing that will cancel out the grounds of the narrator's nostalgia. It is as if the narrator must find out that she fooled herself: current-day Dunnet Landing is far from the real article. In fact, what the narrator mistook for wholesome refreshment offered by a trip to the premodern past appears to the initiated, such as Susan Fosdick, as scarred precisely by modernity's worst effects of standardization: "There, how times have changed; how few seafarin' families there are left! What a lot o' queer folks there used to be about here, anyway, when we was young, Almiry. Everybody 's just like everybody else, now; nobody to laugh about, and nobody to cry about" (428).

Throughout the loosely connected scenes that make up Jewett's novel, this dynamic is repeated time and again, with the effect that *Country* gains its nostalgic feeling not so much from the happy bliss of having found a haven of premodern repose, but from the constant displacement of the nostalgic's desire for the past onto a past removed yet further. Slightly varied, the same open-ended anteriority also runs through Hamlin Garland's early story collection *Main-Travelled Roads* (1891). Garland's premise, however, differs quite starkly from Jewett's. Whereas Jewett's narrator seeks a quiet place in order to be able to write without disturbance, Garland, in his preface to the 1922 edition, perceives the rural landscape as "depressing" and the farmer's lot as marked by "ugliness, ... endless drudgery, and ... loneliness" that urgently calls for reform (vi). And yet, in the collection's best-known story, "Up the Coulee," the narrator, Howard McLane, associates rural life with the exact opposite of grimness. A successful actor, he is returning home from the city after ten years, expecting to find the idyllic place he has construed in his memory: "In his restless life ... he had not lost but gained appreciation for the coolness, quiet and low tones, the shyness of the wood and field" (51). Pursuing his fantasy in the role of regionalism's interloping tourist, Howard's disappointment, unexpected by him but anticipated by the reader, is caused not only by the structure of nostalgia's impossible object but also by objective facts: while the narrator has gathered riches as a star of the burgeoning entertainment industry, his family back home has gone bankrupt. Rural life, indeed, is bleaker than it used to be.

Having realized that in the locale of his youth, time has progressed too, Howard reacts in two interrelated ways: he begins to long for an anterior past of infantile bliss – "Oh, to be a boy again! An ignorant baby, pleased with a block and string, with no knowledge and no care of the great unknown" (65) – and he tries to master the forces that have torn the regional place out of the grasp of the past, and have unjustly ruined his brother while favoring himself: "Why should his brother sit there in wet and grimy clothing mending a broken trace, while he enjoyed all the light and civilization of the age?" (85).

Garland's nostalgic temporality is inflected by his naturalism. Circumstances determine his characters and take on the force of finality – they become accomplished facts – because they play out in the medium of irreversible time. Transposing the iron law of progressive time into a naturalist key, temporality in Garland becomes a matter of the expenditure of limited life energy. In the final scene, Garland dramatizes the effect of time on the body by arranging Howard's face next to his brother's: "The two men stood there, face to face, hands clasped, the one fair-skinned, full-lipped, handsome in his neat suit; the other tragic, somber in his softened mood, his large, long, rugged Scotch face bronzed with sun and scarred with wrinkles that had histories, like saber cuts on a veteran, the record of his battles" (87). This scene may anticipate Theodore Dreiser's portrayal of Sister Carrie's rise and Hurstwood's decline, another naturalist study of parallel lives centered on a spectacular career in theater. But in Garland's story, the degenerating effects of time cannot take away the dignity of

Howard's brother, and indeed, the brother's face appears as the more interesting one, a historical painting in its own right.

Much depends on this sympathetic description of the unlucky brother, for it enables Garland to derive a tragic effect from the passage of time and its sapping of vitality. Howard, at the end of the story, is determined to fight the injustice of chance: "luck made me and cheated you. It ain't right" (86). Yet his wish to correct the force of circumstance proves futile: "'Money can't give me a chance now'," explains his brother. "'I mean life ain't worth very much to me. I'm too old to take a new start. I'm a dead failure. You can't help me now. It's too late'" (87). As the progress of time becomes translated into diminished lifetime and physical decay, the future appears as robbed of contingency: even with money, Howard's brother no longer has a chance.

Once the progress of time becomes coupled, in naturalist manner, to a decrease in life expectancy and vital energy, the established object of nostalgia – a past of idyllic repose – becomes superimposed with an object that is quite different: a personal, even biological, past – youth – in which chance and uncertainty are unlimited. Garland's story gives us exactly this superimposition: while it begins, as we have seen, with Howard's longing for an idyllic past, it ends with the anterior longing for youth: "Both [brothers] were thinking of the days when they both planned great things in the way of an education, two ambitious, dreamful boys" (86).

As we will see shortly, for Cather, too, dreaminess and related states of consciousness like sleepiness and slumber are favorite ways of describing the nostalgia for youth. Indeed, Cather's nostalgia of security builds on a temporality of longing devised by regionalists, and in particular shares elements of Garland's naturalist type of regionalism. Like Garland, she superimposes the nostalgic longing for repose with a longing for a second youth.[10] But the differences are crucial: When Garland creates anterior nostalgia as a longing for youth, he does so by instantly emphasizing the impossibility of reversing the course of time. Youth is off limits. This gives his stories the punch of the tragic. By contrast, Cather, in *The Professor's House*, creates scenes of security that bring to life, and to the narrative present, memories in which the openness of youth becomes accessible in intricate and varied ways.[11] In my account of Cather's concern with security, I have so far emphasized her creation of scenes of order and regularity. Now that we have embedded her in the naturalist variant of regionalism's longing, we can begin to appreciate the second level of nostalgia for security superimposed on the first: her romance with the radical contingency of youthful vitality.

4.3 Security as Radical Contingency

As I have begun to suggest, Cather inherits from literary naturalism the tendency to naturalize the flow of progressive time, endowing it with material reality by linking it to the trajectory of bodily lives from maturation to decay. We can readily guess how sleep fits into this picture. Particularly in Book Three, St. Peter, alone at home while his family travels in Europe, seems to have lost his vital energy almost entirely. His life becomes increasingly dominated by the power of fatigue. Whereas previously he used to laugh "at people who naïvely confessed that they had 'an imagination'" and who talked about "day-dreams," he now finds himself spending his time doing nothing (258). He certainly is not making any progress with the writing task he has set for himself: a preface for a scholarly edition of Tom's diary that includes "a sketch of Outland, and some account of his later life and achievements" (203). (This task, we might say, had to wait for Willa Cather, for whom St. Peter in many ways acts as alter ego.) His energies depleted, even his eloquence falters. During a check-up with the family doctor, the most he can say is, "I simply feel tired all the time" (262). Finally, he nearly perishes by falling asleep in his study during a storm. For years, the little room under the roof of his old house offered him a refuge that allowed him to write his eight volumes on the "Spanish Adventurers," an achievement that has brought him academic recognition and financial success. More importantly, his oeuvre points back to the time of its creation, a period in the Professor's life of awe-inspiring creativity that made his historiographic and stylistic risk-taking resemble his great subject. Now, however, this very room no longer puts him in touch with his adventurers, but instead has come to resemble a tomb. Quite literally so: "The sagging springs [of his old couch] were like the sham upholstery that is put in coffins" (264). On this uncomfortable bedding he is seduced by sleep: "For a long while he slept deeply and peacefully. Then the wind, increasing in violence, disturbed him." Hearing things "banging and slamming about," St. Peter "turned over on his back and slept deeper still" (267). Aware of the danger of his gas stove, he buries himself in sleep as he registers the wind blowing out the flame and slamming shut the windows. The gas nearly suffocates St. Peter. There seems to be a straight line from daydreaming and general fatigue to deep, and finally, eternal sleep.

Surprisingly, however, sleep is also pervasive in "Tom Outland's Story." Climbing up the cliffs toward the mesa-top for the first time, Tom "discovers" the Cliff City: "I saw a little city of stone, asleep. It was as still as sculpture – and something like that. It all hung together, seemed to have a kind of composition" (221). On a literal level, sleep is related to vital force quite like it is for St. Peter: with the dwellers gone, the mesa's deep sleep points to the expiration of life.

And yet there is a world of difference between Tom finding a "city of stone, asleep" and a "city of stone, dead." Exploring the city soon after, Tom and Roddy come to a spring (a sign of life if ever there was one) where they find relics of life stopped in mid-action.

> Beside this spring stood some of the most beautifully shaped water jars we ever found ... standing there just as if they'd been left yesterday. In the back court we found ... several clay ovens, very much like those the Mexicans use to-day. There were charred bones and charcoal, and the roof was thick with soot all the way along. ... There were corncobs everywhere, and ears of corn with the kernels still on them – little, like popcorn. We found dried beans, too, and strings of pumpkin seeds, and plum seeds, and a cupboard full of little implements made of turkey bones. (233)

It is as if there had intervened virtually no time between the disappearance of the ancient culture and its discovery in the present moment; as if the soot in the ovens indicated their being used, like in Mexico, "to-day." Indeed, it seems as if Tom and Roddy might just have to wait a few moments for the return of the dwellers to share a communal meal. In the little city of stone, asleep, the absence of life does not point to mortal finitude, but to the possibility of life reawakening: because nothing is happening presently, anything may happen shortly.

Sleep-sunken though the mesa may be, it initially will not let Tom sleep. Sharing their observations about their find, Tom, Roddy and Henry "talked and speculated until after midnight. ... [A]fter we went to bed, tired as I was, I was unable to sleep. I got up and dressed and put on my overcoat and slipped outside to get sight of the mesa" (222). It is not death that prevents Tom from sleeping, but the vibrant presence of life. The traces of life don't stop at the present moment, but point ahead, into the future. And while this future thrust is of the "dreamy indefiniteness" suggested to Cather by Thomas Mann's *Joseph and His Brothers*, Tom and Roddy do more than dream of a possible future: the deep sleep of the mesa civilization makes Tom and Roddy wide awake with bustling activity, both imaginative and practical. They excavate relics, create an inventory (Tom calls it, in entrepreneurial fashion, their "ledger"), make anthropological inquiries, and ultimately try to get the Smithsonian to "revive" the Pueblo civilization (234).

But all this busyness is no more than a transitional stage. Tom goes on a "fruitless errand" to the capital (256) – a trip that makes it painfully clear to him (and here Cather turns the historical record inside out[12]) that the federal government pays no interest to its "national" treasures – and upon returning, he falls out with Roddy over the latter's selling the relics to a German dealer. In this state of seeming despair, sleep is all that Tom craves: "I went to sleep that night hoping I would never waken" (251). This is the kind of death-wishing sleep that the Professor, as already described, will later replicate when he nearly lets himself be suffocated by his gas oven (see 267). But if sleep, in Tom's experience on the mesa, has an alternative meaning from the moment he "saw a little city of stone, asleep" (221), it is this alternative meaning that he soon after manages to recover. Having searched in vain for Roddy, he returns to the mesa by himself. In his first night after his return he reaches the spiritual climax of both his life and his story:

> [T]hat was the first night I was ever really on the mesa at all – the first night that all of me was there. This was the first time I ever saw it as a whole. It all came together in my understanding, as a series of experiments do when you begin to see where they are leading. Something had happened in me that made it possible for me to coordinate and simplify, and that process, going on in my mind, brought with it great happiness. It was possession. The excitement of my first discovery was a very pale feeling compared to this one. For me the mesa was no longer an adventure, but a religious emotion. I had read of filial piety in the Latin poets, and I knew that was what I felt for this place. It had formerly been mixed up with other motives; but now that they were gone, I had my happiness unalloyed. (253)

In learning how to sleep, Tom undergoes a purification process that gives him a sense of religious rapture – an experience in which he approaches the state of the mesa itself. Sleep has let him in on something strangely nontransitive: "It was possession." Neither does the mesa possess him, nor does he possess the mesa. Possession happens in the form of "It was," a kind of Heideggerian "There Is," which anchors abstract *Sein* in the concretely materialized collective present tense of *Dasein*.[13] Possession happens, in other words, to both Tom and the Blue Mesa. It grounds Tom's being in a relation of existential belonging, a belonging that lacks a proprietor and yet binds him to the here-and-now of a place associated with pastness.[14] In this carefree state, simple and happy, security – originally the cliff dweller's achievement of protection, ritual, and civilizational uplift – comes into its own as his condition. It is a condition I describe as "radical contingency." If security is marked by the removal of worry, the procurement of protection, and the state of bliss, "radical contingency" represents a variant of security in which life is preserved in its state of full potentiality, shielded from any constrictions that come with actuality.

Cather's superimposition of security as a place and time of order on the one hand and of slumbering potential on the other takes up regionalism's stacking up of pasts of increasing anteriority. Cather, however, reverses the direction, moving from the deep past toward the present. And as in the regionalist model, with each step through the different time layers of the past, she alters the referent to whom the past relates. Thus, when the mesa generates a nostalgic experience of secure order and tradition, Father Duchene and Tom refer to what they believe was the past of the Pueblo dwellers, full of reverence for ritual. But when the imagination of bygone security gains its additional layer of evoking potentiality, it is Tom who experiences the mesa by himself, without any interfering reconstruction of the cliff dwellers. The mesa now evokes a potential life that refers to him, not to the Pueblo Indians.

For Tom, security as "radical contingency" not only exceeds the sense of being protected from external danger but also goes further than the transitional stage he has just left behind, that of enterprising (or even entrepreneurial) activity with Roddy: he quits "adventure" and gets rid of the admixture of "other motives." That these other motives existed for him is a concession that itself bespeaks his purification. During his fight with Roddy, Tom had insisted that Roddy's selling of the relics, which belonged to neither one of them, constituted an unforgiveable breach. To which Roddy replied, "I supposed I had some share in the relics we dug up – you always spoke of it that way. But I see now I was working for you like a hired man, and while you were away I sold your property" (249). Now that Roddy has left, Tom's recognition of "other motives" suggests that Roddy was right: in setting the terms of their joint (ad)venture, in deciding, without consulting with Roddy or accepting his diverging view, that the found objects are taboo, he has in fact made Roddy work for him. Once alone, Tom rejects this unwitting adherence to proprietorship. In this newly gained state, the world becomes simplified to a neighborly coexistence with primal elements, a vegetating existence[15]: "Up there alone, a close neighbour to the sun, I seemed to get the solar energy in some direct way" (253).[16]

His physical state is the apparent inversion of the Professor's toward the end of the novel: While St. Peter "simply feel[s] tired all the time" (262), Tom is full of energy: "nothing tired me" (253). And yet, his condition is almost interchangeable with the Professor's, for he spends his days in much the same way as St. Peter – doing nothing. And in fact, this doing "nothing" has a palpable effect on him: nothing *tires him* greatly. So much so that he says, "I used to feel that I couldn't have borne another hour of that consuming light, that I was full to the brim, and needed dark and sleep" (253). Both St. Peter and Tom share a complete breakdown of productivity, and for both, this becomes manifest in relation to Tom's diary: While St. Peter cannot bring himself to write the preface for the scholarly edition, Tom cannot make himself add anything new to his previous busy recording of his and Roddy's explorations. He cannot even take the diary from the place where he stored it before his trip to Washington: "All that summer, I never went up to the Eagle's Nest to get my diary – indeed, it's probably there yet" (253).

I describe Tom's sense of security as consisting in a sense of "radical contingency" because it arises from opting out of an existence that records itself and makes itself available for reflection, opting out of an economy of relics, opting out of the logic of the trace, according to which relics are left behind by people, taken up later by others who again leave them behind, and so on. Tom's experience on the mesa is one of solitary completion: "I ... saw it as a whole." But it is a completion of a very peculiar kind, not characterized by things having been perfected, but by things being kept from beginning.[17]

The rendition of security as radical contingency in Cather's novel proposes a state of being in which possibility is not an ontological given but must be wrested from the present actuality of the material world and defended against the intrusion of future actuality. Contingency here replaces actuality only on the condition that actuality is forcefully pushed out. Security as radical contingency, in other words, is an essentially temporal attempt to rid the world of its worldliness in order to ensure a future of unlimited potentiality. In short, everything is possible, and imaginable, only if nothing is the case.

Around this idea, Cather built an aesthetic program detailed most famously in her essay "The Novel Démeublé." Beginning with her essay's very title, Cather unfolds a calculation of a modernist reception aesthetics, according to which the subtraction of the detailed description of objects, and even of the objects themselves, will produce a gain in the reader's imaginary experience. "The novel," she writes, "for a long while, has been over-furnished. The property-man has been so busy on its pages, the importance of material objects and their vivid presentation have been so stressed, that we take it for granted whoever can observe, and can write the English language, can write a novel" (834). Only if the writer recognizes that "the novel is a form of imaginative art," that "mere verisimilitude" must be abandoned in order "to present [a] scene by suggestion rather than enumeration," can there be hope for great novels to come (836). For "it is the inexplicable presence of the thing not named, of the overtone divined by the ear but not heard by it, the verbal mood, the emotional aura of the fact or the thing or the deed, that gives high quality to the novel or the drama, as well as to poetry itself" (837).

It is quite possible to hear Tom in this account: he and Roddy, propertymen despite themselves, have been extremely busy (the pages of Tom's ledger seem to be even clearer proof of this than the pages of "Tom Outland's Story"), and the importance of material objects and their vivid presentation have been greatly stressed (Tom's diary contains "a minute description of each tool they found, of every piece of cloth and pottery" [258]) – until it is revealed to Tom, his world having been de-furnished and depopulated, that property can be replaced by the "it was" of non-transitive possession. Tom, like the intended reader, begins to live in a world of great auratic value, engulfed in an aesthetic experience of religious intensity. The implication of Tom's solitary summer even goes further than the argument of the essay: Cather not only does not name "the thing or the deed" but also removes them from Tom's world altogether. The relics are gone, sold and resold; Roddy is gone (first Tom does not give him much thought, but later, looking for him among railroad workers, he is distressed that he cannot find any trace of him); Henry has died from a sudden snake attack; even Mother Eve has fallen into the abyss. In short, Tom has taken over the Pueblo dweller's city and has adapted their security to a wholly new experience of sheer possibility based on the absence of anything more actual, more substantial, than solar energy. Security as radical contingency, then, arises from a reworking of the meaning of the Catherian rock. Initially representing security by providing a counterpoint to modernity that is marked by tradition and order, the Mesa, as experienced by Tom, opens into a different dimension of security by preserving life in its state of unlimited possibility, shielded from the contractions necessarily attached to existence in the actual.

4.4 From Contingency to Fate

Tom's immersion in contingency momentarily suspends the progression of time, keeping open all the options for a future by keeping at bay its necessary actualization of potentiality. Where a modernist experimenter like Virginia Woolf, whose *To The Lighthouse* (1926) structurally and thematically echoes *The Professor's House*, would grasp from the inside of consciousness this experience of temporal suspension, Cather instead aims at "the verbal mood, the emotional aura" of the security of contingency.[18] Crucial for such a creation of aura is once again the temporal constellation of nostalgia, which reconstructs the experience of security from the point in time of having lost it. Tom's account is specifically marked as a memory of something in the past: his very wording emphasizes the irreversible progression of time, the irretrievable pastness of the experience described, even if that experience tries to push off the necessary narrowing of potentiality that comes with temporal succession. His revelation of potentiality freed from the actual depends on the pathos of singular and unrepeatable newness: during his "first night" alone on the mesa, he has the experience of wholeness for the "first time." Though the power of firstness seems to extend over a stretch of time that lasts a whole summer, the temporal marker of the first nonetheless implies that the progression of time asserts itself over the attempt of radical contingency to keep the future from restructuring and reactualizing the world.

The nostalgia here is not merely Tom's but also St. Peter's, in the form of a nostalgia both for Tom's experience and Tom himself. As Lisa Marie Lucenti puts it, St. Peter aims "to keep his moments with Tom outside of this temporal process of destruction and reconstruction; he would like to preserve the integrity of a short span of time, in effect, make it timeless" ("Sleeping with the Dead" 246). The Professor's imaginary relation to Tom and his story, however, finds itself surrounded by alternative acts of remembrance: Tom becomes a legend in the Professor's family, told and retold from different angles by the family members. Rosamond and Louie Marsellus, Kathleen and Scott, the Professor's wife Lillian all insist on their own version and deprecate competing claims for memorialization. While Scott admits that "Tom isn't very real to me any more. Sometimes I think he was just a – a glittering idea" (164), his wife Kathleen, in a moment of intimacy with her father, resents her sister Rosamond and Louie for having turned Tom into "chemicals and dollars and cents," and confides to St. Peter: "Our Tom is much nicer than theirs" (177). Louie and Rosamond, on the other hand, aim to memorialize Tom by naming their newly built, decadently large, country mansion "Outland," and installing in it a museum of sorts that will present to Outland tourists "all the sources of [Tom's] inspiration" (122), including his library, pictures, and laboratory (which they plan to remove from the physics department, effectually halting all further research on his invention[19]). And whereas Louie uses a family dinner to dish up the kind of sentimental heroism – "Outland got nothing out of [his invention] but death and glory" (121) – that echoes St. Peter's own admiration for early death ("[Tom] had escaped all ... the meaningless conventional gestures," 257), Lillian, who perceives in Tom a competitor for her husband's affection, criticizes precisely Tom's mythmaking tendencies, his being beholden to the "chivalry of the cinema" (203).

Despite this contestation of memory, Tom and his summer on the mesa are claimed with the greatest vigor by the Professor, not least because St. Peter is subtly present in the narrating voice of "Tom Outland's Story," which superimposes Tom and St. Peter.[20] It is as if Godfrey St. Peter were called upon, by the sheer force of his name, to appropriate Tom's experience of security on the Blue Mesa, to become immersed in the elemental *Dasein* of radical contingency, and thus to finally become the rock itself. Cather does not make explicit the allusion, but it sounds loud and clear: "And I say also unto thee, That thou art Peter, and upon this rock I will build my church; and the gates of hell shall not prevail against it" (Matthew 16:18).

St. Peter seems to take this interpellation seriously, indeed. Taking up his calling to become the rock, he separates radical contingency from its condition of being placed in an irretrievable past. Whereas at the end of Tom's story, we are told, in a voice that flirts with omniscience, that "Happiness is something one can't explain. You must take my word for it. Troubles enough came afterward, but there was that summer, high and blue, a life in itself" (254), St. Peter seems to make a point of not taking the speaker's word for it. Not only does he longingly revisit a moment of youth positioned in the past, in a different life, measured by the unit of the season, but he also aims at literal rejuvenation, carrying over to the present the potentiality made available during that summer on the rock, "high and blue": "Just when the morning brightness of the world was wearing off for him, along came Outland and brought him a kind of second youth" (255).

Trying to make the present radically contingent requires the same de-furnishing and depopulating of the world that Tom accomplished on the mesa. From this perspective, the St. Peters' new family residence, bought with the prize money awarded for the Professor's *magnum opus*, turns out to be of great advantage. Though it is usually interpreted as the imposition of material comfort and debilitating domesticity on the Professor's preferred strenuous life, the new house serves St. Peter as storage space for all the material objects that clutter his life. The new house, in other words, allows him to spend as much time as possible in a version of the old house which, now that it has been emptied out save for his study, might bring him closer to a state of radical contingency. (It is as a *maison démeublée* that Cather honors the old house in the novel's title.[21]) And with Lillian,

Rosamond, and Louie off to Europe for the summer, St. Peter has effectively freed himself from all the obligations that come with what the novel calls "this secondary social man" (259). Extricating himself from all the claims that come with social interdependence – consumption, domesticity, marriage, and even reproduction (Rosamond and Louie, he is informed by letter from France, are expecting a baby) – Godfrey embraces his first name, and, aspiring to become free as a god, believes to have recovered his "original self" (261): "first nature could return to a man, unchanged by all the pursuits and passions and experiences of his life" (261). He persuades himself that he has successfully reverted to being a "primitive" (260) and that his constant fatigue signals his achievement of having become "indifferent" (261) to his life in the actual world. He has, it might seem, arrived at a sense of completion available to those who inhabit a point in time *before* anything has taken shape.

This ideal position of temporal priority, however, is available only as a mental exercise of memory. As the Professor discovers in his moment of crisis, being placed *before* everything is not at all a tenable position in the present, since the present cannot be taken out of the progressive thrust of time.[22] And as the present moment slides into the past, what was a potential future closes in on the new present as its actuality. The attempt to ward off future actuality, in other words, creates a position in which the flow of time becomes experienced as an overpowering and crushing force. Radical contingency turns into mere chance, and chance is precisely what the Professor, at the outset of Book Three, discovers to be the determining factor of his life: "All the most important things in his life, St. Peter sometimes reflected, had been determined by chance. His education in France had been an accident. His married life had been happy largely through a circumstance with which neither he nor his wife had anything to do" (255).

Taken down from the Mesa, contingency falls into mere chance and becomes divorced from security. In its articulation in the regionalist text, potentiality could become associated with security only on the condition of being placed in the past of youthful vitality. Security thus depended on its rendition in a nostalgic mode, on the imaginary recovery of having life before oneself. The Professor's attempt to access a "second youth" and make radical contingency a condition of the present, on the other hand, arrests him in a position that can no longer be grasped as security. Passively exposed to futurity, he has become utterly insecure. Instead of preparing for what the future might bring, life happens to him in unforeseeable strokes of fate. His near-suffocation in his study during the storm is an apt illustration: though there are strong hints that St. Peter welcomes the occurrence as a convenient way to sink into interminable sleep, the narrator (with St. Peter as focalizer) remembers the event as an accident, purging any active involvement on the Professor's part: "Yet when he was confronted by accidental extinction, he had felt no will to resist, but had let chance take its way, as it had done with him so often" (271).

Even the things that make the Professor's life worth living now appear as a matter of sheer fate: "Tom Outland had been a stroke of chance he couldn't possibly have imagined; his strange coming, his strange story, his devotion, his early death and posthumous fame – it was all fantastic" (255). In fact, he is glad that things have turned out the way the have: "he had fared well with fate" (255). He would not gamble on a better life even if he could: "he might not have such good luck again" (255).

Alternating between the wish for total potentiality and the feeling of utter lack of power, St. Peter's trajectory at this point in the novel is so polarized that it comes to be at odds with his primary identifications. Witlessly submitting to the force of fate, he has become alienated from the self that is textually prior to his "original self." After all, St. Peter has made a career writing about the "Spanish Adventurers" – I will come back to the euphemistic quality of this term momentarily – and, as the narrator relates early on in playfully fallacious logic, his subject of study has rubbed off on him: "St. Peter was commonly said to look like a Spaniard. That was possibly because he had been in Spain a good deal, and was an authority on certain phases of Spanish history" (104). An authority on the history of colonial exploration and conquest, St. Peter is an expert on a key modern practice of processing uncertainty and chance, and he has gained his expertise thanks to a sympathetic identification that presumably must have turned himself into a skilled chance-taker. From this vantage point, St. Peter has a spiritual son not so much in Tom but in Louie Marsellus, who is likewise adept at dealing in chance. During his interview with Mrs. Crane in Book One, St. Peter speaks admiringly of Louie's skill in turning Tom's invention into a profitable business: "A great deal of money was put into it, too, before any came back; every cent Marsellus had, and all he could borrow. He took heavy chances. Crane and I together could never have raised a hundredth part of the capital that was necessary to get the thing started. Without capital to make it go, Tom's idea was merely a formula written out on paper" (181). Reverting to primitivism, St. Peter has given up any trace of spirit or skill necessary for testing out the uncertain. His attempt to appropriate radical contingency in the present has turned him into a thoroughly risk-averse man: instead of taking chances, chance happens to him. St. Peter has resigned himself to fateful insecurity.

4.5 Facing the Future, or: The Coming of Berengaria

The novel's final paragraphs find Godfrey St. Peter slowly reconciling himself to life as a matter of action. This is partially thanks to the arch-Catholic family seamstress Augusta, a "reliable, methodical spinster" (106), who has miraculously rescued the Professor from suffocating in his study, whose name evokes the stability of the Augustan *pax romana* (historically allegorized on imperial coins by the goddess *Securitas*), and who acts as a "corrective, a remedial influence" that suggests to St. Peter "proper action" (269).[23] If "Tom Outland's Story" combined two notions of security, one deriving from the observation of tradition and ritual, the other from the recovery of life's youthful potential, and if St. Peter unsuccessfully tried to isolate the second strain and make it work in the present, Augusta reestablishes the primacy of ritual as the source of security. For this devout woman, the rock of security really is the Church.

With Augusta guiding him out of the Biblical "gates of hell," which have almost "prevailed" against St. Peter after all, he gives up his aspirations for radical contingency: "His temporary release from consciousness seemed to have been beneficial. He had let something go – and it was gone: something very precious, that he could not consciously have relinquished, probably" (271). No longer trying to stave off the forward thrust of time, his "letting go" is a step aside, making way for things to come: a gesture familiar from *laissez-faire, laissez-passer*. His new acceptance of futurity, Cather's hopeful ending suggests, will allow him to accept our susceptibility to chance, without becoming stuck in a passive state that helplessly subjects us to the force of fate. This, it would seem, is the chastened compromise between idealism and determinism that allows the Professor to live on instead of awaiting the next opportunity for accident-assisted suicide.

But even though the Professor may find much good sense in Augusta's orientation to life, *The Professor's House* does not prescribe Augusta's ways as a model for St. Peter. The novel does not end with his conversion to faith, nor does it seek a solution in the reverential observation of ritual, whether secular or sacred. Cather, I would suggest, does not give her novel the conservative turn that she herself would perform a few years later, most explicitly in her essays. "Letting go" – a phrase Cather consciously adopts from Robert Frost[24] – is not a recipe for holding on to faith and maintaining tradition, but rather for a pragmatic flexibility regarding the ever-changing givens of the external world. Indeed, "letting go" does not replace the promise of contingency with tradition, but rather sidesteps the destructive dimension of radical contingency. Instead of defining contingency against actuality, which requires the total negation of the actual, "letting go" turns the unavoidable arrival of future actuality into an advantage by welcoming and eliciting the fugacity and ephemerality of the actual, anticipating the continuous sequences of futures.

This affirmation of the contingent as actual comes at a high cost, however, for it exacts a negation of its own: it requires giving up "something very precious," an act so difficult that few will be able to bring themselves to commit it in full consciousness. The "precious" something the Professor lets go is a classic Catherian case of "the thing not named." What is it that St. Peter must give up? Clearly, the most obvious answer would be: his idealized image of Tom Outland. But the name "Tom" does not quite capture the magnitude of this sacrifice; the unnamed thing is larger than that, large enough to unsettle the entirety of St. Peter's social existence. More precisely, the Professor can only return to being a "social man" by remapping his social world in a way that highlights what has only shimmered through the novel's surface.

The basic binary on which the social world of *The Professor's House* is constructed – consisting of Tom Outland and Louie Marsellus as the opposite poles – gets reaffirmed with great clamor throughout Book One (by far the longest section of the novel), but at the same is repeatedly, if subtly, undermined. The affirmation of this dualism is generated by the majority of St. Peter's professed views, as well as by those of his daughter Kathleen and her husband Scott. On this view, Tom is set in relief against Louie: Reviving the civilization of the mythical founders of the Southwest, Tom embodies the ur-American national origin, whereas Louie is the Jewish interloper, the novel's true Outlander, who has, according to Kathleen, "ruined" Rosamond with all his money (148) and with their soon-to-be-born child. Tom is the rugged adventurer, a man who does not care for table manners, whereas Louie is conscious of his appearance to the point of being effeminate. Tom is a philosophical idealist whose sensibility naturally strives for the highest cultural achievements – he is an avid reader of Virgil and Lucretius – whereas Louie is a materialist who is invested in luxury and only appreciates culture for its capital (for the family trip to Europe, he envisions luncheons with Emile Faguet and Anatole France, but neither does he mention having read, or wanting to read, their works, nor does he know much about them: Faguet has died a few years back, in 1916). Finally, Tom primarily inhabits his youthful "original" self – the Professor rarely considers him in his role as Rosamond's fiancé and his own virtual son-in-law – whereas Louie stands at the center of dreadful family life, is exhaustively defined to the Professor in his role as son-in-law, and, just having passed through youth, moreover represents the painful progression of time.[25]

Letting go of Tom, then, also means revising the image of Louie and thus taking apart the scaffolding on which the novel's character constellation depends. A thread runs through the novel that calls into question its basic polarity, and in the very last sentence this thread is brought to the foreground: "He thought he knew where he was, and that he could face with fortitude the *Berengaria* and the future" (271). The *Berengaria* is the passenger liner on which Lillian, Rosamond, and Louie are returning from Europe (Cather herself was one of its passengers in 1923). Cather's choice is not sufficiently explained by the steamer's real existence, however. Routinely picking proper names for their symbolic significance, she clearly decides on *Berengaria* to evoke its broad semantic spectrum.

Berengaria is also the name of the wife of King Richard I, better known as Richard the Lionheart. While critics have noted the reference before,[26] they have neglected that this allusion marks Richard's second appearance in Cather's novel: the mythical story of Richard's encounter with Saladin in Jerusalem during the Third Crusade is evoked earlier in the novel precisely in order to unsettle the negative image the novel has conferred onto Louie. Asked by his students to contribute a tableau vivant for an "historical pageant" in order to commemorate "deeds of an early French explorer among the Great Lakes," the Professor decides on a scene "that has nothing to do with the subject" (140): he casts his sons-in-law as Richard and Saladin and stages their encounter in a scene that might be lifted straight from Walter Scott's 1825 novel *The Talisman*.

In that novel, Scott had taken up the positive treatment of Saladin by Enlightenment historians such as Hume and Gibbon,[27] and had firmly established the Romantic trope of the rational, magnanimous, and admirably noble Saracene leader, in comparison to whom Richard the Lion-Hearted (Scott's spelling) pales considerably: the English Crusader comes across as impetuous, arrogant, and vain, and serves Scott as a vehicle for ridiculing the myth of chivalry. At the very end of *The Talisman*, as Saladin's military and moral superiority can no longer be questioned, and as the vicissitudes of the plot have been resolved with Saladin's help, Richard makes an utter fool of himself begging Saladin to have it out with him in a duel: "Is it fitting that such a royal ring of chivalry should break up without something being done for future times to speak of? ... If not for Jerusalem, then ... yet, for the love of honour, let us run at least three courses with grinded lances?" (234). But Saladin keeps his cool: Having considered for a moment whether to accept the challenge, he declines, characteristically putting the interest of his people before his own vainglory and wittily reminding the crusader of the teachings of the Bible: "your own Scripture saith that when the herdsman is smitten, the sheep are scattered" (234).

The Professor's version of this scene remains true to Scott's liberal Orientalism and poses his two sons-in-law in a tapestry-hung tent, for a conference between Richard Plantagenet and the Saladin, before the walls of Jerusalem.

> [Louie] Marsellus, in a green dressing-gown and turban, was seated at a table with a chart, his hands extended in reasonable, patient argument. The Plantagenet was standing, his plumed helmet is his hand, his square yellow head haughtily erect, his unthoughtful brows fiercely frowning, his lips curled and his fresh face full of arrogance. (140–141)

Though ostensibly a showdown between Kathleen's Scott and Rosamond's Louie, the scene also invites being read as a confrontation between the Professor's other pair of competing sons-in-law: Tom, Rosamond's virtual late husband; and Louie, her actual present husband. Cather makes a point of omitting Scott's name in the passage cited, and throughout the book, Marsellus is measured against Tom at least as much as against Scott. With Scott literally standing in for Tom, the Professor is able to present a picture he might not have consciously countenanced: Tom appears as arrogant, haughty, and unthoughtful, while Louie is reasonable and patient. Just as *The Talisman* offers revisionist pictures of Richard the Lion-Hearted (as foolish and proud) and Saladin (as noble and magnanimous), so the Professor's tableau vivant reimagines Tom's romantic heroism as conceited and foolish, and Louie's ostensible exploitation of someone else's ingenuity as reasonable and dignified. Both of these reinterpretations find support throughout the novel: Tom rushes off to war in the Foreign Legion to defend France and civilization and thus commits the heroic fallacy that in the course of World War I would come to appear ever more naive, and which would later be debunked with great relish by the expatriate modernists.[28] Moreover, Tom himself begins to revise his own myth when he concedes his lack of disinterested magnanimity after his fallout with Roddy, admitting to have acted from mixed motives. Louie, on the other hand, puts to shame the envy of Kitty, Scott, and even the Professor by reliably acting in the most generous manner, and by remaining composed and forgiving when being slighted by the various members of the family.[29]

Understandably, the tableau's familial revisionism fails to grab the students' attention, and Lillian remarks that "nobody saw his little joke" (141). Presumably, she sees the joke in the Professor's casting Louie, the

Jew, as the Muslim leader. But in light of St. Peter's wife approaching on the ship named after King Richard's wife – in other words, in light of Lillian and Berengaria becoming interchangeable names of the "secondary social man's" foundation in marriage – the joke turns out to be on the Professor himself. For if Richard the Lionheart resembles anyone, it is, in fact, Godfrey St. Peter: "standing, his ... square yellow head haughtily erect, his unthoughtful brows fiercely frowning, his lips curled and his fresh face full of arrogance," the King recalls the portrayal of St. Peter early on in the novel. Though the Professor's face is brown, not yellow, the Spaniard-by-scholarship exudes the same haughty pride that characterizes King Richard. In both cases, the sense of cold superiority derives from eyebrows, fierce and wicked-looking: "He had a long brown face, with an oval chin over which he wore a close trimmed Van-Dyke, like a tuft of shiny black fur. ... [His hawk-like eyes] were set in ample cavities, with plenty of room to move about, under thick, curly, *black eyebrows that turned up sharply at the outer ends, like military moustaches. His wicked-looking eyebrows made his students call him Mephistopheles* – and there was no evading the searching eyes underneath them" (104, emphasis added).

Beyond the immediate social world of the novel, St. Peter's inhabiting the position of King Richard has wider implications for the reassessment of adventurous heroism in *The Professor's House*. Cather leaves no doubt about the ethnic differences between St. Peter, the Spaniard (who dons a mustache like black fur), and King Richard I with "his square yellow head." (It is tempting to describe Richard as the stereotypical Anglo-Saxon, except that his Norman ancestry makes this a rather difficult claim.[30]) But this difference in ethnicity only highlights the continuity between Richard I, the crusader, and St. Peter, who identifies with the "Spanish Adventurers." The alignment of the crusader and the conquistadores can be further extended to include the "early French explorer among the Great Lakes" memorialized by St. Peter's students, though the Professor wants to make us believe that this "has nothing to do with the subject" (140). St. Peter, in fact, is associated with the conquistadores and the French explorers even by the Biblical context of his name: not only is he compelled to be the foundation of the Christian Church but, having been told by God "that I should not call any man common or unclean," he sets the precedent for missionary work among the Gentiles (Acts 10:28).

We begin to see, then, the full scope of St. Peter's "letting go": in relinquishing Tom, he must revise his account of Louie, which, taking the relational interdependence of Tom and Louie to its displaced conclusion, demands putting into practice what he unknowingly suggested when staging his tableau: he must recognize himself as Richard Coeur de Lion as envisioned by Walter Scott – a slightly ridiculous, ill-tempered, and aggressive ruler who foolishly believes in the grandeur of knightly honor and adventure. In other words, the Professor is forced to face the true nature of the ideals he has been chasing. If he has had "two romances: one of the heart, which had filled his life for many years, and a second of the mind – of the imagination" (255), he must give up both of them. Having let go of Tom, he must also abandon his romance with the "Spanish Adventurers," and thus with the organizing idea of his life's work.[31]

In its final paragraph, Cather's novel thus amplifies a debate over the meaning of "adventure" that was audible at a low volume even in "Tom Outland's Story." To recall, Tom proclaims to have rejected "adventure" – he finds it to be fraught with mixed motives – and instead seeks a purified experience of radical contingency. Dismissing adventure is a rare step in Cather's oeuvre since for the most part, her characters romanticize adventure as an expression of the youthful vitality the Professor seeks in Tom. Usually, that is to say, adventurism and radical contingency appear as inseparable in Cather's nostalgic staging of the lost past of security. Among her characters, it is only Tom who differentiates between the adventurous exploring – and exploiting – of the world's seemingly unlimited possibilities and the experience of sheer potentiality in its purified version cleansed of the actual. By contrast, the more typically Catherian infatuation with adventure celebrates forays into the uncertain that contain both a material and a spiritual dimension.

This Romantic idea of adventure is articulated nowhere as clearly as in *A Lost Lady* (1923), the prairie novel (and condensed masterpiece of longing) immediately preceding *The Professor's House*. As Niel, the young protagonist in love with his ideal construction of Marian Forrester, imagines it, "The Old West had been settled by dreamers, great-hearted adventurers who were unpractical to the point of magnificence; a courteous brotherhood, strong in attack but weak in defence, who could conquer but could not hold" (58). The "courteous brotherhood" of expansionists settling the "Old West" encapsulates the Romantic vision of adventurous conquest by setting it apart from modern-day capitalist expansion of the "New West" (embodied in *A Lost Lady* by Ivy Peters) and by imagining it as wholly benign: since attack is not followed up by defense, it is as if the deeds of the great-hearted explorers had no consequences at all, as if settling in the West were at once a claim on the real world and an activity as immaterial and impractical as dreaming. In *The Professor's House*, such a starry-eyed vision of adventure is no longer tenable, especially as the Professor becomes once again a "social man" at the side of Berengaria and thus faces the fact of having been Lion-Hearted all along. But as the Professor has realized in Book Three, neither is life possible if the advent of future actuality – the *adventura* – is outright repudiated, especially if this is done not as nostalgic memory of radical contingency, but as present apathy. Early on, he tries in vain to hide his misgivings when he tells his wife, "you're so occupied with the future, you adapt yourself so readily" (153). Now he recognizes that trying to shut out the future is no solution either.

To tease out the orientation to the future suggested by the Professor's new commitment to survival, I propose to take yet another look at the novel's final lines: "At least, he felt the ground under his feet. He thought he knew where he was, and that he could face with fortitude the *Berengaria* and the future" (271). Facing the future is the key to St. Peter's regained entry into the progressive thrust of temporality that entangles him in the double bind characteristic of the will for survival: he exemplifies what I have described in the introduction as a particularly modern stance marked on the one hand by the wish to turn the contingency of the future to his own advantage and thus convert insecurity into security, and on the other hand by an anxiety over the impression that the now cannot be preserved in the face of future contingency, that we are therefore doomed to never overcome insecurity, and that we indeed must never overcome it since the hope for security and the fear of insecurity grow out of the very same contingency. But beyond this double bind of futurity – striving for security and accepting insecurity – Professor St. Peter's facing "with fortitude the *Berengaria* and the future" furthermore suggests that he must also acquire a particular kind of historical sensibility, a skill in which this award-winning historian has been strangely lacking.

The clue for the affirmation of the historical is provided once again by the word *Berengaria*, but this time its suggestiveness comes from a more literal angle. The *Berengaria* is an ocean liner whose career is so remarkable that it strongly invites reflection on the nature of the historical itself: Initially a German passenger liner, the *Berengaria* was built in Hamburg for HAPAG and launched in 1913 as the SS *Imperator*. The US Department of the Navy relates its further history as follows:

> Taken over by the U.S. Navy after the World War I Armistice [under the name USS *Imperator*], she was placed in commission in early May 1919. During the next three months *Imperator* carried U.S. troops home from the former European war zone. . . . USS *Imperator* completed her seagoing Naval service in August 1919 and spent the following three months at New York, where she was decommissioned in late November 1919 and turned over to

the British Government. Renamed *Berengaria*, she spent nearly two more decades as a civilian passenger liner. (U.S. Department of the Navy)

In light of the *Berengaria*'s history, I read the novel's ending as an ironic vision of the need to actively engage the future. Though initially a civilian steamer, its original name *Imperator* bespeaks the imperial nationalism that would result in the catastrophe of World War I. Considering the continuity between civilian and military transportation technology, the *Imperator* must be seen as more than a merely symbolic harbinger of war. But the categories that help historians structure time – war and peace, winner and loser – are constantly undermined by the tenacity of human artifacts. Thus the instruments of the defeated live on in the hands of the winners, and the steamer, still called *Imperator*, carries home the men, dead and alive, whose mission it was to stop the German imperator. And once the war's conclusion has been finalized in a sentencing of justice and the steamer becomes British – as part of war reparations – it changes its name, as if to shed its history, and instead of being an imperator herself, becomes the wife of another empire's mythical warrior-hero who is no less questionable than the Kaiser.

The abounding historical irony exemplified by the *Berengaria*, I would suggest, results from the capacity of human artifacts to outlast the historical contexts of their creation. Anticipating contemporary debates about the anthropocene, Cather highlights the enormous staying power of human material creation and thus suggests the discrepancy between the human capacity to shape the world and the extreme limits of human foresight. Human artifacts – whether the Blue Mesa's pots and cups or a passenger liner – turn ironic when they bespeak their origination in the particular worldview of a given nation or empire and at the same time attest to their makers' inability to imagine future worlds that may be just around the corner and will be materially continuous with present state of affairs. In matters of warfare, this irony is accentuated with particular force: objects that were intended to destroy a particular enemy outlast the initial constellation of the warring parties and become adopted, and repurposed, by the victors. From the bird's eye view, the objects' being recycled signifies that the world continues to run its course. That course, however, is not teleologically determined, but the result of human interventions, the long-term consequences of which are unforeseeably contingent. Nonetheless, it is just such actions that constitute the making of history.

Facing this irony of history, and the *Berengaria*, with fortitude, St. Peter can turn his gaze to the future. What he faces now is not the radical contingency built on sheer negation, but the contingency of the consequences of making history. Acknowledging the consequences of human actions, however unforeseeable and circuitous they may be, sets him apart from the dreamy mythologizer of the "Spanish Adventurers." It also forces him to acknowledge having actively incurred the obligations that have come to structure his life as a "social man." No longer can he bemoan that his life has been determined by fate, no longer can he claim that "one thing led to another and one development brought on another, and the design of his life had been the work of this secondary social man, the lover" (259). The new view that I take Cather to be suggesting maintains that St. Peter has ventured a life, and that its consequences keep coming, not as the imposition of fate, but as the potentiality granted by the uncertainty of the future. If the Professor has undergone a liminal experience of near-death, he has come through not only as a grown-up but as a modern man, indebted to contingency both in searching for security and in accepting insecurity. His newly found capability to appreciate contingency, however, is not really new. It is an ironic revision of his nostalgic longing for the security of radical contingency.

CHAPTER 5

Cold War Liberalism and Flannery O'Connor's "The Displaced Person"

American literature from the early republic to the 1920s, I have so far argued, imaginarily exploited the opportunities slumbering within threat scenarios. In Charles Brockden Brown's republican gothic, the young protagonist, stricken with yellow fever, comes under the suspicion of being more than a physical carrier of the plague: he must counter the accusation of morally corrupting, and thus mortally threatening, the republic. Embodying the threat to security, Arthur Mervyn attempts to restore security by demonstrating that his own actions are disinterested. But taken to its logical conclusion, acting disinterestedly requires breaking the link between intention and consequence. Thus Arthur becomes involved in ever more layers of uncertainty while transforming himself into an actor more and more intricately related to the world and increasingly capable of shaping it.

Some sixty years later, Harriet Jacobs publishes a nonfictional slave narrative that seems to share next to nothing with Brown's novel. Except that for Jacobs, too, insecurity exceeds its deplorable and fear-inducing character and creates opportunities that she seizes with remarkable deftness. While the fictional character Arthur Mervyn turns insecurity into the opportunity to flourish as a republican individualist, nonfictional Linda Brent seizes the insecurity that pervades the fugitive slave's life in the North in order to call into being an imagined community of insecurity. The representation and rhetorical performance of the fugitive's insecurity endows Jacobs with the authority to instantiate a political imaginary.

In the final example explored so far, Willa Cather nostalgically imagines an idyllic state on which the unsettling forces of modernity can have no purchase. It turns out, however, that this antimodern imagination of security is itself deeply attached to the unsettling dynamics of modern times. For the protagonists of Cather's novel, the security imaginarily located on the "blue mesa" unfolds its full appeal only as it becomes associated with a radical contingency in which all the potentialities of the future might still become real. In *The Professor's House*, the imaginary removal of threats arising from modernity allows for an embrace of the uncertainties that were connected with modernity in the first place.

In these three case studies, I speak of security and insecurity in purposefully general terms. The threats I analyze are widely different: they can be as specific as the fugitive's liability to be recaptured and as vague as the unsettling forces of modernity. My point is not to catalog what American writers have perceived to be the gravest threats, but to explore a range of creative responses made possible by threat. What these responses have in common is an appreciation of the open future. While threat itself is never more than a contingency – something that may or may not become real – it is countered by hopes for future states for which uncertainty, contingency, and even insecurity are constitutive.

As we move to the mid-twentieth century, the investment in uncertainty and insecurity takes new yet related forms. But something changes at this point: we witness the emergence of a discourse that explicitly concerns itself with security. In the literary works analyzed so far, the words "security" and "insecurity" are only sometimes used consciously. In the years following World War II, however, security and insecurity become politicized terms, particularly in relation to national security. This also means that a discussion of the presence of security and insecurity in literature must now be placed against the backdrop of this political discourse. For this reason, I begin this chapter by analyzing the reflections on security by some leading intellectuals of the time. This brief excursus into the intellectual history of national security will provide the context for my ensuing consideration of Flannery O'Connor's fiction. O'Connor's works might not have any immediate stakes in the political problem of security discussed by the Cold War intellectuals. Yet security and insecurity structure her literary project in their existential and theological dimension, and as I will show, they do so in ways that are intimately related to the concerns of the Cold War intellectuals.

5.1 Liberalism, Realism, and the Dialectics of Security

During the early years of the Cold War, the term "security" became a buzzword for politicians, intellectuals, and the broader public, and it did so in two contrary ways. It is during the years immediately following World War II that "national security" became an established – and ideologically powerful – phrase. Up to that point, the established terms had been "national interest" and "national defense." In 1947, the National Security

Act and the founding of the National Security Council institutionalized the term (hitherto used occasionally, though not self-reflexively[1]). The corresponding discourse demanded priority for national security in all areas of life, and "national security" became the subject of the hour.[2]

But simultaneously, the term "security" was in heavy use in a different sense as well. Here, security was connoted negatively, as an ideal to be rejected. I argue here that these two understandings of security did not exist side by side, but rather stood in dialogue with each other. The sudden prevalence of the notion of security that we find in the phrase "national security" and that seems to have done the ideological work of resolving the contradictions between American idealism and American power politics can therefore be understood only if it is related to security's other meaning. In this complementary dimension, security stood for an excessive trust in progress and rationality, a political utopianism that had ended up in a kind of dialectic of the Enlightenment. The ideal of security in this sense was seen as harmful because it was an illusion that allowed people to shy away from reality and because it led to catastrophic results once the ideal was put into practice. In the opening pages of *The Vital Center* (1949), Arthur Schlesinger gave voice to the first of these two aspects: "We must recognize that this is the nature of our age ... security is a foolish dream of old men, [and] crisis will always be with us" (10). Reinhold Niebuhr stressed the second aspect. He argued that the philosophy growing out of the Enlightenment, "intent ... upon eliminating the natural hazards to comfort, security and contentment," created "the ironic situation that the same technical efficiency which provided our comforts has also placed us at the center of the tragic developments in world events" (*Irony* 43, 45).

Schlesinger, Niebuhr, and their fellow anticommunist intellectuals consequently began to call for a repudiation of the ideal of security. They associated their critical stance variously with political, moral, and theological "realism." Rarely defined precisely, these variants of realism shared the conviction that evil was ineradicable, that human nature was prone to weakness when tempted by vanity and power, and that plans to engineer a future free of conflict and hardship would run up against the stubborn facts of the human condition.[3] As Richard Pells writes in his classic intellectual history of postwar liberalism,

> Niebuhr, Schlesinger, and [Lionel] Trilling all [argued that both liberal progressives and socialists] overlooked the extent to which people were unmanageable and unpredictable, and both assumed that society could be made to conform to some preconceived plan or ideal. Such innocence about history and human nature no longer seemed charming to the postwar intellectuals;

they preferred a political philosophy that was sensitive to the illogical and accidental elements in social life. (137)

For the individual, this meant that one had to face the messiness of all action, its necessary implicatedness in what the action was designed to oppose. Essentially, the realist view emphasized the tragic character of the modern condition: morally forced to act in a world full of evil, the individual could not help becoming evil's helper.[4]

In including Lionel Trilling in his list, Pells gestures to the fact that the anticommunist rejection of the value of security carried over into the domain of literary aesthetics. In fact, literature became an area that was regarded to be of special importance for the purpose of formulating a response to the dangers emerging from an overly rationalistic ideal of security. For writers as diverse as Whittaker Chambers, Lionel Trilling, and Arthur Schlesinger Jr., literature provided insights, applicable to the political world, in how to face a world dependent on human action yet recalcitrant to human planning. In Michael Kimmage's succinct phrase, "tragedy was a gift that art could give to politics" (164).[5]

Tragic realism thus served as the antithesis to what anticommunist writers interpreted as an inhumane, mechanical, thoroughly rational, and mistakenly optimistic worldview. While they interpreted this worldview as characteristic of the international communist left of the 1930s and the emerging communist bloc of the postwar years, it is important to understand that the early Cold War intellectuals did not simply engage in a strategy of *othering*, as a result of which the Soviet Union would have appeared as the evil foe. This is precisely because their threat construction was more abstract and theoretical, drawing on critical theories of modernity. Since, in their minds, the gravest threat to civilization arose from a philosophical outlook that overvalued instrumental reason and understood the world as raw material to be shaped according to human designs of order, danger lurked everywhere: the communist bloc, the United States, the entire West were at risk, since the reign of radical rationality seemed to be spreading everywhere. Indeed, on one level, the anticommunist critique of the ideal of security ran counter to any easy distinction between "us" and "them," considering that it was to a large degree a self-critique: after all, nearly all postwar anticommunists had been affiliated with the communist left only a few years earlier, either as party members or as fellow travelers.

If it is true that Cold War liberals became supportive of domestic and foreign policies of national security only against the background of rejecting the ideal of security-as-rationality in a self-critical maneuver, we must also revise the dominant explanation of the triumph of "national security." For in this dominant view, security gains political cachet precisely because it helps draw and foster the boundary between inside and outside, friend and enemy.[6] To be sure, Cold War discourse can be seen as the attempt to transpose internal divisions and conflicts into a binary identity logic of "us versus them," and in that sense, Cold War liberals exacerbated the rigidity of Cold War anticommunism. But at the center of Cold War liberalism, we nonetheless find deeply rooted resonances of a post-Romanticist critique of the Enlightenment (what Nancy Rosenblum has called "Another Liberalism"). And this critique located the object to be criticized in the history of the West and thus made the problems represented by communism a property not of "them" but of "us."

If realism was a touchstone for both liberal and conservative anticommunists in their struggle *against* the utopian belief in security, it is also what propelled the *embrace* of security as it appeared in the phrase "national security." In such influential government communiqués as George Kennan's "Long Telegram," cabled from Moscow in February 1946; the Clifford-Elsey Report of the same year; and Kennan's X article published in *Foreign Affairs* in 1947 – all of which were instrumental in establishing the reign of national security – political realism seemed the only possible stance toward the Soviet Union. Since Soviet leaders were perceived as unwilling or unable to work toward a settlement, the aim of ever achieving stable peace became denigrated as unrealistic. Therefore, rather than serving as a synonym of peace, national security became associated with the anti-isolationist and antiutopian position of engaging in the world in order to defend freedom against totalitarian forces. Though defense at times lost its primary connotation of reaction and instead became associated with a proactive stance that aimed to be one step ahead of the totalitarian enemy, national security was nonetheless differentiated from the imposition of order. That the "defense of freedom" was inevitably beset by contradictions and required acts of violent aggression impossible to square with the values of Western democracy was what, in the eyes of Cold War thinkers, made national security a tragic – and, for that matter, all the more humane – affair. To put it differently, national security was seen as a defense strategy of freedom that was necessarily bedeviled by the hazards of chance and inconsistency, and for that very reason appeared as an antidote to, and triumph over, the rationalist ideal of security.

5.2 Flannery O'Connor's Critique of Secular Modernity

The fictional work of Flannery O'Connor may at first glance run counter to the Cold War liberals' insistence on rejecting the ideal of security-as-rationality in order to secure America against what was perceived as the threat of totalitarianism and, more particularly, Stalinism. O'Connor thought of herself as a Southerner and a Catholic, identity components that were conducive to her self-perception as an outsider to mainstream political discourse. Indeed, some scholars have absorbed this view and claimed that she was thoroughly at odds with Cold War liberal ideology. Jon Lance Bacon, for instance, argues that O'Connor undermined the central tenets of containment: her stories affirm neither "the integrity of the American family" (48) nor the fear of foreign invasion (see 79–81).

Such an interpretation, however, rests on a reductive notion of the assumptions organizing Cold War thought. We need to remember that the Cold War liberals targeted both Stalinism and progressivism (the latter term serving as a synonym for the kind of liberalism popular up to World War II). In the view of anticommunist liberals, both Stalinists and progressive liberals were effectively identical in promoting a single-minded belief in rationality, social engineering, and the hope of expunging contingency from life. Thomas Schaub has astutely remarked that "though [O'Connor] viewed her fiction as a dramatic reprimand to liberal assumptions, the revisionist liberalism of the postwar era was in many respects speaking her language" (*American Fiction* 124). Principally aligned with the revisionist-liberal critique, O'Connor focused on the intellectual, moral, and spiritual follies of the liberal progressivism that, in her opinion, had reached dominance in the modern world and particularly in the United States. On this basis, she articulated a critique of security that is commensurate with that of anticommunist liberals.

As remarkable as these continuities are, I inquire into O'Connor's oeuvre not primarily to elucidate yet another version of the critique of security I have outlined so far in this chapter. In what follows, I argue that O'Connor brings to the fore a facet of the Cold War critique of security that has so far remained oblique. She couples violence and security differently than do the anticommunist liberals of her time, and this difference becomes recognizable precisely because she primarily works in fiction rather than political theory or literary criticism.

The Cold War intellectuals theorized violence in principally two ways. First, violence was seen as the systematic and catastrophic outcome of amoral rationality, as exemplified by the atrocities of totalitarian regimes. To the extent that the ideal of security was itself part and parcel of the idealization of rationality, security had to be rejected. It was the surest way to mass death. Alternatively, Cold War intellectuals conceptualized violence as a necessary evil accompanying a realist and tragic engagement in the world. For the realist, violence had to be accepted as an unavoidable element of battling evil, but aggressive impulses could in no way be condoned. After all, that was why evil had to be fought in the first place. O'Connor's stance toward security differs from these two positions. Her understanding of violence emerges from her religious worldview, but it becomes articulated through the aesthetic means of her fiction. As I argue in this chapter, her art effectively embraces the aggression of violence by treating it as a force of redemption. It is this moment of redemption that instantiates true security – that is, security comprises the perpetration or suffering of violence.[7]

O'Connor's affirmation of religion (and of religious authority) functions as a particular mode of critiquing both secular modernity and a notion of security conceived in secular terms. From O'Connnor's binary construction of secularism versus religion follow numerous subordinate and fine-grained binaries central to O'Connor's literary project. Most crucial for the present context, she posits a modern, secular world in which people aim to order the world according to their profane strivings. Rayber, the schoolteacher in *The Violent Bear It Away*, may be the bluntest example in all of her fiction: he believes in the social sciences, is committed to reform through education, and has even chosen a wife (now deceased) who fits his convictions: she is referred to, derisively, by Old Tarwater as the "welfare-woman" (*Violent* 333, 334). Sheppard in "The Lame Shall Enter First," Hulga in "Good Country People," and Thomas in "The Comforts of Home" closely follow O'Connor's archetype. Connected to their misguided trust in rationality is their utter lack of self-awareness, which keeps them from comprehending the limits of controlling and shaping the future. As Frederick Asals has observed, "O'Connor's people are among the least introspective in modern fiction, with minds at once so unaware and so absurdly assured that they have refused to acknowledge any deeper self" (*Imagination* 95). Yet, in the long run, their single-minded worldview is untenable: it runs up against the divinely ordered cosmos. Awareness of and respect for the latter constitutes O'Connor's alternative to secularity. That other life requires the submission to God's rule, the acceptance of his authority and order, and the abnegation of the ideal of mastery. The religious person has learned to live insecurely by giving himself or herself over to God's will.

Throughout her work, O'Connor has recourse to two different, conflicting theological conceptions. On the one hand, her novels and short stories, but particularly her essays and letters, assert the authority of a God-given, timeless order underlying the given world. The divinely created world, which is opposed to a humanly created order, thus demands proper respect and love. This position may be called O'Connor's sacramental stance, and it agrees most neatly with her professed Catholic orthodoxy.

But at a closer look, her fiction tends to curiously undermine this sacramental stance in that it resists the representation of sustainable lives of grace. What such a life might look like is pointed to by symbols (the peacock of "The Displaced Person," the bull in "Greenleaf") and in the revelatory experiences of some of her characters (Mrs. Turpin's vision of the procession in "Revelation").[8] But for next to none of her characters does the alternative to the rational striving for security take shape with any degree of solidity. As some of her most acute readers have pointed out, there is a heretic streak running through her work that has been described as Manichean, Jansenist, or Gnostic.[9] Whatever the precise name, this position builds on the opposition between the worldly and the otherworldly and orders these two poles in an unequivocal hierarchy. Whereas a properly developed sacramental vision affirms the divine order embodied in the given world, her heretic position emphasizes the fallen nature of creation and does so by identifying the secular world with the ills of modernity.

O'Connor pushes her characters in the direction of the divine nature of the world by exposing them to sudden outbursts of violence. The irredeemably fallen world of the secular must be left behind, traded in (as it were) against a higher world in a process of painful purification. O'Connor thus rehearses a transcendent version of cultural critique and endows it with an affective force: as I will detail, she creates a readerly and writerly affect of a religiously bolstered wrath directed against the given world. O'Connor's most powerful fictions aggressively turn this violent wrath against her secular characters, who come to recognize, in the moment of their destruction, God's grace. Divine security and the most extreme physical insecurity become one and the same.

Interweaving her Catholic sacramentalism – the tradition of revering God's creation in its immanent worldliness – with a heretic streak, O'Connor makes the divinely saturated material world appear as the grotesque symptom of human shortcoming. This duality finds its expression when O'Connor, in her lecture "The Catholic Novelist in the Protestant South," ties together the "facts" of creation, the perverse, and mystery:

> Our sense of what is contained in our faith is deepened less by abstractions than by an encounter with mystery in what is human and often perverse. We Catholics are much given to the instant answer. Fiction doesn't have any. Saint Gregory wrote that every time the sacred text describes a fact,

it reveals mystery. And this is what the fiction writer, on his lower level, attempts to do also. (863)

For O'Connor, the facts of creation reveal mystery and thus a divine presence; but in order to get a palpable sense of the divine, fiction needs to showcase the perversity of these "facts." The perverse is at once the apex of the divine and the sign of creation's fallen state.[10] It points, at one and the same time, to grace and the fall from grace. Because of this simultaneity, the scaffolding of O'Connor's cultural critique – the opposition between the commitment to a man-made order of rationality ("rational security") and the submission to a God-given cosmic order ("divine security," which equals "secular insecurity") – is continuously shaken in her fiction. This is so, first of all, because rationality lacks a viable alternative. It seems impossible to truly submit to God's order if that order exists in eruptions of violence and is thus no order at all. Secondly, the purifying impulse of her heretic stance is expressly active and aggressive. It cultivates a rage that aims to destroy the worldly. Like the rational project of security, this is an attempt to shape the world. The result is a religious variant of what I called, in my discussion of Charles Brockden Brown, an "agency dilemma": if the security threat consists in the rational ordering of the world, how can that threat be disarmed without amounting to yet another effort at ordering the world? O'Connor sidesteps this dilemma by inverting the rational project: in order not to build her own world, she emphasizes the sheer negativity of destructive violence.

In the following pages, I will look closely at "The Displaced Person," by far the longest story of her 1955 collection *A Good Man Is Hard to Find*, since here O'Connor radicalizes her critique of security-as-rationality by calling into question whether worldly forms of insecurity – political and economic precariousness – truly deserve to be regarded as instances of insecurity at all. In "The Displaced Person," it is not just that characters are shocked out of their self-satisfied complacency – their belief in the rational attainability of security and their concomitant illusionary feeling of security – by being forced to open their minds to introspection and an awareness of God; even material insecurity, as experienced by stateless refugees and dispensable labor, comes under the scrutiny of the religious attack on the worldly. O'Connor's story aims to make us understand that such forms of political and economic precariousness pale against the insecure existence under divine rule. In fact, they begin to look like another self-satisfied illusion.

5.3 "The Displaced Person" and the Angel of World History

The first thing to be noted about "The Displaced Person" is the story's autobiographical backdrop. In the fall of 1951, a Polish family consisting of Jan and Zofia Matysiak, their twelve-year-old son Alfred, and his younger sister Hedwig arrived in central Georgia. The Matysiaks belonged to a group of displaced persons (DPs) that at the time was known as "the last million": "a multinational group of Jewish and non-Jewish asylum seekers unwilling or unable to go home" after the quick rush of repatriation from spring to fall 1945, during which time six to seven million DPs returned to their country of origin, in many cases forcibly (Cohen, *In War's Wake* 4–5). After his family had moved from camp to camp, Jan Matysiak's application to relocate his family to the United States was finally accepted in 1951, and they ended up in the small town of Gray, Georgia. According to Brad Gooch, "They traveled twenty miles each Sunday morning to the nearest Catholic church … where they met [Regina] O'Connor," Flannery O'Connor's mother (*Flannery* 239). As Gooch phrases it, "By the fall of 1953, alert to reasonably priced labor, Regina had them resettled at Andalusia," the estate on which she lived with her Lupus-stricken daughter (239).

In "The Displaced Person," Flannery O'Connor dramatizes the arrival of the Matysiak family, now renamed Guizac, in the microcosmic farm community of Andalusia. Crafting a story out of the Polish family's presence in midst of her familiar rural setting, O'Connor drew upon one of her favorite plot lines: she rendered Mr. Guizac, the eponymous Displaced Person, as an intruder into an established social order, which in the end is violently shattered. Whether O'Connor rehearsed this pattern with the Misfit in "A Good Man is Hard to Find," Johnson in "The Lame Shall Enter First," or Sarah Ham in "The Comforts of Home," in each case she authorized variants of the same Catholic interpretation: the intruding figure, in radically unsettling the established way of life, is in the end not merely a destructive but rather a redemptive force that allows her characters to accept grace – to the extent that they survive. Sometimes the intruder is a devil, sometimes a saint. In "The Displaced Person," he is a Christ figure whose death, as O'Connor put it in a letter, "did accomplish a kind of redemption in that he destroyed the place, which was evil, and set Mrs. McIntyre [who is comparable to O'Connor's real-world mother in that she owns the farm] on the road to a new kind of suffering" (*Letters* 970). As O'Connor remarks herself in this gloss, redemption and destruction are by no means mutually exclusive. Nor is violence in her work limited to physical destruction.

Given her decision to devote her art to one recurring theological topos – the violent breaking in of grace – O'Connor generally seems to have had little artistic use for world-historical matters. Aside from a few exceptions, such as "The Geranium" and "Judgment Day," her novels and stories are confined to the South, and while her characters lead lives saturated with mass media, they appear largely unconcerned with national, not to mention international, affairs.[11] Occasionally O'Connor picked up on the Civil Rights Movement – for instance in "Everything that Rises Must Converge" and "Judgment Day" – but the references remained allusions rather than explicit reflections of a political (and politically contested) reality. The trace of history we do repeatedly find in her works comes in the form of a shadow presence of World War II: her first novel, *Wise Blood*, and her story "A Stroke of Good Fortune" feature characters who have to readjust to southern life after their return from war. The war itself, however, does not enter these texts. The fact that "The Displaced Person" breaks with this rule may mainly have to do with the autobiographical roots of the material. Whatever the reason, "The Displaced Person" stands out in her oeuvre as the one work in which her intruder is a kind of angel of world history; it is as if, in coming to Georgia as a holocaust survivor, he fixed the gaze of the story's characters on what Walter Benjamin called, in allusion to Paul Klee's *Angelus Novus*, history's "piling wreckage upon wreckage" (Benjamin, "Theses on the Philosophy of History" 257). This acuteness to the world-historical events of the holocaust and its aftermath also forced O'Connor to provide the microcosmic South of her story with a historically specific social structure whose economic and racial foundations take on bodily concreteness in response to the Displaced Person's intrusion.

Thematically, O'Connor's text is concerned with the problem of security and insecurity on three levels, which I'll spend some time spelling out. On one level, the Displaced Person is connected to the problem of economic insecurity under capitalism, particularly job insecurity. In the political discourse of the time, the problem of Displaced Persons was often discussed under the heading of "surplus labor" (Cohen, *In War's Wake* 100–125), and in O'Connor's story, surplus labor is exactly the role in which the Displaced Person appears on the Georgia farm. O'Connor stays close in this respect to her real-world model: just as her mother had hired Jan Matysiak with an eye to cheap and efficient labor, the fictional Mr. Guizac threatens to take away the local population's jobs because he is quite simply the more efficient worker. Surplus labor thus gets translated into the heightened insecurity growing out of labor competition. On a second level, the Displaced Person is a victim of totalitarianism and embodies the precariousness of statelessness, i.e., the lack of protection by the state. A being without rights, the Displaced Person shows the fundamental political insecurity that at first glance would seem to mark the antithesis to citizenship in democratic America. But at a closer look, O'Connor raises the question whether political insecurity may not extend to any communal body, including rural Georgia. Finally, on the third level, the Displaced Person unsettles the story's characters in their complacency and self-satisfaction. Politically and historically specific forms of displacement here become allegorized as our true ontological position, which O'Connor defines as limited, fallible, sinful, and in dire need of God's grace. Thus, insecurity here means coming to terms with the transient nature of our worldly selves and the insignificance of our interests. The upshot of this allegorization is that O'Connor's story in the end does not respond to the first two types of insecurity by striving for a greater level of economic and political security but by emphasizing the importance of learning to be properly insecure. We may see in this final move a macabre reinterpretation of the "*angel* of history," who, in looking at the human wreckage of the past, resigns himself to the transcendent forces pulling him away. Doing so, the angel, half-divine, denies and undoes his other half: his materiality, and by implication that of the human rubble he has been facing.

After developing these three dimensions of the theme of security and insecurity in O'Connor's story, I will relate the thematic treatment of security to the way O'Connor's story mobilizes aesthetic effect and affect. While her characters have to learn to accept insecurity, their learning comes not as a gradual process but as a violent shock. This violence is not contained to the represented world: rather, O'Connor works hard to turn the reader into an affective accomplice of the narrator who will condone and indeed long for the violent action by the time it transpires. Teaching her characters insecurity thus becomes an aggressive act and pact between narrator and reader. Insecurity in O'Connor's story isn't merely passive suffering, but an active achievement. Through her aesthetics of wrathful aggression she comes to wholeheartedly embrace violence. As already mentioned, it is specifically in this regard that she goes further than Cold War liberals, who brought themselves to openly condone violence only to the extent that they defined it as tragic.

5.4 Economic Insecurity

In "The Displaced Person," O'Connor addresses the unsettling power of capitalism by critically drawing on a line of thought well established in southern conservatism. O'Connor's work echoes the writings of the Southern Renascence, the literary and intellectual movement of the 1920s to 1940s, which combined a modernist aesthetic with a conservative, anti-industrial social vision. The essay collection *I'll Take My Stand!* from 1930 may be the clearest instance of conservative modernism upholding the South as a viable alternative to modern America by virtue of the region's rural and purportedly tradition-based social structure. Many of the so-called Twelve Southerners, such as John Crowe Ransom, Allen Tate, and Robert Penn Warren, previously had been members of the Fugitives, a circle of modernists at Vanderbilt, who, in their journal *The Fugitive*, had tried to prove wrong H. L. Mencken's biting dictum that the South was the "Sahara of the Bozart." In *I'll Take My Stand!*, the Fugitives' concern with southern high culture was transposed into a full-fledged conservative pastoralism, which insisted that if the South had to modernize, it had to do so carefully and within bounds, so that it could remain a bulwark against industrialism and the cultural ailments that followed from it.

For the South to work as a defense against the onslaught of the progressivism of mainstream America, its cultural and social tradition had to be recovered first. As Allen Tate claimed in his contribution to *I'll Take My Stand!*, the Southerner could only "take hold of his Tradition ... by violence" ("Remarks" 174). What the South needed to embrace was reaction, which Tate described as "the most radical of programs; it aims at cutting away the overgrowth and getting back to the roots" (175). Nonetheless, this violent program ultimately served the goal of holding on to a substance. As editor Louis Rubin put it in his introduction to the 1977 reissue of *I'll Take My Stand!*, "there *was* a southern tradition worthy of preservation ... it was that of the good society, the community of individuals, the security and definition that come when men cease to wage an unrelenting war with nature and enjoy their leisure and their human dignity" (xx). It was, then, part of the rhetoric of the Southern Agrarians to oppose the South to the remainder of America by regarding it as the only possibility for security in a world increasingly uprooted by industrial capitalism and the spirit of progressivism.[12]

Reading the essays of *I'll Take My Stand!* today, it is striking just how uncritical a stance the contributors managed to take up regarding the purported harmonies of southern rural traditionalism. If slavery was addressed at all, it was mostly in the apologetic tone exemplified by John Crowe Ransom, who wrote: "Slavery was a feature monstrous enough in theory, but more often than not, humane in practice." "The fullness of life," as Ransom called it, extended to "the different social orders," and "all were committed to a form of leisure," and in fact, "labor itself was leisurely" ("Reconstructed" 14). Ransom's denial of the realities of slavery reveals a structural opposition in the Agrarians' worldview between capitalism and the racial order: the resistance to industrial capitalism and to the ideology of progress went hand in hand with the insistence that agrarian society was either antithetical or at least irreducible to market principles. This meant that work was not fully caught up in the logic of the labor market but constituted a kind of leisure. And this in turn implied that the racial hierarchy that traditionally had maintained the peculiar institution was in no way a shameful exception to an otherwise commendable vision of the full life; it was a perfect instance of this life. The experience of slavery could be construed as a relief from the pressures of the labor market – an argument that goes back at least as far as George Fitzhugh.[13] Thus Agrarians implicitly constructed a dualism between inhumane industrial capitalism and a humane rural order that had been traditionally built on slavery and that, after emancipation, managed to keep its humane character by conserving the old racial order.

O'Connor takes up the opposition between modern capitalism and the allegedly benign racial hierarchy of the agrarian South, but she does so in a markedly satirical voice. In O'Connor's story, the Displaced Person is perceived by the farm workers as disrupting the local, rural order. This disruption fuses the economic and racial order in the same way the two merged in the Southern Agrarians' vision. Mr. Guizac poses an economic threat by heating up the competition in the labor market. O'Connor highlights the anxiety resulting from job insecurity by choosing as her focalizer, in the story's first part, a white laborer, Mrs. Shortley, who is the dairyman's wife and helps the farm owner, Mrs. McInytre, manage the household. In Mrs. Shortley's fearful visions, the Displaced Person will bring devastation to the farm. For her, the DP cannot be detached from the concentration camp footage of piled-up, disjointed bodies that she once saw in a newsreel. Though she realizes that her own livelihood is threatened by the arrival of the Polish family, she tries to pass on her fear to the two black farm hands, Astor and Sulk. "There's about ten million billion more just like them," she tells the two black men and claims moreover to have overheard Mrs. McIntyre say, "This is going to put the fear of the Lord in those shiftless niggers!" (290). At the end of part I, however, it is not the black workers who get fired but Mrs. Shortley's husband. Hurriedly leaving the farm, Mrs. Shortley suffers a stroke in the car. Buried beneath boxes and bedding, with her husband's head, her daughter's leg, and her own knee grotesquely jumbled together, she reenacts the concentration camp footage in her moment of death (304–305).[14]

Part II of the story establishes that what's truly disruptive about the Displaced Person cannot be understood merely by reference to the economy. The southern economic order only begins to make sense once Mr. Guizac's transgression is understood as a disturbance of the racial order. He shakes hands with the black workers and attempts to arrange an interracial marriage between his cousin, who is still in a camp somewhere in Europe, and Sulk, the younger of two black men. The outrage at Guizac's innocent plan for miscegenation is tremendous, but, interestingly, his racial trespass is counterbalanced by the reaffirmation of boundaries in the *economic* field. This boundary line determines the proper place for economic competition. It turns out that the intensification of competition is permitted as long as it is confined to white labor, which is an area already defined by market principles. Black labor, on other hand, becomes demarcated, in the course of the action, as off limits to market pressures. This distinction is established at the outset of part II, in the dialogues between Mrs. McIntyre and Astor, the older of the black workers. Repeatedly, Mrs. McIntyre hints that Astor's position may be as precarious as Mrs. Shortley's. "We've seen them come and seen them go – black and white," she tells him, and: "I have somebody now who *has* to work." But Astor simply remains silent, and when he finally does reply, he recycles his employer's clichéd sentence, "We seen them come and we seen them go" (306). In his usage, the pronoun "We" emphasizes the bond between Mrs. McIntyre and himself as the bedrock of agrarian stability. More precisely, his bond is less with Mrs. McIntyre than with the Judge, her deceased husband, who acted as the supreme country patriarch and for whom Astor started to work long before Mrs. McIntyre met the Judge. Astor thus derives authority from embodying a link to the old southern tradition. He also makes clear that the DP's displacement is nothing extraordinary, but – understood as the replaceability of labor – rather the normal condition of white farm workers. From his duel of words with Mrs. McIntyre, Astor emerges victorious, having established that black workers are not economically replaceable, but rather indispensable for the South to remain intact. In this light we begin to understand Mrs. McIntyre's reaction to Guizac's misstep. She accuses the foreigner not of being different, but of being just like the other white workers. "They're all the same. It's always been like this" (311), she complains to herself, and later, as the narrator tells us, she repeats her discovery to the priest: "She said she had found out they were the same whether they came from Poland or Tennessee" (321). The problem, in her view, lies with the unreliability, the essentially fraudulent quality of labor, which equally victimizes her and "her" blacks. In her confrontation with

Guizac, Mrs. McIntyre makes this explicit: "I will not have my niggers upset. I cannot run this place without my niggers. I can run it without you but not without them" (314). The black workers, it seems, are a fixture of the land, an inherent quality of the South. They may no longer be chattel personal, but they still seem like real estate.[15] From the logic of the labor market, this makes no sense at all, but this is exactly the point: black labor must be inefficient and uneconomical. In resisting the logic of capitalism, it guarantees the South's identity as capitalism's agrarian other. We see, then, that O'Connor's story draws out the racial-economic foundation of the Southern Agrarian ideal: modernization, which takes the form of the intrusion of capitalism, may be necessary to some extent, but it must be hindered from confounding the racial order, which underwrites the South's economic and cultural identity.

5.5 Political Insecurity

Mrs. McIntyre's insistence, in the story's second part, that Mr. Guizac is like all the others is borne out only insofar as he is grouped with white labor. Part III reestablishes him as an outsider and thus leads back to the emphasis on displacement as political insecurity that characterizes part I. Initially, the farm population views the DP as an outsider because he is from Europe, that place where people have never "advanced or reformed," where they are "always fighting amongst each other. Disputing. And then get us into it," as Mrs. Shortley tells her husband in a peculiar kind of pillow talk (297). For the Shortleys, being from the Old World means coming straight from some kind of state of nature, from an unending civil war that is as chaotic as the pile of bodies in the concentration camp images. In a sense all Europeans seem to be Displaced Persons. And since in the mess of violent chaos one cannot tell apart good from evil, it is wholly unclear, and even pointless to distinguish, whether DPs are victims of totalitarianism or perpetrators. As far as Mr. Shortley can tell, Guizac is "just exactly who I been fighting" in the war: even his eyeglasses are just like those of the man who threw a grenade at him (323). And now this man has taken Mr. Shortley's job. Worst of all, Mrs. Shortley fears that "the ten million billion of them [are] pushing their way into new places over here" (291) and that the Guizacs – or, as she calls them, "the Gobblehooks" – "like rats with typhoid fleas, could have carried all those murderous ways over the water with them directly to this place" (287).

O'Connor, never reluctant to employ heavy-handed irony, is using the very wording of her narrator to indicate that Mrs. Shortley's visions will come true, though in a different manner than her character expects. Comparing the Gobblehooks to rats with typhoid flees strongly hints at the appropriation of Nazi discourse by Mrs. Shortley. O'Connor spends a good amount of her story's final part detailing the ways in which Mr. Shortley puts pressure on the locals to ostracize, exclude, and finally kill the Displaced Person. The Georgia farm, it appears, has turned into a New Europe.

In fact, the ultimate irony lies in the fact that the xenophobic and ignorant views of the Shortleys are perhaps not such an unjust analysis of the larger problem of political insecurity in the nation-state system exemplified by post–World War I (and post–World War II) Europe. In an interesting way, O'Connor's story here intersects with Hannah Arendt's argument, unfolded in *The Origins of Totalitarianism*, that all nation-states produced minorities that, once considered the "scum of the earth" by their country of origin, were everywhere considered "human beings and nothing else," i.e., no longer part of any human community or polity (*Origins* 302). Particularly after World War I, with the demise of Czarist Russia and Austria-Hungary and the creation of succession states with highly mixed populations, all European nation-states, no matter whether "totalitarian" or "constitutional," rendered a portion of their population stateless. And as Arendt insists, resonating with the imagination of the Shortleys, "these rightless people are indeed thrown back into a peculiar state of nature. Certainly they are not barbarians; some of them, indeed, belong to the most educated strata of their respective countries; nevertheless, in a world that has almost liquidated savagery, they appear as the first signs of a possible regression from civilization" (300).

Political insecurity, O'Connor's story suggests, cannot be explained by the state's declaring certain persons as stateless and unprotected by citizenship rights. Political insecurity rather results when communities identify groups or individuals that may be killed by common consent. Here, too, O'Connor's story is not so far away from Hannah Arendt's analysis of the origins of totalitarianism in relation to Displaced Persons. Arendt argues that the nation-state will always produce displaced populations because nation-states tend to be driven by an imperial urge, while the nationalism of the nation-state requires a strict representational correspondence between nation and state. But the state can only push through its policies of expulsion and extermination if the national community already tacitly agrees with these policies. Simon Swift explains Arendt's point this way: "Rights are the work of the state, but can be guaranteed only by the existence of a genuine political community. This means that when the critical public opinion of a nation chooses to look the other way, that state might take away the rights of some of those who live within its borders" (*Hannah Arendt* 85). Although Arendt and O'Connor draw very different conclusions about the insecurity growing out of political displacement, they share the emphasis on the community's exclusion of minorities as preceding the state's turning citizens into Displaced Persons. While Arendt, the political philosopher, also makes the reverse argument that true protection has to be formally guaranteed by a genuine political community,[16] O'Connor does not follow her dramatization of the fundamental political insecurity of outsiders with any reflection on how such precariousness might be attenuated. Instead, she introduces a third form of insecurity that is framed by a metaphysics conceptualized in Catholic terms.

5.6 Religious Insecurity

At the end of O'Connor's story, the Displaced Person is run over by a tractor in a kind of sacrificial killing. Mr. Guizac's death is gruesome precisely because it is not a murder but an accident in which landscape, machine, and the passively onlooking Southerners seem to cooperate in a silent understanding that amounts to cosmic harmony.[17] However, in an ironic reversal typical of O'Connor's endings, that sense of harmony does not reaffirm the status quo, but rather expresses the redemptive qualities of the Displaced Person's death. Thus, after the accident, Mrs. McIntyre, Mr. Shortley, Astor, and Sulk experience their own displacement, either by leaving the farm or, in the case of Mrs. McIntyre, by suffering a stroke that leaves her paralyzed, blind, speechless, and helpless: "in some foreign country," as the narrator phrases her thought. O'Connor's point seems to be that we are to accept our theological and ontological displacement. Our true position in life is marked by insecurity. But here the crucial question arises: What follows from such an acceptance? Does O'Connor's story suggest that a life that is duly aware of our fundamental insecurity – understood as the human condition, conceptualized in religious terms – will make available responses to the economic and political dimensions of insecurity? Does the recognition of insecurity perhaps lead to an ethical program for living "in some foreign country," a program that would involve a conception of the polity as promoting heterogeneity by requiring each citizen to inhabit a position of exile or displacement?[18]

O'Connor's story follows none of these routes. She rather transforms economic and political insecurity, i.e., social forms of displacement, into mere allegories for spiritual displacement. Neither the problems of losing one's job through labor market competition, nor political expulsion and lack of legal protection have any real significance in the end. For what O'Connor's characters learn in their shocks of violent revelation is precisely that political and economic displacement itself needs to be displaced onto the religious level. Worrying about one's job or the lack of rights is ultimately a preoccupation that acts as a stumbling block to the recognition and acceptance of grace. What O'Connor draws on here is the traditional Christian understanding of security, which I have alluded to repeatedly. Security designates not merely a project of creating, or an achievement of having reached, a state of being in which there is nothing to worry about. Since Augustine, Christian thinkers have predominantly approached "security" through the opposite meaning contained in the words *sine cura*: carelessness and recklessness. Here security describes a feeling that arises from unwarranted feelings of safety and, speaking in religious terms, from an overestimation of human, and an underestimation of divine, power. In this sense, Mrs. McIntyre's suffering at the end of the story weans her from the "security" – or spiritual recklessness – of her mundane outlook on life, and therefore amounts to an experience of a particular kind of care (a "curity" rather than "security"): she has begun to care for human helplessness and isolation. We could say that she has come to care for her insecurity.

If these formulations seem a bit excessive in exploiting the ambiguity of the two opposing meanings of security – freedom from worry versus carelessness – my reason for using them is that O'Connor's story is itself exploiting this ambiguity in suddenly exchanging the meaning of security. Thus, the political and economic insecurity she evokes by focusing on a Displaced Person and surplus labor is revealed at the end to be no real insecurity. We might say that the reason why this is so is that the story initially presents insecurity as a problem and thus implies the desirability of security. But insecurity appears as a problem only because the story is focalized through Mrs. Shortley, Mrs. McIntyre, and Mr. Shortley. O'Connor's story is driving toward the final reversal of their assessment of insecurity. The moment in which political and economic insecurity become allegories of our real insecurity, the story moves beyond their aversion to insecurity, toward its embrace. In fretting about worldly problems, O'Connor's characters were without concern for their true condition. It is the violence that typically befalls O'Connor's characters at the end of her stories that allows them to move from *sine cura* to *cum cura*, as it were. They are shocked into a revealing glimpse of the fact that they cannot take care of themselves, just before that fact fatally asserts itself.

The violence in O'Connor's story contains several dimensions. There is physical violence: the cracking of Mr. Guizac's backbone, Mrs. McInytre's own paralysis. These two instances differ in function: the meaning of the Displaced Person's death remains open (it could either reestablish the old order, or lead to every one else's transformation) until it is coupled with the violence done to Mrs. McIntyre (her paralysis), which is the truly typical instance of O'Connor's violent ending. For this reason, my following analysis focuses on Mrs. McIntyre's violent demise and largely decouples it from the Displaced Person's death. Beside the physical dimension, we also encounter violence in the narratological displacement necessary for effecting the moment of allegorization, which is a moment of revaluing insecurity. If insecurity appears as a problem from her characters' view, O'Connor typically uses the moment of revelation for a change in outlook of her characters as well as for a switch in narrative position. Thus, the final insight is told from a distanced, omniscient narrative position that has moved beyond the limits of her characters. In "The Displaced Person," the shift occurs at the very beginning of the final paragraph, just as the narrator ironically turns Mrs. McIntyre into a Displaced Person, lost "in some foreign country." Here is the transition:

> She felt she was in some foreign country where the people bent over the body were natives, and she watched like a stranger while the dead man was carried away in the ambulance.
>
> That evening, Mr. Shortley left without notice to look for a new position and the Negro, Sulk, was taken with a sudden desire to see more of the world and set off for the southern part of the state. The old man Astor could not work without company. Mrs. McIntyre hardly noticed that she had no help left for she came down with a nervous affliction and had to go to the hospital.... Not many people remembered to come out to the country to see her except the old priest. He came regularly once a week with a bag of breadcrumbs and, after he had fed these to the peacock, he would come in and sit by the side of her bed and explain the doctrines of the Church. (326–327)

The story ends by unmistakably proclaiming the superiority and permanence of God's order, with the priest caring for the peacock and the doctrines of the Church getting the last word. This triumphal assertion of divine power grows out of the narrator's novelistic roundup of the characters' dispersed futures, which is possible only from the omniscient perspective. And the adoption of this perspective is logically connected to the physical and mental demise of the preceding focalizer: Hardly noticing her surroundings, forgotten by pretty much everyone but the priest,

Mrs. McIntyre has been reduced to the point where she simply can no longer function as the narrative instance. Her revelation – her spiritual displacement – is tantamount to the narration doing away with her.

5.7 Insecurity and Aggression

In what sense does this change of focalization amount to an act of violence? I suggest that in combining this narratological shift with the thematic rendition of violence, O'Connor brings to its climax a readerly and writerly aggression toward her characters built up over the course of the story. O'Connor uses a number of interconnected techniques to generate this affect. They concern the means by which her narrator characterizes the story's cast of characters (with the crucial exception of the Christ-like Displaced Person and his institutional representative, the priest) as close-minded, self-assured, and resistant to any kind of change. These characters display an almost total lack of sensibility that amounts to stupidity, deserves no kind of empathy, and can only be overcome with sudden force. A further means to the same end of enragement builds on these characterizations: the narrator herself enacts the lack of empathy by distancing herself from the characters in biting irony. This distanciation becomes necessary because the characters' loathsomeness cannot be neatly confined within the diegetic world, but threatens to infect both narrator and reader. The narrator systematically plays characters off against each other by letting them mutually discredit each other. This technique sets traps for the reader, who is invited, by means of laughter, to join one character in disapproving of another. In turn, the narrative persistently reveals the disapproving character to be a mere copy of the one disapproved. Indirectly, this revelation incriminates the reader as well: having been led by one character to deride another, the reader is no better than either.[19] This all-out attack by O'Connor makes it necessary for the reader and narrator to create a bond that confirms their difference from the characters. This assertion of difference becomes certified through the narrative transcendence beyond the characters' limitations, which in turn becomes possible through the violent ending that meets the characters' old ways. I will now detail how this dynamic unfolds.

A key criterion of sensibility (or lack thereof) in O'Connor's stories, resonant with her theology, consists of the characters' capacity for vision. While Hazel Motes's blinding himself in *Wise Blood* is an act of true asceticism that appears as the only way out of the pervasive pseudo-religious evangelicalism and depraved craving for cheap sensation, in "The Displaced

Person" shortcomings of vision are themselves the sign of utter obtuseness to the spiritually charged material world. Exemplary of the entire story, the first paragraph confronts us with the tension between a symbolically perceptive narrator and a visually ignorant character:

> The Peacock was following Mrs. Shortley up the road to the hill where she meant to stand. Moving one behind the other, they looked like a complete procession. Her arms were folded and as she mounted the prominence, she might have been the giant wife of the countryside, come out at some sign of danger to see what the trouble was. She stood on two tremendous legs, with the grand self-confidence of a mountain, and rose, up narrowing bulges of granite, to two icy blue points of light that pierced forward, surveying everything. She ignored the white afternoon sun which was creeping behind a ragged wall of cloud as if it pretended to be an intruder and cast her gaze down the red clay road that turned off from the highway. (285)

Beginning in an omniscient mode, O'Connor makes the reader look at the peacock and Mrs. Shortley from a distance. Moving up the hill, they appear one next to the other: first the peacock, then Mrs. Shortley. Significantly, the narrator makes us aware that this is the reverse order: the peacock, though appearing first on the page, is following behind. Woman and peacock appear as deeply entangled to the point where it becomes unclear who the protagonist of the sentence's action is. As early as the second sentence, we are told what they look like – a "complete procession," which confirms their mutual complementarity. A few sentences down, by contrast, O'Connor switches to a focalized view: we see Mrs. Shortley not seeing any of this. Completely unaware of her organic embeddedness in her surroundings, her cold eyes engage in the objectifying, quantifying act of the surveyor. Her way of seeing is a way of ignoring. Not only does she fail to notice the sun, but, with her "unseeing eyes" (290), she also consistently overlooks the peacock (itself "a tail of suns," as the priest remarks, [289]). She denies the very procession as a part of which she is introduced. What she does perceive instead is the isolated phenomenon of the car in which the new Polish tenants arrive, greeted with unusual respect by Mrs. McIntyre, the farm owner. Mrs. Shortley, in short, only sees competition and only feels jealousy: "These people who were coming were only hired help, like the Shortleys themselves or the Negroes. Yet here was the owner of the place out to welcome them. Here she was, wearing her best clothes and a string of beads, now bounding forward with her mouth stretched" (285).

In "seeing with unseeing eyes," Mrs. Shortley is like all the other characters of the story, save the priest and the DP. In fact, her limited vision makes her a paradigmatic character of O'Connor's fictional worlds. This failure of vision points to O'Connor's fusing theological doctrine with cultural critique: seeing properly, as demonstrated by the priest, requires attention to the symbolic richness of the individual element of nature, its capacity to point beyond itself to the sacramentally embodied, immanent order of the divine.[20] The key is the symbol's power to generate a vision of wholeness that exceeds the use-oriented gaze of rationality. Much like the Romantics' use of symbolism, O'Connor's religious symbolic vision acts as the antidote to instrumental reason. In making her characters lack this kind of vision, O'Connor not merely renders them critically and theologically deficient; she also makes them ethically impoverished because they completely lack respect for others – Mrs. Shortley literally has no re-*spect* for the peacock.

Limited vision as the sign of a lack of generosity, of self-satisfaction and resistance to change, is reinforced by the characters' clinging to clichéd ways of speaking, rendered in a southern vernacular. In the "Displaced Person," the farm population becomes a community by trading back and forth worn-out sentences, many of them handed down from Mrs. McInytre's late patriarchal husband. Among these stock phrases are "One fellow's misery is the other fellow's gain," and "The devil you know is better than the devil you don't" (299). But more broadly, almost every sentence her main characters utter is a cliché intended to confirm their self-satisfaction. There are moments in which O'Connor's characters reach absurdly comical levels of close-minded self-delusion, as when Mrs. Shortley muses about the odd colors of the curtains in the Polish family's shack: "They can't talk … You reckon they'll know what color even is?" (287). For the most part, however, O'Connor's ridiculing her characters' idiotic idiom is less comical than aggressive, an affective preparation for, and justification of, the violence and shift in narrative focus with which the story ends. Doesn't the greatest satisfaction "The Displaced Person" has to offer come precisely at the end, when Mrs. McIntyre loses her voice – and we are relieved of her southern tongue?[21]

The aggression cooked up by O'Connor is highly ambivalent, particularly because the southern idiom serves the dual purpose of setting apart the narrator from the characters while also binding O'Connor's work to the South and its cultural traditions. Indeed, O'Connor said as much when she claimed, in her lecture "The Catholic Novelist in the Protestant South," that "the Southern writer's greatest tie with the South is through his ear. … A distinctive idiom is a powerful instrument for keeping fiction social. When one Southern character speaks, regardless of his station in life, an echo of all Southern life is heard" ("Catholic Novelist" 855). O'Connor uses the discourse of her characters to stir up a desire to destroy the very southern life to which she, as a self-proclaimed Southerner, aims to tie herself by means of that same discourse. To a large extent, the burden of resolving the resulting paradox is borne by the allegorical transition from worldly concerns to spiritual awakening. The tie to the South, in other words, can be affirmed in the act of creating the wish to destroy it only because what follows the destruction of her Southerners is their entry into their "true country." Here we reencounter O'Connor's dual tendency of affirming creation by rendering it grotesque and by downright destroying it.

O'Connor's ambivalence does not stop at the South, understood as a place, but extends to virtually all Southerners. In a move reminiscent of the Cold War intellectuals' turn against their former political convictions, this implicates O'Connor herself, as well as the narrator of her text. Throughout her stories, we again and again feel her authorial disdain for young Southerners with intellectual and artistic ambitions who feel superior to the old country ways, such as Hulga in "Good Country People," Julian in "Everything that Rises Must Converge," and Asbury in "The Enduring Chill" – figures, in other words, who eerily resemble O'Connor.[22]

"The Displaced Person" lacks such a figure, but it subtly extends her disapproval to the narrator and reader by eradicating, at certain moments, the distance between narrator, reader, and character, only to implicitly indict the narrator and reader along with the character in the next moment. For this purpose, O'Connor resorts to a device common in her works: the creation of character doubles, which expose each other's limitations while nonetheless remaining limited themselves. Such doubles rest less on the model of the uncanny *Doppelgänger* (though these exist in her writing as well, most pointedly in the shadow-devil who follows and eventually rapes young Tarwater in *The Violent Bear it Away*[23]), than on mimetic duplicates (mostly women), whose similarity in outlook establishes the reality of conformism. We may think of Ruby Hill and Laverne Watts in "A Stroke of Good Fortune," Susan and Joanne in "A Temple of the Holy Ghost," Mrs. Pritchard and Mrs. Cope in "A Circle in the Fire," and Mr. Head and Nelson in "The Artificial Nigger." The effect of these doubles can be studied in a scene from "The Displaced Person" in which Mrs. Shortley wittily replies to Mrs. McIntyre's thinly veiled threat of firing her. Instead of responding directly, Mrs. Shortley regains her employer's favor by citing one of the Judge's favorite sayings: " 'However,' Mrs. Shortley remarked, 'the devil you know is better than the devil you don't,' and she had to turn away so that Mrs. McIntyre would not see her smile" ("Displaced"

299). This smile is endorsed by the narrator – indeed, Mrs. Shortley here takes over the narrator's role of mocking another character – and, read in its fuller context, it is one of the comical moments in the story and intended to elicit the reader's smile as well. Yet immediately following this shared smile with Mrs. Shortley, the narrator heightens the exposure of her character's limitations by revealing Mrs. Shortley's deep-seated, and thoroughly ignorant, xenophobia, which climaxes in her vision of a war of words between the Polish and the English language (300). Showing that Mrs. Shortley deserves the exact same contempt that Mrs. Shortley has just conveyed (with full authorization by the narrator) about Mrs. McIntyre, the narrator implicitly indicts the reader (as well as herself) for having sided, a moment earlier, with Mrs. Shortley.

What André Bleikasten has called O'Connor's "misanthropy" ("Heresy" 142) is thus directed at everyone involved in her acts of fiction, including narrator and reader. O'Connor's response to this self-produced predicament is twofold. For one thing, she tries to reestablish the distinction between the characters and the narrator through the use of tone. Not only do her narrators differ from the characters through the absence of the vernacular and the contrast between seeing and unseeing narration. Her narrators also speak in a disdainfully ironic tone that sets them apart from the characters even when the story is focalized through a character. In effect, the narrator manages to see through the character's eyes and to simultaneously comment on the character. We get a sense of this narrative technique by returning to a passage quoted earlier, in which Mrs. Shortley reacts to a newsreel of the Holocaust:

> This was the kind of thing that was happening every day in Europe where they had not advanced as in this country, and watching from her vantage point, Mrs. Shortley had the sudden intuition that the Gobblehooks, like rats with typhoid fleas, could have carried all those murderous ways over the water with them directly to this place. If they had come from where that kind of thing was done to them, who was to say they were not the kind that would also do it to others? ("Displaced" 287)

Mrs. Shortley's thoughts make her so odious because they contain all the elements which, in O'Connor's universe, characterize secular short-sightedness: the smug sense of superiority, the belief in progress, the dull fear of the other. But in the narrator's language, bits and pieces of the character's diction are coupled, in free indirect discourse, with the sophisticated, almost Jamesian, grammar that marks the narrator's skill in getting to the intricacies of consciousness. Thus, on the one hand, we read expressions like "Gobblehooks" (instead of Guizacs) and comparisons of refugees to rats; on the other hand, these expressions are placed inside a sentence whose elaboration exceeds the mental powers of the character: "Mrs. Shortley had the *sudden intuition* that the Gobblehooks, *like* rats with typhoid fleas, *could have* carried." O'Connor's narrator manages to distance herself from the character by getting closer to the character's mind.

Building on this narrative distanciation, we can furthermore reconstruct O'Connor reestablishing the difference between characters and narrator/reader by allowing narrator and reader to create the afore-mentioned bond with each other. The distance between narrator and character becomes the reader's possibility to regain a sense of distinction vis-à-vis the characters. And this sense of distinction is based on the very repulsiveness of the characters. Thus, in a logic that duplicates the sacrifice of the Displaced Person in the story, this bond is created at the expense of her characters, so that O'Connor's endings become scenes of ritual violence which crush her characters, allow narrator and reader to surpass the characters' perspective, and thus confirm their difference from the characters. To put it differently, O'Connor allows narrator and reader to fend off her misanthropy by sacrificing her characters.[24]

But if O'Connor ends her stories by making her characters suffer from sacrificial violence in order to allow the reader to cope with the author's attack on him or herself, we nonetheless should not lose sight of the centrality of her Catholic frame of meaning. As already cited in part, André Bleikasten once remarked provokingly, "one may wonder whether her Catholicism was not, to some extent, an alibi for misanthropy" ("Heresy" 142). Indeed, to some extent. The fact that her characters' suffering is functional for the reader's experience of the text does not lessen the story's insistence that Mrs. McIntyre's purgatorial misery establishes the rightful reign of insecurity. If we bring together the story's pedagogical thrust, according to which the Displaced Person's death allows the other characters to begin to care for their own insecurity, and the aggression vis-à-vis these characters that is built up in the course of the story, we begin to see that for O'Connor the pedagogy of her fiction in fact requires violence. This pedagogical violence, which is designed to procure the respect for our insecurity, would remain ineffectual if we didn't feel that the characters deserved their punishment. The fact that they deserve it is certified by the readerly contempt produced throughout the story. "The Displaced Person," like so many of her stories, stages and enacts a type of violence which appears as necessary in order to live the kind of onto-theological insecurity her religious vision demands.

I have focused in this chapter on the ways in which O'Connor's fiction dismisses the quest for worldly security and instead promotes the recognition that as limited and sinful human beings, our only chance for redemption lies in the acceptance of our insecurity. It might seem, then, that O'Connor relates in an entirely antagonistic way to the intense preoccupation with security in the early Cold War. As national security became the anxious concern of more and more Americans and as the American state became restructured along the lines of the "national security state," O'Connor embraced her southern and Catholic identity in taking a stand against the wrong-headed, God-denying desire for security.

This, however, is only half the story. O'Connor's critique of worldly security creates a position that is much more ambivalent than it may at first seem. And it is this ambivalence that principally aligns her with the Cold War intellectuals considered at the outset of this chapter. Anticommunist writers such as Schlesinger, Niebuhr, and Trilling rejected a rationalist ideal of security and instead embraced a realist politics mindful of the need to engage in a messy struggle against evil. For them, security was an uncomfortable term, difficult to untether from excessive rationality. But on the condition that "security" became instead attached to the defense of a world of chance, uncertainty, and insecurity – values that had come to be defined as the essence of freedom – the critique of rationalist security could be squared with the promotion of skeptical and tragic security.[25]

Similarly, O'Connor did not let matters rest at calling for a sharpened awareness of our condition of insecurity. In fact, in her fictional world, insecurity is not something given – a universal *conditio humana* of vulnerability – but something that humans must be brought to realize. In O'Connor's aggressive vision, they must be chastened and humbled, hated and violently attacked, until they finally submit to God in their moment of demise. In other words, the submission to insecurity must be violently secured.

If the Cold War intellectuals availed themselves of the concept of security by redefining it as the defense of insecurity, O'Connor, in related fashion, committed herself to a struggle for insecurity under God. Insecurity became her *telos* in the fight against the security threat of secular rationalism. Precisely because the properly pious position of insecurity could not be taken for granted, it had to be ensured with violent means. If the rational ordering of the world epitomized the evils of modernity, the countermeasure could only lie in irrationally disordering it. In O'Connor, the Cold War intellectuals' analysis of the dialectic of the Enlightenment – which continued to stand in the service of a chastened Enlightenment – became itself dialectic. Her works feed on a desire for a world in which the Enlightenment apocalyptically undoes itself and the grotesque distortions born of modernity express the mystery of the divine. O'Connor, then, drives to a radical conclusion the imaginary uses of insecurity we have observed among all the literary writers discussed so far in this book. As was the case with Brown, Jacobs, and Cather, for O'Connor the concern with security leads to the embrace of the possibilities enabled by insecurity. But for O'Connor, the possibilities embraced are no longer those of life. Insecurity, instead, becomes the essence of grace and finds its consummation in death.

CHAPTER 6

In the Future, Toward Death
Finance Capitalism and Security in DeLillo's Cosmopolis

My readings of the postwar liberals and Flannery O'Connor aimed to show that a deep attachment to insecurity runs through the early Cold War discourse of national security. While Trilling, Schlesinger, Niebuhr, and other anticommunist writers held up insecurity – political, existential, and aesthetic – as a value that set the free world apart from the rationalist ideal of security purportedly characteristic of totalitarian society, O'Connor approached insecurity from an expressly religious vantage point. The violent breaking in of grace freed characters, and ideally author and reader as well, from the falsities and superficialities of a naively optimistic culture of progressivism. Awakened to a proper sense of our existential vulnerability (a vulnerability that her stories establish by directing violent aggression against her characters), O'Connor's characters embrace insecurity as an authentic existence under God – even if this existence can be realized only in the moment of violent death. Influenced by Christian existentialists ranging from Søren Kierkegaard to Jacques Maritain and Pierre Teilhard de Chardin, O'Connor linked insecurity to a philosophical and religious outlook focused on the elementary questions of existence.

As I argue in this chapter, Don DeLillo's oeuvre is similarly driven by a quasi-existentialist quest for a life that is acute to the physicality of the body and to a temporal orientation of being toward death – though that quest seems forever bound up with frustration. The concern with authentic existence is particularly pronounced in his recent novels *Cosmopolis* (2003) and *Point Omega* (2010), which, significantly, move the theme of security to the center of the narrative.[1] Whereas in previous novels, including *Players* (1977), *The Names* (1982), *Libra* (1989), and *Mao II* (1991), DeLillo had obliquely touched on security as a topic subordinated to terrorism, these recent novels turn priorities around and treat death-dealing assassins as a function of security. No longer do these novels focus primarily on the figure of the terrorist; instead their protagonists are obsessed with their private security apparatus (Eric Packer) or they work as consultants for the security strategists of the state (Richard Elster). If the concern with security allows DeLillo's recent narratives to pay attention to insecurity and thus to explore the longings for the authentic, then *Cosmopolis* – on which this chapter concentrates – shows that such longings become particularly urgent in a world dominated by the abstractions of finance capitalism. Finance capitalism, DeLillo suggests, has made life intensely virtual, and as a consequence the problem of the real begins to matter with renewed vigor. Once life has been thoroughly "financialized," however, it is no longer possible to simply "return to the real," to use Hal Foster's resonant phrase. Yet rather than dampening the appeal of security, this caveat only boosts its promise. Security manages both to counteract the virtuality of speculation (in that it brings into focus our physical vulnerability) and to join forces with the virtual, for similar to the risk-driven world of finance capitalism, security acts on the present by creating scenarios of the future which are by definition mere potentials. I conclude my study of the aesthetic uses of security by discussing Don DeLillo's recent fiction, then, because it allows us to reconstruct the imaginary appeal of security in what is still aptly called a postmodern condition of late capitalism.

Shortly after September 11, 2001, DeLillo published an essay in *Harper's*, "In the Ruins of the Future," in which he asserted that terrorism had put an end to finance capitalism's power to shape global consciousness. In making this claim, he unwittingly joined pundits – many of them conservative – who gleefully seized on 9/11 to pronounce that "the age of irony ha[d] come to an end" (Roger Rosenblatt in *Time*), or that "the end of postmodernism" had arrived (Julia Keller in the *Chicago Tribune*). But DeLillo's recent novels, I maintain, carefully keep a distance from the narrative of a future-crazed, morally irresponsible postmodern generation that finally, thanks to the terror attacks, has sobered up to seriousness. Instead, these works point us to the fact that the cultural, social, and economic trends toward the immaterial and virtual are subtended by desires for the real without thereby enabling a simple recovery of the real. A case in point, *Cosmopolis* leaves highly ambiguous how speculative finance and speculative security are related to each other. Does the rapid-fire spread of security discourse bespeak a turn toward a new realism that serves to attenuate postmodernism's infatuation with the sign, or does it merely cloak the abstractions of the virtual in a language game of concrete physical violence? An analogous question can be asked from the opposite direction: Does the reliance of security on projections of the future present proof that today's power is exerted from within the realm of the probable and uncertain – that virtuality has colonized our world – or does it serve as a reminder that the virtual is no less real than the actual, and that ultimately financial risk is as much about physical lives as is security? In *Cosmopolis* such questions are generally not decided one way or the other: DeLillo's works may best be described as novels of ideas, but it is seldom clear which among the contradictory set of ideas wins the author's approval. It is rather the battles of ideas themselves that contribute to the character of his works. In order to get closer to the character of *Cosmopolis*, I begin by briefly suggesting how it works against DeLillo's reactions to the attacks of September 11, 2001 in "Ruins" and in his 2004 novel *Falling Man*.

6.1   9/11 – Traumatic Loss of the Future?

> In the past decade the surge of capital markets has dominated discourse and shaped global consciousness. Multinational corporations have come to seem more vital and influential than governments. The dramatic climb of the Dow and the speed of the Internet summoned us all to live permanently in the future, in the utopian glow of cyber-capital, because there is no memory there and this is where markets are uncontrolled and investment potential has no limit.
>
> All this changed on September 11. Today, again, the world narrative belongs to terrorists. ("Ruins" 33)

These opening lines of "In the Ruins of the Future" relate what soon would be known as 9/11 in terms of radical and all-encompassing rupture: "All this changed …" It is striking that DeLillo combines two rather different claims here. He implies that the attacks would reverse the supremacy of the markets over governments – the state would return with a vengeance, no doubt in the guise of the security state – and he further suggests that after this change of guard, the future would play a diminished role. In this reasoning, after the attacks, the public mindset would no longer be dominated by the future-orientation of the financial markets because "the world narrative" now belongs to terrorists, who are prepared to face – and bring on – imminent death. Instead of speculating about the future, their willingness to die reasserts the immediacy of the present and real. Conjointly, state and terrorists change global consciousness: we realize the inappropriateness of wanting to construct a future to our liking and likewise become aware of the importance of the protection by a strong state. DeLillo seems to be uncertain whether these changes are for the better or for worse. What matters is that they are real.[2]

Falling Man (2007), DeLillo's contribution to the emerging genre of the 9/11 novel, approaches the question of the future from a similar position. While the terrorists embrace an eschatological readiness to die – "The time is coming, our truth, our shame, and each man becomes the other, and the other still another, and then there is no separation," DeLillo's fictionalized Mohammed Atta is preaching to his conspirators (80) – the inhabitants of DeLillo's post-attack America have in effect lost the future and exist in a state of temporal belatedness, of shock and traumatic repetition: "These are the days after. Everything now is measured by after" (138), as the narrator puts it.

The novel's male protagonist, Keith Neudecker, who was in the World Trade Center during the attack and witnessed the impact in his own office, seeks solace in playing poker. Creating a refuge in the temporal structure of the poker game, he gambles not to win but to keep on playing. The ritual character of the poker game, to which Keith adheres with conscious discipline, in effect suspends time. The outside of the casinos – whose windowless rooms are shielded even from the natural rhythm of daylight and dark – nearly ceases to exist altogether: "This was never over. That was the point. There was nothing outside the game but faded space" (189).

Keith's estranged wife Lianne, who watched the towers fall on TV, experiences a different sort of trauma. Rather than being shocked by the immediate impact, she suffers a second-order trauma, a fear of losing her identity and memory. She gives therapeutic writing lessons to a group of Alzheimer's patients, who write storylines of their lives in order to hold on to a sense of self. As they turn to the attacks, their capacity for storytelling falters – "No one wrote a word about the terrorists" (63) – and Lianne fears succumbing to the disease herself. Her father, himself Alzheimer-stricken, committed suicide when the disease began, and her mother, Lianne fears, is also betraying early symptoms. "With a certain symmetry" (29), Keith commits to poker as Lianne commits to her storytelling group. While for Keith the outside of the game diminishes to faded space, Lianne fears the future as her own fading.

Put sympathetically, *Falling Man* aims to represent not 9/11, but rather the difficulties in representing it.[3] In more skeptical terms, however, the novel reiterates the narrative of rupture rehearsed in "Ruins," according to which a craze for speculation has been displaced by a reawakening to the authentic and real. Put differently, *Falling Man* tells the story of how a concern with risk gave way to a preoccupation with security. While during the boom of the new economy there was a consensus that uncertainty was good, in the new millennium uncertainty appears as bad. Before 9/11, "global consciousness" connected uncertainty to markets and profits; afterwards, uncertainty became associated with terror attacks. Keith and Lianne pay the price for having been the profiteers of a society fixated on the future. Hit by the force of terror – which puts an end to future schemes by insisting on imminent death – they are shoved into the traumatic time of suspended futurity.

Yet, as I already suggested at the outset, DeLillo's recent works are generally acute to the fact that security, too, makes manifest a concern with the future. DeLillo recognized this as early as 2003 in a comment on the Iraq war:

> I think the curious psychological subtext to the war in Iraq was to return America to its sense of the future, a feeling that had been damaged by the events of September 11. ... We're using our technological imperative in order to win a struggle that concerns the past and the future. This is not something that's at all overt, but I think the element exists at some level of our exertions against terrorists and the Iraq situation as well. We want to live in the future. (Bertodano)

Point Omega's protagonist Richard Elster, whom DeLillo's narrator addresses by the Cold War moniker "defense intellectual," repeats the point when explaining his philosophy of security: "A great power has to act. We were struck hard. We need to retake the future. The force of will, the sheer visceral need. We can't let others shape our world, our minds" (30).[4] The reign of the future, it becomes clear, did not end in 2001 – neither in our world nor in DeLillo's.

DeLillo's 2003 novel *Cosmopolis* – written in part before the attacks – moreover refuses to sever the logic of risk from that of security and instead shows them to be tightly interwoven. Here, security's relation to the future shares little with Richard Elster's dream of being able to determine the shape of the world to come. As I will argue, the contemporary imagination of security as it emerges from *Cosmopolis* is not concerned with eradicating uncertainty but rather appropriates from risk the engagement with uncertainty. But whereas risk aims to manage uncertainty, security acts as a check on the fantasy of management. Security, more precisely, is revealed to be a mode of confronting an uncertainty that arises from the unmanageable fact of death.

Cosmopolis follows asset manager Eric Packer during the course of a day in April in the year 2000, just before the collapse of the boom of the 1990s, which we are implicitly asked to interpret not merely as the end of a millennium, but as the millennial end of an epoch. Wandering through his luxury triplex apartment located on the top floors of what seems to be modeled after Trump Tower ("the tallest residential tower in the world" [8]), Packer begins his day by deciding on a whim to "get a haircut" (7) in the neighborhood of his childhood – a self-destructive wish considering that "getting a haircut" has recently come to refer to taking heavy financial losses.[5] His armored limousine takes him from luxury to shabbiness along Forty-Seventh Street all the way to its western tip in Hell's Kitchen. Backtracking his career from splendor to humble beginnings, DeLillo sends Packer on a homeward journey resonant with the classical tradition. Keeping with the episodic structure of the Homeric epic, Packer is intermittently joined by his "chief security," "chief of technology," and "chief of theory." Perennially stuck in traffic, his daylong trip leaves him enough time to have several meals in restaurants, spend time in hotels, have sex with four different women, watch the assassination of the International Monetary Fund's managing director on the screens of his car, begrudge the US President his even larger security apparatus, become witness and target of an anti-globalization protest, take part in the funeral procession of a Sufi rap star, attend a techno rave, and squander "his personal fortune in the tens of billions" (121) – in addition to the more than seven hundred million belonging to his wife (124) – in the financial markets. All through the day, Packer's security team receives more or less unspecified threats. Though originally all efforts are made to prevent harm, ultimately Packer will seek out his assassin, who will duly serve his office and thus complement Packer's financial ruin. The novel comes to a close as its two thematic axes – currency speculation and security management – reveal a shared longing for death.

6.2 The Time of Risk

In order to make sense of the novel's engagement with security, it will first be necessary to explore in some detail how DeLillo narrates the temporality of risk in the financial economy. Focusing on the dealings of a megarich currency trader allows DeLillo to flesh out what it might mean to "liv[e] in the future," as one of the characters puts it (78).[6] To get at that meaning, DeLillo juxtaposes two registers of representation. On one level, Packer's behavior captures certain features of financial trading, including stock forecasting and a typical hedge fund operation, in which selling short (speculating on falling prices) is "hedged" by going long (speculating on rising prices). This representation can be called realistic in the narrow sense that it refers to standard procedures of real-life finance capitalism. Notably, DeLillo's novel differs from most contemporary representations of finance capitalism in popular culture, such as the movies *Wall Street* (1987) and *The Wolf of Wall Street* (2013), in that his protagonist stays within the limits of normal, legally sanctioned procedures. Gordon Gekko and Jordan Belfort, on the other hand, have rigged the game: they have amassed their enormous wealth through insider trading, securities fraud, and money laundering, and they thus represent aberrations (no matter how common they may be) to a financial system that itself stays on the margins of the narrative.[7] DeLillo's decision to focus instead on the systemic workings of finance capitalism allows the novel to ponder the significance of "living in the future" on the basis of standard procedures. But on top of that, DeLillo also presents us with a fictionalized version of the risk economy in which the discourse of real-life finance capitalism is poetically distorted, exaggerated, or pushed to its logical conclusions through aesthetic means. In what follows I focus on this second level.

As we will see, on this level *Cosmopolis* emphasizes what inhabiting the future would *feel* like. Taken to its most radical conclusion, DeLillo's novel suggests, the future-orientation of the markets leads to a sense of timelessness. As life becomes entrenched in the virtuality of the future, the future ironically begins to recover its premodern function as sheer fate. But in contrast to the premodern subject, the postmodern subject of DeLillo's novel encounters the future's blows as if in a ghostly state of numbness and shock. As I detail in what follows, DeLillo creates the effect of the timeless, ghostly, and uncontrollable future by combining aesthetic strategies on the level of plot structure, style, motifs, and dialogue.

Regarding plot structure, *Cosmopolis* riffs on the tradition of the Homeric epic; more precisely, DeLillo references the *Odyssey* in its modernist, nineteenth-century, and classical variants. In this way the novel's plot structure contributes to the sense of suspended temporality. From James Joyce,[8] DeLillo adopts the condensation of the Homeric voyage into a single day. DeLillo further emphasizes Packer's restlessness by adopting from the Victorians – particularly from Tennyson, who builds on Dante – the idea that the Odysseus-figure is a restless seeker who cannot find peace after his homecoming. His determination "to strive, to seek, to find, and not to yield" (Tennyson, *Poems* 90) might be heroic were it not ironically undermined by the fact that it is this very restlessness that will drive him to take a final, most likely fatal, voyage. In Tennyson's "Ulysses," just as in *Cosmopolis*, that voyage is an anticipated more than an accomplished fact: a path towards demise, the last step of which is suspended in mid-air, just like time itself.[9]

In the context of temporality, the most important adaptations of the epic come from the *Odyssey* itself. Again, there are detailed parallels. David Cowart observes, for instance, that both Odysseus and Packer stay with three women before they (re)unite with their wives.[10] But more significantly, it is the adoption of the epic's loose and episodic structuring of incidents that leads to a particular perception of time. In *The Specter of Capital*, Joseph Vogl keenly observes that while the modern novel is concerned with the rules that provide order for singular events, in *Cosmopolis* events appear "as external forces and hardships that ultimately take a turn for the worse as they interconnect and escalate in a fateful way" (6). Vogl emphasizes the convergence between the events of the novel and the utter failure of Packer's investments: "The erratic course that draws DeLillo's protagonist from one incident to another and on to his death is shadowed or doubled by a wild run on the currency market: 'against expectations' (8), the Japanese yen climbs ever higher until nothing can stop its rise: Packer Capital's holdings are wiped out and its CEO is ruined" (7–8, page number in quote refers to the edition cited here). Life in times of financial markets, according to Vogl's take on DeLillo, has regressed into archaic conditions with the result that humans must interpret seemingly inexplicable calamities as blows of fate. The epic is the proper genre for this helplessness vis-à-vis the world out there, even if it is humans themselves who have created the uncontrollable monster of the financial market.

But the episodic structure of *Cosmopolis* culminates not merely in an erratic course of events to which Packer is subject; it moreover establishes a particular temporality in which episodic elements fail to create a rational sense of time. The episodic character of incidents I'm stressing here does not mean that the epic in general, or this novel-epic in particular, is without a plot. But on the other hand, scenes tend to be cut short and turn into shredded, disconnected memories. The text's episodic nature brings the sense-making capacity of narrative to its limits, even while the overall narrative thrust of the homecoming plot continues to move forward. This narrative leveling effect has ramifications for the novel's temporal order. Because there is no recognizable structure of cause and effect between successive events, the order of the novel's incidents remains random. Which of the women did Packer meet first? Did he stop by the techno rave before or after he watches the assassination of the IMF managing director on his screen? The reason why the temporal order is difficult to reconstruct is that these events happen on the same logical plane, the same sheet of time. Their order of telling is a matter of space (literally, space on paper), not of time.

Fredric Jameson, famously, had seen in this drive toward spatialization a key characteristic of postmodernity: "our daily life, our psychic experience, our cultural languages, are today dominated by categories of space rather than by categories of time" (*Postmodernism* 16). But in DeLillo, this observation only gains significance when it is linked to the complementary idea that once technology and media allow us to bridge physical space, and thus to overcome the material impediments imposed by space, it is time – particularly the future – that becomes the key concern of life. This is the phenomenon that Zygmunt Bauman emphasized about postmodernity (or, as he prefers to call, "liquid modernity"):

> The change in question is the new irrelevance of space, masquerading as the annihilation of time. In the software universe of light-speed travel, space may be traversed, literally, in "no time"; the difference between "far away" and "down here" is cancelled.
>
> ...
>
> Time is no longer the "detour to the attainment," and thus no longer bestows value on space. The near-instantaneity of software time augurs the devaluation of space. (*Liquid Modernity* 117–118)

DeLillo's epic plot structure shows that both of these explanations – a drive toward spatialization (Jameson) and a drive toward temporalization (Bauman) – are dialectically bound up with each other. The instantaneity of "living in the future" gives rise to a spatial ordering of what used to be temporal progression.

This temporal levelling effect is reinforced by a similar effect in the dimension of style. The reception of *Cosmopolis* in the press was anything but enthusiastic, and one of the recurring criticisms directed at DeLillo had to do with his tendency to inflate the banal to the near-sublime. As John Updike complained in *The New Yorker*, "DeLillo's fervent intelligence and his fastidious, edgy prose ... weave halos of import around every event, however far-fetched and random" ("One-Way Street"). Even more damning was James Wood in *The New Republic*, who detected in DeLillo's style an excessive pathos that results in a rhetorical insolvency comparable to Packer's financial ruin. Since, throughout the book, "DeLillo's prose races ahead of the actual importance of its subject," near the end, "when he seeks to raise some moral equity," his "already half-mortgaged language" leaves him "without the means" ("Traffic").[11]

Updike's and Wood's descriptions are perceptive, but their inflexible fidelity to the normative horizon of literary realism, centered on plausibility and psychological character development, blinds them to the function DeLillo's style has for the aesthetic rendition of futurity. The de-hierarchized sequence of events, each of which glows in a "halo of import," is less a failed attempt at realism than yet another means of undermining the narrative time of plot. Rather than progressing and developing, *Cosmopolis* strings together moments of high intensity that, in their seriality, become monotonous and begin to cancel each other out. One may or may not appreciate this effect in a novel, but it does contribute to DeLillo's aesthetic rendition of "living in the future" as a state in which the future no longer supplies a horizon of contingency for the present.

These considerations of narrative structure and style at least partially concern the aesthetic effect of the book and thus address the aesthetic experience of the reader. Matching his reception aesthetics with the corresponding production aesthetics, DeLillo devises aesthetic strategies on the level of motif and dialogue. Two sets among his repertoire of recurring motifs suggest that the "global consciousness" of "living in the future" (as DeLillo phrased it in his post-9/11 essay "In the Ruins of the Future" [33]) calls into question the very idea of the future.

The first of these concerns the characters' interaction with the materiality of signs. The fascination with the sign, word, or letter is likely to be familiar to every reader of DeLillo, since it runs virtually through his entire oeuvre. To name just a few instances, it centrally (and comically) features in the football/campus novel *End Zone* (1972), in which a group of college football players are riveted by a class on "the untellable," which requires students to memorize Rilke's ninth *Duino Elegy* in German – on the condition that they neither know nor learn the language. "The theory is," explains one student, "if any words exist beyond speech, they're probably German words, or pretty close" (181).

In *The Names* (1982), the materiality of language moves to the very center of the novel (and to its title). Here, an internationally operating cult kills people whose names have the same initials as the place they inhabit. The conceit is that such a doubling destroys the proper name's mystic unity of word and referent. While it exerts a strong pull on several characters, the cult's philosophy appears as ludicrously esoteric. As an alternative, however, the novel proposes the kind of literature written by the protagonist's aptly named son Tap, which – like the cult – thrives on the materiality of letters and sounds. Tap's playful misspellings, his father marvels, "seemed to contain curious perceptions about the words themselves, second and deeper meanings, original meanings" (311).

White Noise (1985) similarly carries the materiality of information in its title, and in a scene that has become iconic, protagonist Jack Gladney has an experience of the "postmodern sublime"[12] when he inserts his card into an ATM machine. After he has "tapped out" his request, the numbers on the screen confirm the balance he has estimated, and he is overcome by a sense of systemic and cosmic harmony: "I sensed that something of deep personal value, but not money, not that at all, had been authenticated and confirmed.... The system was invisible, which made it all the more impressive, all the more disquieting to deal with. But we were in accord, at least for now. The networks, the circuits, the streams, the harmonies" (*White Noise* 46). As in the previous examples, the medium far exceeds the message, and the sense of harmony with the invisible system results in a heightened experience of the self: Gladney has been "authenticated and confirmed."

The prevalence of this motif has in recent years played a key role in claiming DeLillo as a writer invested in the mystical and religious (a line of interpretation often keen on calling into question whether the interpretive frame of postmodernism, taken for granted by the majority of critics, is appropriate for DeLillo at all). According to this reading, when DeLillo's characters focus on the materiality of language, habitual operations of signification (the generation of meaning by means of the conventional, and forever slippery, matching of word and thing) make way for a deeply spiritual, numinous experience, fleeting though it may be. From the immanence of the material – the shape of letters, the pure sound of words – arises an experience of transcendence: the "original meanings" of language.[13]

In *Cosmopolis*, it is the materiality of economic information as it appears on the screens inside Packer's limousine that seems to transport the characters toward immanent transcendence – or perhaps more precisely, toward an erotic experience. Packer's "chief of theory," Vija Kinski, goes furthest in emancipating the aesthetics of data from the information it contains. Having joined Packer in his car after emerging from the Church of Saint Mary the Virgin – which "was curious but maybe it wasn't" (78) – she confesses: "Oh and this car, which I love. The glow of the screens. I love the screens. The glow of cybercapital. So radiant and seductive. I understand none of it" (78). Her very sentences, insistent in their rhythm, fragmented in grammar, convey her sense of rapture. It is at this moment that Kinski – paid for producing ideas, i.e., sentences, about matters she claims she cannot penetrate – ruminates on the future:

> The idea is time. Living in the future. Look at those numbers running. Money makes time. It used to be the other way around. Clock time accelerated the rise of capitalism. People stopped thinking about eternity. They

began to concentrate on hours, measurable hours, man-hours, using labor more efficiently. ... It's cyber-capital that creates the future. ... Because time is a corporate asset now. It belongs to the free market system. The present is harder to find. It is being sucked out of the world to make way for the future of uncontrolled markets and huge investment potential. The future becomes insistent. (79)

As Updike put it, DeLillo's "characters spout smart, swift essays at one another" ("One-Way Street"). The device of the "chief of theory" pushes this tendency to self-reflexive extremes: Kinski's outburst has just enough lucidity to be read as a theory of time and informational capitalism. She quite accurately sketches the transition from time as a function of efficiency in industrial capitalism to time traded as a good in the credit economy of finance capitalism. But as she reflects on "living in the future," what starts as an erotic, seductive experience of looking "at those numbers running" becomes transformed into an ominous vision of life in a lethal vacuum: the present "is being sucked out of the world" and makes place for markets whose lack of control sounds distinctly sinister. The vertiginous future that becomes palpable on the computer screens no longer offers any sense of present tense. It has turned into a dark power that insists on its own rule and that activates the disquieting potentials which Jack Gladney, in *White Noise*, had vaguely sensed standing in front of the ATM. Vija Kinski's theory of time and finance capitalism is thus subtended by an experience of the materiality of the sign that goes against DeLillo's strain of semio-spiritualism: the sense of living in the future that arises from the contemplation of prices, charts, and other economic information no longer offers the self a sense of authentication and confirmation because it destroys the anchor of a present that is needed as the referent of authentication and confirmation. While Packer's financial speculation aspires to match the present with the future, Kinski's theoretical flight of fancy rids the future of the present, leaving the self in a state of dizzying powerlessness.

The second dominant cluster of motifs in *Cosmopolis* insists on the outmodedness of the present world, its being in the process of rapidly sliding into the past. Packer complains throughout about the obsolescence of the present and the words that catalog it. The list of outdated names ranges from "office," "automated teller machines" (the nod to *White Noise* is impossible to miss), and "skyscraper." The latter is DeLillo's cue to bridge the diegetic pre-9/11 world to the reader's post-attacks reality in making Packer muse – with an ominous perverseness recognizable to the reader but not to the character – that the towers of the World Trade Center "looked empty ... They were made to be the last tall things, made empty, designed to hasten the future ... They weren't here, exactly. They were in the future, a time beyond geography and touchable money and the people who stack and count it" (36). While the Twin Towers' presence in the novel places it in a bygone, pre-attack era, the particular kind of appearance that the World Trade Center makes has moreover become self-consciously outmoded on the level of prose: the provocation of the looming towers featured prominently in DeLillo's previous novels *Players* (1977), *Mao II* (1991), and *Underworld* (1998).[14]

The list of outmoded things and concepts spread throughout the novel is even more encompassing than that of words: it includes stretch limousines, whose disappearance will signal that the "global era officially ends" (91), shooting at presidents ("I thought there were more stimulating targets," Packer grudgingly states [20]), physical money, Packer himself (at the techno rave he realizes that "an era had come and gone without him" [127]), the past (which is itself "disappearing" [86]), and even the emergence of the new ("There's no more danger in the new" [8]). Obsolescence is a vortex that sucks up the coordinates of being, including the primary objects, actors, and concepts that make up the novel. The world of *Cosmopolis* empties itself out to the point where it affects the literary text itself. The theme of growing outdated metaleptically jumps onto the level of the novel: as DeLillo employs and reemploys the hallmarks of virtuality – from the abstractions of finance capitalism, the glow of screens, and the evaporation of space, down to the well-worn topos of the Twin Towers that strive toward their own annihilation – *Cosmopolis* turns into a novel of negation. "Living in the future" is represented as a state of being "no longer," and the proper form for such a passé world is a literature that palpably and self-consciously begins to fatigue itself. In presenting a world in negation, it negates itself.

In order to render the presence of the future as the negation of the present, DeLillo adds to the above cluster of motifs a peculiar form of speech that hovers between dialogue and monologue and that is frequently interrupted by the short question "what?" – a stylistic element DeLillo uses far more excessively in this novel than in any other. In the course of the text, the interrogative "what?" takes on a range of subtly different meanings. Most commonly, "what?" does not so much express a search for meaning (and is in that sense a literal question) as it registers a slight moment of hesitation, a stutter within the expression of an idea. At one point Packer says, "That I'm a powerful person who chooses not to demarcate his territory with singular driblets of piss is what? Is something I need to apologize for?" (39). In a slight variation, the question "what?," located early on in a sentence, marks the entire idea to follow as inadequate. Here is how Packer aims to seduce his wife: "Looking at you, what? I'm more excited than I've been since the first burning nights of adolescent frenzy" (49). "What?" contradicts the message, redirecting attention from the immediacy of sexual excitement to the inadequacy of its representation. The interrogative itself produces the sense that what follows has already been devalued.

As mentioned earlier, when the characters interrupt themselves by "what?," their speech undoes the distinction between monologue and dialogue.[15] In most cases, the question is addressed neither at themselves nor at their listeners, but at language itself. It might not be an exaggeration to say that language is talking to language, just like money, in the words of the "chief of theory," "is talking to itself" (77). It is in this domain of self-referential language that self and other are co-constituted and co-situated. In *Cosmopolis*, all language is in this literal sense *colloquial*. Or as Alison Shonkwiler puts it, in *Cosmopolis* all "discourses are universally available at once. All discourse here is free and indirect" ("Financial Sublime" 273). DeLillo invokes the familiar postmodern idea of the subject's textual makeup. Characters, as Michael Shapiro phrased it with respect to DeLillo's early novels, "operat[e] more as linguistic vehicles than self-contained and controlled identities" (*Reading* 131). How, then, is this brought to bear on Packer, and how does it tie back to the question of temporality?

DeLillo's hero adopts and purifies a tendency that is observable in admixed versions in the major finance moguls that populate American literature and film. In American fiction, the speculator has most lastingly been established by the naturalist novel. Curtis Jadwin, in Frank Norris's *The Pit* (1903), and Frank Cowperwood, in Theodore Dreiser's *The Financier* (1912), *The Titan* (1914), and *The Stoic* (1947), may ultimately lose the battle against natural forces and the inscrutability of Lady Luck. Nonetheless, either they manage to test those forces because they themselves possess a natural energy and a degree of willpower that far exceeds that of their contemporaries (Jadwin), or they combine amoral determination with an attunement to the wily ways shared by nature and the markets (Cowperwood).[16] In the world of both *The Pit* and *The Financier*, speculating is ultimately indistinguishable from gambling. But while in *The Financier* gambling is primarily a matter of luck, in *The Pit* it is a habit that takes full possession of the gambler. Having fallen victim to gambling in wheat prices, Curtis Jadwin eventually is conquered by wheat itself: first it creeps into his mind – he is tormented by an inner voice that screams "Wheat – wheat – wheat, wheat – wheat – wheat" (204) – and then it asserts its supremacy by creating a harvest yield that ruins Jadwin's corner of the market. And yet, despite falling prey to addiction that undoes his autonomy and rationality, Jadwin is a master of speculation, and this mastery takes an intersubjective form: he is an unusually authoritative figure who naturally commands the will of others, as can best be seen in the control he exerts over his wife. He is a worthy opponent of nature, and his fall only adds to his majesty. Read in strict accordance with the doctrines of naturalism, his failure signifies the supremacy of external forces. In fact, however, it carries a trace of *hamartia* lifted straight from classical tragedy.

The naturalist tradition of creating a textual balance that places the financial hero between charisma, prestige, and authority on the one hand (natural forces working in and for the hero) and addiction, powerlessness, and greed leading to inevitable ruin on the other (natural forces working against him) gets further developed in later works ranging from Tom Wolfe's *Bonfire of the Vanities* (1987) to popular movies such as the aforementioned *Wall Street* (dir. Oliver Stone, 1987) and *The Wolf of Wall Street* (dir. Martin Scorsese, 2013). Several critics were indeed quick to align *Cosmopolis* and Eric Packer with Tom Wolfe's "masters of the universe."[17] But in contrast to this tradition of the exceptional – and often exceptionally wicked – financial hero, Packer blends into his world, if in a manner wildly out of proportion. This is made concrete early on in the novel when Packer, standing outside his apartment building, feels "contiguous with it. ... They shared an edge or boundary, skyscraper and man" (8). Even his state of the art limo looks entirely standardized: walking across First Avenue, he is confronted with "lines of white limousines ... identical at a glance" (9). He watches the drivers who are each awaiting their own Eric Packer: "they waited for the investment banker, the land developer, a venture capitalist, for the software entrepreneur, the global overlord of satellite and cable, the discount broker, the beaked media chief, for the exiled head of state of some smashed landscape of famine and war" (10).[18]

Packer is by no means wholly at odds with the hero of the naturalist tradition: he is propelled by primal forces of appetite and aggression, by a "predatory impulse, the sense of large excitation ... the sheer and reeling need to be" (209). But to the degree that these energies are directed toward speculating on the future, they find no social outlet, no intersubjective reverberation; instead they become absorbed, and subdued, in the abstract universe of information which glows on his screens. If Jadwin succumbs to wheat and at the same time is a charismatic financier, Packer lacks the second of these dimensions. Absorbed in the run of numbers, he lives an isolated, secluded life. Outside of his limousine anti-globalization protestors may be raising hell, but from inside his sound-proofed car, nothing becomes any realer than images on screens. He has surrounded himself with media geared at extending and stimulating the senses, but his temporally and stylistically leveled world feels overwhelmingly deaf, dumb, and cold. In other words, neither does Packer stick out of the pack of wolves, nor does he build up the intersubjectively confirmed ego boasted by figures like Jadwin, who is tellingly known as the "Great Bull" (230) – a designation that exceeds the technical meaning of speculating on rising prices. Deprived of vitalizing sense impressions, Packer instead moves, in a description from DeLillo's first novel *Americana* (1971), "from first person consciousness to third person" (270).

The separation of speech from subjectivity, the rendering of all discourse as free and indirect, captured by the eruption of "what?" in the characters' speech patterns, thus finds confirmation in the flattening and emptying out of DeLillo's protagonist. The impersonality celebrated by postmodern theory appears remarkably bleak in *Cosmopolis*. Packer, no longer a unified subject, has been plugged into the stream of information running across his screen. But instead of being released into immanent transcendence, he falls into a state of anesthesia in which "living in the future" is experienced as the stalled time of instantaneity.

Packer's world is stunning in both senses of the word, and as we have seen over the last few pages, DeLillo makes palpable its lifelessness by range a of aesthetic techniques, including an epic plot structure of suspended temporal progression, a style of monotonous pathos, a motif-language that turns the material sign into a determinist imperative rather than a ground for immanent transcendence and that further sketches the present as fading into obsolescence, and finally a transpersonal colloquialism that causes language to stumble over its own outmoded inadequacy and that reduces interpersonal dialogism to the abstract exchange of signs. By this set of strategies, *Cosmopolis* conveys the impression that the financial temporal imaginaries of "living in the future" create a present without a future and a future without a present. The temporal order of financial risk keeps the speculator imprisoned in a state deprived of any future horizon and therefore without any sense impressions that could pierce the subject. What Packer spitefully observes about the US president turns out to be a self-description: "He was the undead. He lived in a state of occult repose, waiting to be reanimated" (77).

6.3 The Time of Security

So far I have exclusively considered the ways in which *Cosmopolis* creates the time of risk. In fact, however, DeLillo confronts the time of risk with a different temporal order, which I call the time of security. The makeup of this alternative temporality and its relation to the time of risk will be the subject of this chapter's remaining pages. While the novel spells out the time of risk as a phenomenology of "living in the future," according to which the temporal progression of past-present-future is replaced by a disorienting and sense-numbing suspension of progression, the time of security keeps the end in sight: its horizon is limited by the existential scope of threat.

It might seem, then, that taken together, the logics of risk and security create a sense of balance. The financial markets work according to the logic of risk: here, Packer seeks to profit from the uncertainty of the open future. Physical life, by contrast, is approached from the logic of security: here, Packer tries everything to ward off uncertainty.

Indeed, this sense of balance is evoked early on in the novel. Packer confidently bets against the yen and simultaneously delights in the effectiveness of his security apparatus. We get detailed descriptions of the special security features of Packer's stretch limousine, and we see him communicate at length about the diagnosis of threats. Packer continuously seeks reassurance from his security team that his networks are "secure" (12) and "safe from penetration" (22). But as the novel continues – and particularly as it enters its second half – it becomes clear that security plays a key role in *Cosmopolis* not as a counterpoint to uncertainty, but rather as a way of restoring a sense of reality that has been lost in the abstractions of finance capitalism. The security apparatus is less an occasion for peace of mind than a motive force that turns the imagination to potential threats. Security – its technology, personnel, and the practices carried out by them – gives rise to a heightened sense of insecurity. It no longer counterbalances financial uncertainty with physical safety, but rather creates an acute sense of danger that might help break through the shock-absorbing shields of virtuality.

In the course of the novel, security, in fact, not only awakens the imagination to the insecurity of threat and danger but also gives this imagination a particular value. Rather than producing fear, insecurity becomes a source of thrill and excitement. When his "chief of security" recommends extra security measures in light of the threat to the president and the attack on the managing director of the IMF, Packer muses (in the words of the narrator), "How did he feel about additional security? He felt refreshed. The death of [IMF director] Arthur Rapp was refreshing. The prospective dip in the yen was invigorating" (35).

At one point, Packer has a private moment with a female bodyguard in a hotel room. It is a sad affair of super-safer sex. The attempt to get into physical touch is literally obstructed by what seems to be a fetishization, on Eric's side, of the guard's protective gear: "She wore her ZyloFlex body armor while they had sex. This was his idea. She told him the ballistic fiber was the lightest and softest available, and the strongest as well, and also stab-resistant. At some level she would never be naked" (111). The fetish turns out to lack sexual charge, however, and Packer is left unsatisfied. Instead he commands her to shoot him with her stun gun: "The voltage had jellified his musculature for ten or fifteen minutes and he'd rolled about on the hotel rug, electroconvulsive and strangely elated, deprived of his faculties of reason" (115). By turning his security apparatus against himself, he has finally consummated the act.

From that moment on, he will systematically reverse the direction in which the technology of security is targeted. It is only logical that in Packer's eyes, his real "enemy" (147) is not the assassin who is supposedly out to kill him, but rather his "chief of security," Torval. And it is strictly in line with this reversal that he will take Torval's high-tech gun, use it to casually shoot Torval, and leave the corpse and the weapon behind. If it is the function of the security apparatus to awaken him to the thrill of insecurity, fulfilling that function ultimately requires obliterating the apparatus itself.

In the early parts of the novel, the thrill of insecurity emerges from taking extra security measures that are linked to economic potential ("the prospective dip of the yen"). Later, as the excitement of insecurity emancipates itself from the apparatus that nominally stands in the service of security, it becomes tied, little by little, to taking financial hits. Insecurity and economic failure begin to work in concert.

After the stun gun encounter with his bodyguard, Packer goes on a spending spree, borrowing huge quantities of yen. Maximizing the risk of his supposedly hedged transactions prolongs the orgasmic effect of the electric shock:

> The yen spree was releasing Eric from the influence of his neocortex. He felt even freer than usual, attuned to the registers of his lower brain and gaining distance from the need to take inspired action, make original judgments, maintain independent principles and convictions, all the reasons why people are fucked up and birds and rats are not. (115)

Packer manages to free his orgiastic high-risk dealing from the "inspired action" and "original judgments" that are the hallmark of the successful speculator, but his investments do not stand quite yet in the service of loss. Their extreme riskiness still situates them in the uncertainty of the future that hovers between prospective gains and losses. Later, however, Eric Packer has an experience that recalls and inverts Jack Gladney's communication with the ATM: hearing a rapturous chant at the funeral service of a Sufi rap star, "Eric's delight in going broke seemed blessed and authenticated" (136). While Gladney had felt authenticated because the system confirmed his own estimate of his account balance, Packer feels confirmed by his steep trajectory toward bankruptcy.

Shortly before, at the close of the novel's first part, Packer ecstatically watches the stock ticker and feels "purified in nameless ways to see prices spiral into lubricious plunge. Yes, the effect on him was sexual, cunnilingual in particular, and he let his head fall back and opened his mouth to the sky and rain" (106). At this point, the "joy at all misfortune, in the swift pitch of markets down," becomes connected with, and is only topped by, existential insecurity: "But it was the threat of death at the brink of night that spoke to him most surely about some principle of fate he'd always known would come clear in time. Now he could begin the business of living" (107).

Eric Packer, it becomes obvious, is on an epic voyage toward purity and clarity, toward a state of being that will allow him to break through the "occult repose" of the "undead" brought about by speculating on the future. Engaging in risk has trapped him in a temporal state that DeLillo had captured in *Americana* with the help of Augustine: "And never can a man be more disastrously in death than when death itself shall be deathless" (21, 99).[19] Packer can only escape this disastrous state by giving himself over to passivity vis-à-vis insecurity and threat, which is to say, to fate. The reversal of the security apparatus, in short, will entail aiming for a relation to the future that the invention of security was meant to overcome. The aim of Eric's journey is the recovery of death from deathlessness. Only if death is resurrected can life become "the business of living."

Packer's quest evokes the preoccupation with authenticity in existentialism and, more broadly, the philosophy of existence, but it does so in a specific sense. According to a line of thought that leads from Kierkegaard to Heidegger and Sartre (and that should include Emerson), authenticity consists of an attitude toward life and death that must actively be achieved. Such an achievement is precisely what Packer's Odyssey turns out to aim for. However, for these philosophers, authenticity must be wrested from the forces of social conformity. But in Packer's world of the market, everyone tries to beat the herd. Authenticity, defined as nonconformity, is what the speculator excels in. That is why for Packer, moving toward authenticity requires more than freeing himself from the force of public opinion. It rather involves breaking free from the Augustinian condition of deathless death.

This is not the place to reconstruct a tradition of philosophical thinking about death as it comes to bear on DeLillo. I limit myself to the observation that the stance toward which Packer moves resonates specifically with Heidegger's notion of *Sein zum Tode* ("being-toward-death").[20] This concept ought not be confused with thinking about the fact that all of us must die. It rather involves an attachment to life in its scope of possibilities that grows out of the awareness of one's very own personal finitude and mortality. From the perspective of one's own mortality, death does not appear as a contingent possibility of the future, but as a certainty that reaches into present life, even if it remains "indefinite" when the moment of death will arrive.[21] It is this stance toward death as both certain and indefinite that sets apart authentic (*eigentlich*), first-person being from the generalized being that Heidegger grasps with the German word *Man* (a universalized third-person singular) and that DeLillo associates with the abstract and timeless third-person consciousness that flourishes in the environment of speculation. Toward the end of the novel, then, Packer moves toward a reinstatement of death, time, and the historical. He seems to reestablish the possibility of a life that is mindful of the future but diverges from "living in the future" insofar as it does not trivialize or even deny death. The existentially reanimated hero mounts the time of security against the time of risk.

However, *Cosmopolis* creates a number of ambiguities in Packer's existential pursuit that it ultimately leaves unresolved: the novel asks whether it is possible at all to break out of the time of risk once life has been thoroughly financialized. Moreover, *Cosmopolis* suggests that the "business of living" in the face of death has a tendency to move just a little closer to the edge and become a suicidal death wish. Finally, tying these two problems into one, DeLillo raises the question whether the time of security must not be incorporated into the time of risk if being-toward-death is to serve survival rather than self-annihilation. In order to get nearer to these ambiguities, I will look closer at the novel's final pages.

In the drawn-out closing scene, Packer has sought out his prospective murderer in an old warehouse. A thinly veiled *Doppelgänger* of Packer's who has moreover doubled himself – he goes by the names of Benno Levin and Richard Sheets – he presents himself, hardly persuasively, as the counterforce to the virtual. Earlier in the novel he boasts, "I still have my bank that I visit systematically to look at the last literal dollars remaining in my account" (60) and in his *Confessions* – self-consciously styled after none other than Augustine – he enacts a multitude of outcasts who emblemize the authentic. He impersonates Ralph Ellison's Invisible Man – "I steal electricity from a lamppost" (57) – and claims to be an inhabitant of the Waste Land: "I collect things ... from local sidewalks. What people discard could make a nation" (57). Levin acts as the embodiment of the real but his body is no more real than Packer's or that of the women with whom Packer practices, what one might call, "just sex, don't touch." He duplicates Packer moreover in that he, too, is caught in a colloquialism that dissolves the speaking subject into a universal third person. As he confesses, "I am speaking to someone and hear the sound of my voice, third person, filling the air around my head" (57–58).

In trying to move from the inauthentic toward the authentic, Packer aims to project the pathological and evil onto his double and thus create something that can break through to the real and will help him comprehend his own mortality. "As is usual with the Doppelgänger trope," observes David Cowart, "the one reifies the other's unconscious," and "Levin hypostatizes the something pathological in Packer's heart all along" (*Don DeLillo* 221). However, *pace* Cowart, Levin never credibly "reifies" into anything at all; he never becomes more than yet another set of voices in the choir of third persons and thus leaves Packer thrown back on himself to find his first-person viewpoint of authentic being-toward-death.

The only avenue left open to Packer is once again to turn what's left of his security apparatus against himself – this time, against his own body. His meandering verbal confrontation with Levin leading nowhere, he casually, half-consciously, holds his hand over the barrel of his gun and pulls the trigger. A "scorch mark" (197) of blood beginning to spread across his hand, he gets a first inkling of an existentialized alternative to the all-encompassing cosmopolis of globalized capitalism:

> The pain was the world. The mind could not find a place outside it. He could hear the pain, staticky, in his hand and wrist. He closed his eyes again, briefly. He could feel himself contained in the dark but also just beyond it, on the lighted outer surface, the other side, belonged to both, feeling both, being himself and seeing himself. (201)

Even this world of pain retains a trace of its mediality. Pain is a sound – not a sheer, immediate presence of feeling – whose place, it seems, is elsewhere. It travels across airwaves and, once picked up, remains intermixed with the white noise of static. Whether there is a world outside the sign, outside of mediated information, in which there is room for truly authentic being-toward-death, is rendered questionable. Pain itself is both a whole world and mediated.

The capacity of death to lead to authenticity becomes even more dubious as Levin moves toward fulfilling his task of shooting Packer. Packer sees his own death on the crystal screen of his high-tech watch – before he has heard the shot. "His hand contains the pain of his life, all of it, emotional and other, and he closes his eyes one more time. This is not the end. He is dead inside the crystal of his watch but still alive in original space, waiting for the shot to sound" (209). Death – the ultimate instance of authenticity, the experience that, according to Heidegger, no one can experience in your place – becomes yet another projection of the future that flickers on a screen. His own death, it seems, has not brought Packer a single iota closer to breaking out of the time of risk. In fact, it can hardly be called his own death at all. What is more, the reduction of death to a digital projection seems to fulfill the longing for immortality aspired to by the conquering of the future under the aegis of risk. "It is happening now, an evolutionary advance that needed only the practical mapping of the nervous system onto digital memory. It would be the master thrust of cyber-capital, to extend the human experience toward infinity as a medium for corporate growth and investment, for the accumulation of profits and vigorous reinvestment" (207).

Yet, DeLillo insists on ambiguity and simultaneously reinforces belief in the power of pain to create a pathway to authentic finitude: "But his pain interfered with his immortality. It was crucial to his distinctiveness, too vital to be bypassed and not susceptible, he didn't think, to computer emulation. The things that made him who he was could hardly be identified much less converted to data" (207). In fact, to the extent that the novel's final pages do credit pain with providing a way out of finance capitalism's temporal imaginary, death comes to seem more appealing than the life that is mindful of death. Situated in the space between seeing his death and hearing the shot, the text registers Packer's suicidal thrust: "Maybe he didn't want that life after all ... What did he want that was not posthumous?" (209). It dawns on him that the loss of his fortune will have real consequences, that he will be "starting over broke, hailing a cab in a busy intersection filled with jockeying junior executives, arms aloft, bodies smartly spinning to cover every compass point" (209) – and that he no longer has "the predatory impulse" (209) for renewed upward mobility into the spheres of abstraction and virtuality.

For Packer, breaking with the virtual – a project that initially aimed to recover a life of the senses numbed by virtuality – seems to lead straight to an "empire of the senseless" (to use Kathy Acker's phrase). It is an empire that is final, total, and definite: cosmopolis has become necropolis. Alternating between virtual life and death, Packer is incapable of imagining how to move from virtuality to virtue, i.e., how to free himself from the abstractions of finance capitalism in order to re-embed himself in a social world in which values are not abstracted and purely self-referential but tied to collective interest.[22] Torn between virtuality and death itself, Packer seems to have lost his way toward the "business of living." Yet, the final lines of the novel warrant another look precisely in this respect, for they seem to redirect the suicidal momentum to survival:

> His hand contains the pain of his life, all of it, emotional and other, and he closes his eyes one more time. This is not the end. He is dead inside the crystal of his watch but still alive in original space, waiting for the shot to sound. (209)

In two senses this moment is, of course, precisely the end. In Benno Levin's "Confessions," inserted earlier in the narrative, Levin ponders Packer's corpse on the floor of his warehouse apartment. From this we already know he will die this very instant. And, in a variation of the ending of *Arthur Mervyn*, the course of events and the text metaleptically come to share their ending. While the first-person narrator in *Arthur Mervyn* announces to put aside his pen and finishes the novel just as the chain of tumultuous events makes way for the eventless happiness of marital bliss, the story of Packer's voyage is coming to its last sentence as he sees the image of his death. And yet, in *Cosmopolis*, finality comes in a decidedly indefinite manner. It arrests the interval between image and sound and keeps Packer waiting indefinitely.

Peter Boxall has claimed this moment to mark a radical openness: "[Packer] occupies a transitional space that does not know yet whether it is a transition. He occupies a place of pure potential, a space of possibility, that holds itself open for the briefest of periods, waiting for the shot to sound" (*Possibility* 232). But in what sense can we speak of "a place of pure potential, a space of possibility" if we know that Packer is mistaken, that this truly is the end? In Boxall's reading, potential and possibility open up "for the briefest of periods" in which it is still unclear to Packer whether the transition actually is a transition. Simply put, as long as the future moment of the shot has not arrived, Packer cannot know for sure that it will happen. Given the knowledge of the reader, potentiality, in Boxall's interpretation, is no more than ignorance on Packer's part.

In the alternative interpretation I propose here, Packer, at the very end, returns to "the business of living" in the face of death. The projection of his death on his watch is not interpreted by Packer as an uncertain sign of the future, but instead as a fact. It is because of the discrepancy between the visual and the aural fact that he becomes keenly alive. The sentence "This is not the end" has a note of surprise and appreciation derived from the conviction that it *is* the end. Possibility and potentiality do not refer to the question whether the shot will sound or not; they arise from the certainty that it will, but has not yet. Possibility and potentiality, in other words, refer to a particular position toward life and death: life becomes possible in an authentic manner only once death has been accepted as a fact.

This attitude I have earlier associated with the time of security, i.e., with a temporality that is mindful of the individual's finitude and that leads to an attachment to life in its excitable, sensory, and unmediated dimension. But if I earlier suggested that Packer's security breaks through the time of risk and establishes its own temporality, these last lines of the novel force us to rephrase this relation. For Packer's recovery of life-in-waiting is made possible by the camera and screen inside his watch – the most avant-garde media technology of the financial risk economy and its corresponding temporal imaginary. Recalling his economic transactions, Packer's watch makes the future available by presenting its projection as a fact: the watch prophetically shows you not what time it is in the present, but what the future will bring. In the economic realm, treating the projection of the future as a fact led to disastrous results. Not only did it produce self-defeating prophecies but it also engulfed him in the numbness of virtuality. But what gets projected onto Packer's very personal timepiece is not the future development of prices, but the certainty of his death. Security thus breaks open the time of risk by adopting its aspiration to access and conquer the future.

In the final analysis, the time of security in *Cosmopolis* cannot produce an alternative temporality to the deeply entrenched logic of the world of finance capitalism. What it can do is transpose the temporal imaginary of late capitalism into an existential key in which questions of future investment become questions of finitude and mortality. DeLillo thus dramatizes a crucial appeal of security in the cultural imaginary: the encounter of threat afforded by the concern with security comes to appear as the gift of death. If this gift reinstates the privilege of dying, it simultaneously restores the possibility of living a life oriented to the future. For while modernity may be characterized by contingency, chance, and the open future, these uncertainties are never to be taken for granted. After all, the project of modernity has consisted not just in the emancipation from old dogmas but also in the attempt to master and overcome (through techniques such as risk management) the uncertainties gained from that emancipation. DeLillo's novel suggests that the cultural fascination with security – which is a preoccupation with insecurity – in the end aims to restore the openness enabled by the modern worldview by perverting the modern project of making the future secure.

Epilogue

The preceding chapters have aimed to demonstrate that in order to understand the centrality of the logic of security for American life, it is not sufficient to approach it as an antidemocratic political tool that operates through the concerted stimulation of the affects of fear and terror. To be sure, critiques of the politics of securitization are valuable and necessary in order to make us understand how the logic of security has been used as a matrix for wielding power that is applied to ever more realms of contemporary life. This is especially the case in our neoliberal era, in which security provides the normative, and insecurity the descriptive, justification for a politics organized around a revamped rationality of risk. At present, our lives are structured by two different logics of risk. One variant informs the ideological construct at the core of neoliberalism, i.e., of the self-reliant and rational individual who is in charge of taking care of her own life, rather than relying on provisions by the state, and who is asked to comprehend this burden of individualized responsibility as freedom.

The other rationality of risk, which operates inside the frame of security and insecurity, has evolved from probabilistic thinking (which balanced possible gains with possible losses on the basis of statistics and probability) into an anticipatory framework centered on the preemption of merely possible, and indeed highly improbable, futures. No longer about potential losses and gains of the risk-taking *homo oeconomicus*, this new logic of risk has come to work hand in glove with a logic of security that declares scenarios of threat as situations that demand a decisionist politics in order to avert the perceived threat from actualizing. Louise Amoore has given us the best account of this type of risk logic: "[I]t acts not strictly to prevent the playing out of a particular course of events on the basis of past data tracked forward into probable futures but to preempt an unfolding and emergent event in relation to an array of possible projected futures. It seeks not to forestall the future via calculation but to incorporate the very unknowability and profound uncertainty of the future into imminent decision" (*Politics of Possibility* 9). The emerging politics of risk accepts uncertainty as the condition for political decisions that intervene, sort out, lock up, or kill, in order to prevent futures whose shape does not need to be clearly defined. As virtually every commentator on this politics of risk points out, all of these acts – violent, undemocratic, and not even rational – are carried out "in the name of security." And increasingly, as Amoore discusses throughout her book, this risk logic of preemptive securitization forms alliances with the risk-embracing rationality of *homo oeconomicus* (11).

As dire as this picture and as trenchant as this critique may be, what we get here is not the whole story of security and insecurity. In literary fictions, the interplay of threat, insecurity, and response often takes rather different shapes. Amoore herself is aware of this. As she points out, resistance to, and critique of, the "politics of possibility" pose particular challenges, since "the politics of possibility appears to occupy the same terrain – of unknown subjects, acting upon the excess, thinking nonlinear relations – that has for so long provided resource for politics and critique" (155). What critique must do in the face of the harnessing of uncertainty to purposes of securitization is to find ways of "sustaining potentiality itself, [of keeping] open the indeterminate, the unexpected place and the unknowable subject" (157). It is by turning to imaginative literature (Jennifer Egan's *A Visit from the Goon Squad*, Joseph O'Neill's *Netherland*, and Herman Melville's "Bartleby the Scrivener") as well as installation art (Meghan Trainor's *With Hidden Numbers*) that Amoore finds heartening models for how to defend potentiality against its cooptation. In these works, potentiality remains "slippery and evasive": "it is the domain of the unanticipated effect, surprise event, and chance encounter" (161).

By turning to literature (and installation art) for the articulation of critique, by investing art with the promise of replacing "the politics of possibility" with a "potential politics" built on indomitable surprise and chance (158), Amoore stays faithful to a modernist line of critique that sees in the aesthetic a last refuge of resistance and a resource for a different way of life. Indeed, in the now budding field of literary security studies, this approach to literature as a place of resistance to the politics of security is very prominent.[1]

The position I have developed in this book is distinctly different. Rather than seeing "the unanticipated effect, surprise event, and chance encounter" as that which literature mounts against the politics of security, I conceptualize the literary poetics of insecurity and the contemporary politics of security as part of a larger modern practice of conceptualizing uncertainty through the interplay of threat and possibility. And if the politics of security, based on the suspension of rights and law, is a subset of this larger modern handling of uncertainty, this in turn also means that the modern cultural practice of security cannot be reduced to the death-dealing politics of security. Its scope is much broader: it allows for the articulation of a model of agency in which the future moves within the purview of the shapeable without therefore ever fully coming under control. My argument, then, is neither that what literature tells us about insecurity and potentiality is how to resist the politics of security (though a contrastive comparison of the two allows for that perspective), nor that the literary staging of security and insecurity serves to affirm that politics (though this happens[2]). I rather move beyond the binary of resistance and co-optation in order to frame security as a foundational modern cultural matrix of contingency management, the manifestations of which are not limited to the politics of the security state.

The Poetics of Insecurity, for this reason, aims to detail, with the help of literature, some of the ways in which security provides an occasion to imaginatively confront the uncertainty of the future, particularly the insecurity that emerges from perceived threats of malevolent forces. The experience of facing potentially harmful futures – always *potential*, since all futures are possibilities, not accomplished facts – brings forth an imagination of widely different scenarios that are in one way or another enabling.

To get a handle on these generative capacities of security, two analytical steps are necessary. First, security needs to be severed thematically from terrorism and other recognized types of security threat so that we can come to regard it as a broader pattern of responding to the uncertainties characteristic of modernity. Indeed, it should be remembered how recent an invention the now habitual connection between security and terrorism is. "Security" initially became a politicized term in the United States during the Great Depression, with the invention of "social security" constituting a key element of the New Deal. Soon after, at the end of World War II, the term moved closer to its present context when it became a buzzword in the phrase "national security."[3] At that time, the threat scenario was shaped by the Cold War; terrorism played virtually no role. Yet even during the eras of social security and Cold War national security, the concept of security gave expression to a concern with uncertainty and threat – in short, with a future perceived as open. Security is a logic and practice of processing contingency that by far precedes the problem of terrorism. It even precedes the self-reflexively charged use of the term "security." The presence of security in contemporary (political) culture needs to be understood against this broader context.

As a second analytical step, critical attention needs to be directed to fictional narratives of security because they provide access to the imaginary experiences afforded by security. The literary narratives I have discussed in this book allow us to specify more clearly in what senses the confrontation with, and response to, insecurity can be said to be enabling. Hanging in the balance between the openness – and thus the partial shapeability – of the future and the presence of threat, the imaginary experiences triggered by security produce stories of discovery and recovery. As stories of discovery, the works I have considered allow for individual or collective self-realization in ways that could not be articulated before. Charles Brockden Brown's *Arthur Mervyn* turns uncertainty into a virtue and thus valorizes experiments in individual action and the creation of networks beyond sanctioned social circuits; Harriet Jacobs transforms the insecurity of the fugitive slave into the foundation of a transracial Northern community united against "the slave power." As stories of recovery, the fictions that star in this book make it possible for individuals and collectives to revive and revitalize dimensions of meaning and ways of living that seemed to have been lost. Such recoveries are always problematic: they tend to be pervaded by a potentially suffocating sense of nostalgia (Willa Cather's *The Professor's House*), they struggle violently against the present state of things in order to achieve an experience of redemption (Flannery O'Connor's "The Displaced Person"), or they depend on the realization that the recovery of an authentic being-toward-death requires reconciliation with the present in order not to turn suicidal (Don DeLillo's *Cosmopolis*). Each of these stories of recovery have a brush with death, and each provides evidence of how in the cultural imagination the encounter with threat, precisely in getting in touch with the end, can open horizons of meaning that are larger than the self.

The texts I have explored in this book, then, open a view onto security as a way of "combining the elements of certainty and uncertainty in life," to use the terms Georg Simmel used to dissect the structure of adventure ("The Adventurer" 193). As in Simmel's analysis of the adventure, the literary poetics of insecurity produce stories in which the seizing of opportunity to create our own world is joined by our "abandon[ing] ourselves to the world with fewer defenses and reserves than in any other relation" (193). This radical abandonment to uncertainty is caused (or enabled) precisely by threat, and it is this abandonment, in conjunction with the transformation of passive victim into active responder, that is instrumental for creating experiences of individual and collective self-transformation.

Throughout this book I have conceptualized this dialectic of activity and passivity generated by the encounter with threat as underwriting a modern conception of agency. But if taken to the extreme, abandonment suggests a way of engaging the future that moves beyond the limits of this very idea of agency. Don DeLillo's recent works are a case in point. In *Point Omega*, from 2010, the so-called defense intellectual Jon Elster embraces a version of Pierre Teilhard de Chardin's idea of the omega point that reverses its inbuilt direction, similar to the way in which Eric Packer, in *Cosmopolis*, changes the direction of his security apparatus by pointing it at himself. For Elster, the idea of the omega point is no longer, as it was for Teilhard, to capture a process of evolution that will move toward an upward union of human and divine consciousness. Instead, for Elster, "point omega" (the reversed word order points to the reversal of the concept, as David Cowart has observed ["The Lady Vanishes" 47]) captures the moment at which humanity is integrated and dissolved into the material world. Elster aspires to overcoming, rather than raising and enlarging, consciousness: "Ask yourself this question. Do we have to be human forever? Consciousness is exhausted. Back now to inorganic matter. This is what we want. We want to be stones in a field" (52–53).

The relation of humans to stones is a theme DeLillo had already explored at length in *The Names*, from 1982; he revisits it in his recent *Zero K*, a novel in which he focuses on the problem of mortality and immortality more centrally than in any of his previous works. While the protagonist's father and stepmother are at the forefront, as investors and customers, of a scientific and commercial project aimed at achieving immortality by freezing the body (which, in effect, amounts to a mere claim of triumph over death by entrusting suspended life to an unknown future), the protagonist, his girlfriend, and her son Stak ponder a rock displayed in a museum and muse on the future of the human species. "Stak talked to the rock. He told it that we were looking at it. He referred to us as three members of the species H. sapiens. He said that the rock would outlive us all, probably outlive the species itself" (216).

DeLillo's concern here is with a conception of the future that differs from that encapsulated in the logic of security insofar as it fantasizes about the end of human times, about a post-human age in the literal meaning of the word, rather than about the challenges posed, and emerging possibilities afforded, by harmful potential futures. The foretaste of this post-human future lies in the stern resistance of the rock to Stak's attempts at interspecies contact on human terms. Stak can talk to the rock, he can touch it, he can define it, but he will not get the rock to respond to him.

The rock stands as a testament to the *futur antérieur*, or future perfect, of homo sapiens, to humanity's *will-have-been*. It defiantly resists interpretation and yet, thanks to this very obstreperousness, tells a story of a future in which the world will no longer answer to human efforts at mastery. In this regard, DeLillo's most recent novels join the conceptual problem of security to the thriving discourse of the Anthropocene and implicitly ask how security and the Anthropocene are related conceptually.

As Kate Marshall and others have pointed out, several contradictory fantasies resound in the concept of the Anthropocene: "the first side being a kind of ultimate egocentrism or anthropocentrism," which results conceptually from the Anthropocene's definition as a geological epoch marked by human impact ("What Are the Novels" 525); and "the second side being what could seem like a radically non-anthropocentric fantasy of extinction, for the achievement of the legible anthropocenic layer not only implies a posthuman future archeologist, but also contains the popular dream of 'the world without us' somehow able to overgrow the ruins of a tarnished modernity" (525). Encapsulated in these versions of the Anthropocene, then, are stories of radical, destructive agency (humanity having fallen yet again by having spoiled the gift of nature) and humanity's passively suffered retribution, which will, in the best of cases, allow for the world's recovery without the human villain.

The moral terms in which I have cast the interplay of these two fantasies can perhaps explain the "desire for catastrophe" displayed by influential voices of Anthropocene discourse across the disciplines.[4] Writing from a socialist position, Canadian activist and scholar Ian Angus, for instance, sees the Anthropocene as a sure sign that humanity is doing away with itself if it is not finding the right way any time soon: "The extermination of humanity is the ultimate concomitant to capital's destructive force of development" (*Facing the Anthropocene*, n.p.). Science studies scholars Christophe Bonneuil and Jean-Baptiste Fressoz write with even greater urgency when they argue that "the Anthropocene is also (and perhaps above all) a Thanatocene" (*Shock of the Anthropocene*, n.p.) and conclude that "thinking the Anthropocene, finally, means abandoning the hope of emerging from a temporary 'environmental crisis.' The irreversible break is behind us, in that brief and exceptional moment of two centuries of industrial growth. The Anthropocene is here. It is our new condition" (n.p.).

Literary scholar Roy Scranton has perhaps gone the furthest in sounding out this desire in his long essay, "Learning to Die in the Anthropocene" (a version of which appeared initially, to much acclaim, in *The New York Times*). He writes, "the greatest challenge we face is a philosophical one: understanding that this civilization is already dead. The sooner we confront our situation and realize that there is nothing we can do to save ourselves, the sooner we can get down to the difficult task of adapting, with mortal humility, to our new reality" (23). In his title and throughout his text, Scranton invokes Michel de Montaigne's essay "That to Philosophize is to Learn to Die." Montaigne himself paraphrased Horace, Cicero, and Lucretius (among others) in making the case for losing the fear of death by accepting that "you are in death while you are in life" ("Philosophize" 78). As philosophical Stoics, Montaigne and his predecessors insist on approaching life as being-toward-death (as Heidegger would put it). In Montaigne's hands, this amounts to a lesson in how to stop worrying about the wrong things. But this is not at all the tone struck by Scranton. When he speaks of "confronting the end of the world as we know it" (*Learning to Die* 20) and asks, "[H]ow do we make meaningful decisions in the shadow of our inevitable end?" (20), his sublime vision of catastrophe echoes, and negatively reconfirms, humanity's outrageous geological agency, despite the fact that he also calls on us "to accept human limits and transience as fundamental truths" (24). Anthropocene discourse, in these examples, tells a story of human guilt and casts the shuddering vision of human extinction in a tone of – ultimately liberating – repentance. In this manner, even the post-human future remains anthropocentric.

Most shuddering about this vision is in fact the claim that it is not a vision but already our reality. Abandon all hope! is the slogan of this discourse, not because Anthropocene discourse is a justification of political complacency – it surely is not – but because hope requires a view of the future as open. And this is not the notion of the future suggested by the Anthropocene. "The Anthropocene," Ursula Heise suggests, "is a kind of speculative fiction, in that it focuses on the reality of a terraformed planet … which has already arrived in the present on our own planet" (*Imagining Extinction* 219). The future, in other words, is already here; it is an accomplished fact.

From a political perspective, Anthropocene discourse has clear advantages. Declaring the posthuman future to be our present allows for the rhetorical ontologization of politics: the decentering of the human no longer needs to be defended as a goal; it can be asserted as our new reality. But what is of interest in the present discussion is not the politics of the Anthropocene, but rather its relation to security on the level of cultural meanings and imaginary appeals. On this level, the concept of the Anthropocene has transformed insecurity into catastrophic certainty. While it makes appeals to responsibility and action (and in this sense shares with certain strands of security discourse a debt to existentialism), it decouples them from contingency, uncertainty, and openness. Anthropocene discourse posits catastrophe both as our past (the posthuman future has already begun, therefore the cataclysm lies behind us) and as our inevitable future (which is why we are called upon to imagine a future without the human species). From these two sides we are asked to face the ending (the literal *catastrophe*) of the human tragedy. Though the Anthropocene may not exactly provide an effect of catharsis, it does hold out a vision of awful resolution.

As DeLillo's works suggest, visions of the Anthropocene overlap with fictions of insecurity. Perhaps the Anthropocene can even be regarded as an outgrowth of the imagination of insecurity. But the poetics of insecurity and Anthropocene discourse could not differ more sharply regarding the question of resolution. In this respect, the fantasies spawned by the Anthropocene in fact resemble those of a perfectly ordered society of security. Each is the shadow image of the other: complete devastation, perfect order. Thus both of them come to represent the antithesis to the cultural logic of insecurity. As American writers of the last two hundred years suggest, engagements in the uncertain future have drawn their appeal not merely from the prospect of turning weakness into strength but also from recognizing the value of insecurity. Since the imaginary appeal of security arises from the manifold opportunities that grow out of our vulnerability, vulnerability itself becomes a prized resource for the imagination. The writers discussed in this book therefore concur that if there is one state that is hostile to the imagination enabled by insecurity, it is the *achievement* of security itself. When happenstance makes way for happiness, when threats are preempted by total predictability, when the open future is taken over by an eschatological timelessness, and when the future has displaced the present, security ceases to be a problem. It is at this point that writing and reading come to an end.

Notes

1 Introduction

1 While I borrow the phrase "Age of Security" from Stefan Zweig, I reverse its original meaning. In his autobiography, written in exile in 1942 shortly before taking his life, Zweig reflected on the stability of the period prior to World War I – a period that, to him, deserved being called "the Golden Age of Security": "When I attempt to find a simple formula for the period in which I grew up, prior to the First World War, I hope that I convey its fullness by calling it the Golden Age of Security. Everything in our almost thousand-year-old monarchy seemed based on permanency, and the State itself was the chief guarantor of this stability" (*The World of Yesterday* 1). In the current context, the Age of Security does not denote a past in which security had been achieved, but rather the present pursuit of security in the face of the perception of an all-pervasive insecurity.

2 As Peter Burgess points out in *The Ethical Subject of Security*, the normative aim of undoing insecurity is also the common thread that runs through the various strands of security studies in the social sciences. "The sciences of security, from the frivolousness of the pre-modern scholarship to the challenge of probability and statistical uncertainty, to the new sciences of security management, all conceptualize insecurity as something to overcome, an experience whose time can and should be put to an end, as though security, in an anti-Hobbesian way, were itself some kind of natural state of things, the beginning and end of humanity" (1). The procuring of security is both the legitimation of the "sciences of security" and the promise they make over and over.

3 The critical literature on these two areas has grown significantly in the last decade. See, for instance, Lentricchia and McAuliffe, *Crimes*; Clymer, *America's Culture*; and Houen, *Terrorism*; and, for the 9/11 novel, Gray, *After the Fall*, and Däwes, *Ground Zero Fiction*.

4 I will have more to say about the classical tradition of *securitas* later in the chapter. For philological studies of security, see Schrimm-Heins, "Gewissheit und Sicherheit" (part I and II), Kaufmann, *Sicherheit*, Conze, "Sicherheit, Schutz," and – most recently and most comprehensively – Hamilton, *Security*.

5 The phrase "culture of fear" was popularized by sociologist Barry Glassner in his study *Culture of Fear: Why Americans are Afraid of the Wrong Things* (1999). See also his article "Narrative Techniques" for a summary. For an emphasis of the production of fear in the media, see Altheide, *Terrorism and the Politics of Fear*. For a useful social history of fear in the United States, see Stearns, *American Fear*. For a cultural-historical overview of modern fear, see Bourke, *Fear*. Jean Delumeau's *Sin and Fear* (1990) remains the classic historical account of the social functions of fear from the thirteenth to the eighteenth century.

6 For the thesis of fear as a background feeling, see *The Politics of Everyday Fear*, edited by Brian Massumi.

7 For different versions of this argument, see for instance the editors' introduction to *Cultures of Fear: A Critical Reader*, in which Uli Linke and Danielle Taana Smith argue that "Cultures of fear have a political grounding: negative emotions like fear or terror are produced and sustained to govern populations within the carceral spaces of militarized societies" (4–5). Corey Robin's often brilliant *Fear: The History of a Political Idea* similarly emphasizes the political uses of control to which theorists and politicians alike have put fear.

8 In the section "Fear as a Mode of State of Mind" from *Being and Time* (1927), Martin Heidegger writes: "That in the face of which we fear can be characterized as threatening. Here several points must be considered. ... 4. That which is detrimental, as something that threatens us, is not yet within striking distance [in beherrschbarer Nähe], but it is coming close. In such a drawing-close, the detrimentality radiates out, and therein lies its threatening character. 5. This drawing-close is within what is close by. Indeed, something may be detrimental in the highest degree and may even be coming constantly closer; but if it is still far off, its fearsomeness remains veiled. If, however, that which is detrimental draws close and is close by, then it is threatening: it can reach us, and yet it may not. As it draws close, this 'it can, and yet in the end it may not' becomes aggravated. We say, "It is fearsome." 6. This implies that what is detrimental as coming-close close by carries with it the patent possibility that it may stay away and pass us by; but instead of lessening or extinguishing our fearing, this enhances it" (§30; Trans. Macquarrie and Robinson, 179–180).

9 John Hamilton summarizes Cicero's distinction as follows: "Whereas *salus* targets a palpable threat, *securitas* addresses the tribulations that arise from within the soul" (*Security* 51).

10 This conception differs from Elisabeth R. Anker's proposal, in her monograph *Orgies of Feelings: Melodrama and the Politics of Freedom* (2014), to interpret the political discourse of security through the generic prism of melodrama. She argues that in this discourse scenes of looming victimhood hold out a promise of freedom for the virtuous and unjustly injured. This norm of freedom is centered on liberal and American interpretations thereof, i.e., "as self-reliance, as unconstrained agency, and as unbound subjectivity," and it is embodied by the violent state (9). Anker's argument is an important step beyond the "culture of fear"-thesis and its claim that the regime of securitization hinges on political scare tactics. But the narrative trajectory of Anker's model suggests

that threat and insecurity are overcome in the course of their transformation into freedom, whereas in my model, "security" depends on the continuing coexistence of threat and the possibilities emerging out of threat.
11 Reinhart Koselleck has influentially described the transition of the early modern period as the increasing enlargement of "the difference between experience and expectation ... more precisely, ... *Neuzeit* is conceived as *neue Zeit* only from the point at which eager expectations diverge and remove themselves from all previous experience" (270). Expectation, Koselleck usefully suggests, is structured differently from experience. While experience can be metaphorically understood as a "space" because it refers to a past that is taken to be complete, expectation grasps the future as a horizon, which metaphorically points to the future's contingency. The horizon of expectation "is the future made present" (259), but its presence remains impossible to pin down: "The horizon is that line behind which a new space of experience will open, but which cannot yet be seen. The legibility of the future, despite possible prognoses confronts an absolute limit, for it cannot be experienced" (260–261).
12 On Augustine's theodicy, see Meister, "Problem."
13 The classic text is Bercovitch, *American Jeremiad*. For the centrality of the jeremiad relating to the discourse of terrorism and national security, see Murphy, *Prodigal Nation*.
14 There is yet another sociological discourse of risk which has been made popular above all by Ulrich Beck and his concept of "risk society" (see *Risk Society* and *World at Risk*). That discourse tends to mute the economic foundations of risk and downplays the ambiguity of possible gain and harm. Instead, "risks" designate harmful future events of a broad variety, particularly those brought about by technology. The theoretical debates of this discourse largely turn on the question to what degree risks are objectively given or discursively constructed. Conceptually, this discourse tends not to differentiate between the logics of risk and security. Niklas Luhman, for instance, reconstructs security as the absence of risk, a foil against which risk is measured but which is itself never substantiated. He must thus conclude that "security as a counterconcept to risk remains an empty concept ... similar to the concept of health in the distinction ill/healthy. It thus functions only as a reflexive concept" (*Risk* 20). Michel Foucault's concept of risk – though very different from Luhmann's in that it considers risk in the context of governmentality – similarly bundles it together with security as a particular type of rule. For Foucauldian studies of risk and security, see Ewald, "Two Infinities of Risk" and "Insurance and Risk," as well as *Risk and the War on Terror*, a recent essay collection edited by Louise Amoore and Marieke de Goede. For a good overview of the various theoretical positions based on the negative understanding of risk, see Lupton, *Risk*.
15 In using these terms, it is never quite clear whether the evocation of existential threat can be contained on the metaphorical level. May a crisis in data security not escalate into a matter of physical threat (or at least the very real loss of money) and only for this reason lay claim to being a necessity?
16 On this point, see Esposito, "Beyond the Promise of Security."

17 On the entrepreneurial self, see Bröckling, *Das unternehmerische Selbst*.
18 Among the many classic studies that have explored the perceived threats emanating from the fluid social structure in eighteenth and nineteenth-century America, see Cawelti, *Apostles of the Self-Made Man*, and Halttunen, *Confidence Men and Painted Women*. Halttunen captures the ambiguity of insecurity by pointing to the similarities between the representations of confidence men and their victims in popular culture: "The contaminating powers of the confidence man sprang from his social formlessness, his marginality, but his youthful victim was also socially formless, liminal. The confidence man was selfish, self-aggrandizing, but the youth too was seeking to make his fortune in the 'open society'" (32).
19 For an account of the changing functions of fiction of nineteenth-century US fiction, see Fluck, *Das kulturelle Imaginäre*. For a related account that focuses on the literature of the early republic, see Scheiding, *Geschichte und Fiktion*.
20 In *The Game of Probability*, Rüdiger Campe traces the relation between these two different meanings in eighteenth-century European thought and literature. As he writes, "Two things turn out to be essentially related in this mode of investigation: the interpretation of theories of gaming chance as the theory of probability, and the phenomenologization of verisimilitude. They nevertheless form two separate threads of development: one is cognitive and the other relates to representation" (9). At this point, a possible objection might arise regarding the difference between novel and romance, and the contention, upheld by American literary criticism during much of the twentieth century, that American literature of the nineteenth century was dominated precisely not by the (realist) novel but by the romance, which made ample use of unrealistic elements for purposes of symbolism. Prime examples would be Brown's sleepwalkers in *Edgar Huntly*, Melville's strange universe of islands in *Mardi*, and Hawthorne's witches in "Young Goodman Brown." While it is true that many American writers, beginning with Brown, often insisted on the need to set an American tradition of romance against the English novel of manners, Brown himself, in the essay quoted here, makes clear that the romance, like the novel, relies on both dimensions of probability: that which enables acts of conjecture and that which provides the basis for conjecture via representations that make the fictional world familiar to the reader.
21 Gallagher takes the phrase "ironic credulity" from Felix Martinez-Bonati, *Fictive Discourse* 35.
22 My argument here ought not to be confused with Namwali Serpell's recent appraisal, in her *Seven Modes of Uncertainty*, of an ethics of literary uncertainty. "Literary uncertainty" in her approach refers to states in between knowing and not knowing that result from particular textual strategies. The modes of uncertainty she explores are all couched within fictionality and do not concern the question of how fictionality itself requires an attitude useful in a world marked by contingency. Whereas at this point in my argument I am addressing what it takes to be invested in a fiction, she is concerned with how particularly fictions, once we have become invested in them, provide for agonistic reading

experiences. Throughout her book, her analyses focus on the affordances of literary form for particular kinds of unsettling reading experiences; my own readings in the following chapters concentrate on the ways in which threat scenarios create openings inside a given literary world. Her and my approach overlap insofar as these openings – particularly in Jacobs and O'Connor – can only be understood by considering how their creation is made dependent on specific acts of reading afforded by the text.

23 The literature on "narrative identity" is expansive and interdisciplinary. Among the most important texts are Ricoeur, "Life: A Story in Search of a Narrator," Somers, "The Narrative Constitution of Identity," and Ezzy, "Theorizing Narrative Identity."

24 One might object that the transgressive tendencies of narrative are counteracted by genre. This, however, would misunderstand the site of transgression. Transgression here initially does not refer to the violation of readerly expectations that are based on genre, but rather to the logical makeup of fictional narratives: any narrative fiction needs a coherent and ordered world in which and against which events can take place. Genres create horizons of expectation for how a fictional world is ordered and how transgressive events play out in and against that order. At a closer look, however, transgression cannot be contained to the structural dimension of diegesis and event but bleeds into the question of genre. This is because generic expectations can never be fulfilled entirely if a story is to be narratable. To recall Ricoeur, each narrative must activate "a thousand contingencies"; thus each iteration of a generic pattern must break with the readerly expectation created by that pattern, if only in the minutest details. As Derrida famously put it, "Madness is law, the law is madness" ("Law of Genre" 81).

25 Coleridge, whose idea of the "willful suspension of disbelief" takes up a central place in Gallagher's discussion, himself suggests the proximity between reading fiction and dreaming. The difference between them is precisely the role of will: "It is laxly said that during sleep we take our dreams for realities, but this is irreconcilable with the nature of sleep, which consists in a suspension of the voluntary and, therefore, of the comparative power. The fact is that we pass no judgment either way: we simply do not judge them to be real, in consequence of which the images act on our minds, as far as they act at all, by their own force as images. Our state while we are dreaming differs from that in which we are in the perusal of a deeply interesting novel in the degree rather than in the kind" (Coleridge, *Shakespeare Criticism* I, 116).

26 On the articulation effect of the imaginary, see the introduction to Fluck's *Das kulturelle Imaginäre*.

27 In his literary and cultural history of the accident, Ross Hamilton comes to a similar result, but from a different conceptual perspective. For Hamilton, the concept of the "accidental" brings together – as it did for Aristotle – two different meanings: extraordinary events and elements of a character or thing that do not belong to its substance. In the eighteenth-century novel, Hamilton argues, accidental events and accidental qualities come to interact in a manner

that leads to a character's self-actualization: "Accident rose to prominence as a site of self-transformation, and the mutable nature of accidental qualities responded to the new sense that aspects of personal identity could shift over time" (*Accident* 134). The main differences between the concepts of accident and security are ontological and temporal: security imagines threat as a possible future, whereas the accidental event, in order to qualify as accident, must have already happened. Both, however, are disruptions of established orders, and it is from this disruptive quality that their transformative potential accrues.

28 For a critique of the current state of security studies, particularly regarding its variant in literary studies, see "Aestheticizing Insecurity," my response to a special issue of *American Literary History* on the theme of *Security Studies and American Literary History*, edited by David Watson.

29 Foucault addressed security most extensively in his 1977–1978 lectures at the Collège de France, collected as *Security, Territory, Population*. In these lectures, Foucault extends his historical typology of power, adding the "security dispositif" to juridical rule and discipline. Security, for Foucault, is a technology of power that is shaped by liberal principles of circulation and laissez-faire. The second now dominant critical approach to security comes from the discipline of International Relations. The so-called Copenhagen School has influentially proposed that security is a social construct based on a particular speech act (also called a "securitization"). In such a speech act, an "enunciator" claims that his or her group is faced by an existential threat; this serves to legitimate extraordinary measures (see Buzan, Waever, and de Wilde, *Security*). In order to explain what makes a securitizing speech act successful, Buzan et al. combine speech act theory with Pierre Bourdieu's concept of "cultural capital": "A successful speech act is a combination of language and society, of both intrinsic features of speech and the group that authorizes and recognizes that speech ... Among the internal conditions of a speech act, the most important is to follow the security form, the grammar of security, and construct a plot that includes existential threat, point of no return, and a possible way out – the general grammar of security ... The external aspect of a speech act has two main conditions. One is the social capital of the enunciator, the securitizing actor, who must be in a position of authority, although this should not be defined as official authority" (32–33).

30 See the following two clips for representative samples of the rich archive of amateur coverage stored online: www.youtube.com/watch?v=pyjQnEPA5is and www.youtube.com/watch?v=Vuedg_-Dn1Y (last visited January 25, 2015).

31 This climaxed in the conviction, among a portion of the online community, that a twenty-two-year-old Brown university student, who had been missing for a month, was one of the bombers. Soon after, his body was found in the Providence River; apparently he had committed suicide.

2 The Virtue of Uncertainty

1 The most canonical studies of this debate include Bailyn, *The Ideological Origins of the American Revolution*; Pocock, *The Machiavellian Moment*;

Wood, *The Creation of the American Republic*; and Appleby, *Capitalism and a New Social Order*. Wood and particularly Appleby argue against the position, embraced most fervently by Pocock, that the early republic is thoroughly republican in the classical sense. This debate by historians has changed the field of early American literature and particularly the scholarship on Charles Brockden Brown. Indeed, the rediscovery of the republican heritage, which, to many scholars, seems to hold the promise of providing a politically compelling alternative to liberal capitalism, may be chiefly responsible for the recent flourishing of Brown studies. Most major studies have therefore placed themselves in relation to the republicanism-versus-liberalism debate. Currently, the republican approach is the dominant one. Pioneering work in this line includes Michael Warner's *The Letters of the Republic* and Christopher Looby's *Voicing America*. More recent examples include Bryan Waterman's writings on Brown (particularly his monograph *Republic of Intellect*), as well as Stephen Shapiro's *The Culture and Commerce of the Early American Novel*. With the publication of the Hackett edition of Brown's novels, edited by Shapiro and Philip Barnard, and the projected scholarly edition of Brown's non-novelistic writings (edited mostly by prominent proponents of the recent emphasis on the republican Brown), the republican position seems to be on the way to becoming an institutionalized consensus.

2 The term "market revolution" refers to the transformation from controlled mercantilism to market capitalism. See Sellers, *The Market Revolution*, and Larson, *The Market Revolution in America*.

3 The idea of refinement through commerce is most immediately associated with Scottish Enlightenment thinkers, particularly Adam Ferguson and Adam Smith. See Pocock's *The Machiavellian Moment* and his later essay, "Virtues, Rights, and Manners: A Model for Historians of Political Thought." In the latter he develops the crucial role that the concept of "manners" played in accommodating commerce. Pocock's focus on manners informs Philip Gould's reading of *Arthur Mervyn* in relation to the yellow fever (see his "Race, Commerce, and the Literature of Yellow Fever in Early National Philadelphia"). See also Wood, "Interests and Disinterestedness," for the prominence of the refinement argument among Federalists during the making of the Constitution. Like commerce, debt and credit proved capable of being reconciled with republican virtue by being seen as providing a social bond of confidence. Pocock focuses on the debates on credit during the Augustan period (see chapter XIII of *The Machiavellian Moment* 423–461). See also Baker, *Securing the Commonwealth*, for an analysis of the definition of credit as social bond in the literature of the early republic. Regarding *Arthur Mervyn*, Baker argues that "the corruption that comes with indebtedness and economic insecurity promotes communal union precisely because it encourages a process by which readers and auditors of narratives come to sympathize with others" (120).

4 It did not take long for Brown to grow uncomfortable with the writing and reading of novels. In September 1803, Brown retroactively rejected and disowned his prolific novelistic output. In the first issue of the *Literary Magazine*,

he claimed: "I should enjoy a larger share of my own respect at the present moment if nothing had ever flowed from my pen, the production of which could be traced to me" ("The Editor['s] Address" 4).

5 Andreas Kalyvas and Ira Katznelson have emphasized that Madison pursued the same agenda with respect to religion. Against the republican tradition of seeking to create civic unity among the citizens with the help of an established civic religion, Madison sought to institutionalize freedom of religion in order to make religious pluralism prosper. "Turning the logic of the civic religion doctrine on its head, Madison proclaimed that publicly sponsored religion degrades civil society by creating 'a spiritual tyranny' and by upholding 'the throes of political tyranny'" (Kalyvas and Katznelson, *Liberal Beginnings* 111).

6 Skinner is quoting from *Discourses on the First Decade of Titus Livius*, in *Machiavelli: The Chief Works and Others*, trans. A. Gilbert, 3 vols. (Durham, NC, 1965. 175–529). See also Pocock's summary of Machiavelli's premises: "If politics be thought of as the art of dealing with the contingent event, it is the art of dealing with *fortuna* as the force which directs such events and thus symbolizes pure, uncontrolled, and unlegitimated contingency.... The republic can dominate *fortuna* only by integrating its citizens in a self-sufficient *universitas*, but this in turn depends on the freely participating and morally assenting citizen. The decay of citizenship leads to the decline of the republic and the ascendancy of *fortuna*" (*Machiavellian Moment* 156).

7 Security is a concern of republicanism because the republic is constantly threatened by the weakness of human nature, which exposes it to the caprices of *Fortuna*. Security is not, then, a concept that gains political relevance only with the advent of liberalism, as a growing theoretical consensus would have us believe. For a critique of this position, see my "The Aspiration for Impossible Security." In *Liberalism and the Culture of Security*, Katherine Henry paradigmatically argues that while republicanism defined citizenship through active participation in the polis, security, understood as the need for protection, became the liberal foundation of citizenship. The close affiliation of security with liberalism underestimates the degree to which the specter of tyranny is part and parcel of republicanism.

8 For authoritative versions of this argument, see, in particular, Warner, *Letters of the Republic*, and Barnard and Shapiro, "Introduction." For a recent reading of the prevalence of uncertainty through the structural figure of the network, see Margolis, "Network Theory Circa 1800."

9 For these dates, see Barnard and Shapiro, "Introduction" ix, xvii.

10 For these dates, see Barnard and Shapiro, "Introduction" ix, xvii.

11 In the *Poetics*, Aristotle sees the difference between historian and tragic poet in the ontological status of their referents. While the historian records particular facts ("what has been"), the poet describes probabilities based on what one might expect from a given character ("what may be"): "The poet and the historian differ not by writing in verse or in prose. The work of Herodotus might be put into verse, and it would still be a species of history, with metre no less than without it. The true difference is that one relates what has happened,

the other what may happen. Poetry, therefore, is a more philosophical and a higher thing than history: for poetry tends to express the universal, history the particular. By the universal I mean how a person of given character will on occasion speak or act, according to the law of probability or necessity; and it is this universality at which poetry aims in the names she attaches to the personages" (*Poetics* IX, 1451 b, p. 35).

12 Shortly before Brown's variation on Aristotle's distinction, William Godwin composed his own take on this question in his essay "Of History and Romance" (1797), which remained, however, unpublished until 1987. According to Godwin, historians and fiction writers are forced to conjecture about the motives behind actions. "But we never know any man's character. My most intimate and sagacious friend continually misapprehends my motives. He is in most cases a little worse judge of them than myself and I am perpetually mistaken" (466). For Godwin, then, conjecture is a necessary evil, which dooms to failure the endeavors of historians and romancers alike: "The result of the whole, is that the sciences and the arts of man are alike imperfect, and almost infantine" (467).

13 Jacob Bernoulli's *Ars Conjectandi*, published posthumously in 1713, built on Leibniz in tackling a problem ignored by earlier thinkers of probability. Earlier theorists, such as Blaise Pascal, Pierre de Fermat, and Chevalier de Méré, had been concerned with the a priori problems of probability as they pertain to games of chance. In games of dice, for instance, the probability of different outcomes can be computed so that there is no need to throw the dice to estimate the outcome. Bernoulli, on the other hand, addressed problems of a posteriori probability as they occur in everyday life, where we do not have all the relevant information and in fact don't even know how much information there is to be considered for estimating outcomes of situations. Bernoulli proposed the "law of large numbers" as a means of reaching "moral certainty." Moral certainty differs from absolute certainty and requires a common standard so that something can count as certain – for instance, in courts – while allowing for a margin of error. The concept was first developed by Leibniz (see Hacking, *Emergence* 146). In the law of large numbers, limited sample data is used to make inferences about the whole: the more individual cases we take into consideration, the greater the probability that they come close to the average. Predictive errors cannot be avoided, but the higher the number of trials, the higher the probability that that error is smaller than a given percentage. See Bernstein, *Against the Gods* 122, and Stigler, *History of Statistics* 63–70.

14 The literary *ars conjectandi* I am extracting from Brown differs from that espoused by the early probability theorists precisely in regard to the acceptance of a remainder of chance. For a thinker like Bernoulli, moral certainty was good enough: it simply didn't matter that absolute certainty was unattainable. Indeed, the emergence of probability theory must be seen in the context of what Lorraine Daston has called "Fortuna's demise" ("Fortuna and the Passions" 27): "in the annals of seventeenth-century philosophy, and most

especially in the writings of the probabilists, there was no error more vulgar than admitting the reality of *Fortuna* and her boon companion, Chance" (26).

15 For some of the most trenchant discussions, see Orians, "Censure of Fiction in American Romances and Magazines: 1789–1810," and Davidson, *Revolution and the Word*, esp. 38–54.

16 In *Die Fiktion der wahrscheinlichen Realität*, Elena Esposito has elaborated on the occasionally noted fact that the novel and the concept of probability both emerged in the second half of the seventeenth century. This, she argues, is no sheer coincidence: both fiction and probability theory are reactions to the uncertainties evolving from the dissolution of the classical world's cosmological and social unity. By *doubling reality*, both respond to the centrifugal forces that break apart what Esposito, using the terminology of Niklas Luhmann, calls "the congruence of the factual, social, and temporal dimension" (*Fiktion* 27; my trans.). Probability and fiction present us with worlds that differ from the reality in which we live, yet that are therefore not simply untrue. They are real in a different sense than reality, as models of real reality that reach back into real reality.

17 This is the gist of Winfried Fluck's history of the changing functions of American literature, presented most comprehensively in *Das kulturelle Imaginäre* (1997). He charts how the aesthetic experience of early American fiction produced an excess in the reader's imaginary that contradicted literature's official didactic purposes and eventually would move beyond such real-world-obligations altogether. Brown is a transitional figure in this development: For Fluck, "Brown's tentative emancipation of the imaginary" marks a point of no return which soon after will lead to the "elevation of fiction to the privileged medium of knowledge" (82, my trans.). For a related take on the changing functions of the early American novel, see Scheiding, *Geschichte und Fiktion*. Scheiding argues that during the period of the early republic the subversion of the utility doctrine of literature had been fully realized, just as much as the turn to epistemological skepticism had been completed (13). He thus relocates to the early republic intellectual developments usually attributed to the 1850s. Scheiding further holds that the rise of fiction went along with a devaluation of historiography. This claim clearly resonates with Brown's differentiation between history and romance discussed above. Discussing Brown's essay, Scheiding concludes that "Brown unsettles the dominant aversion to fiction in the literary system of the early republic by demonstrating that historiography operates with poetic means" (210, my trans.).

18 In Part II, section 3 of his *Philosophical Enquiry*, Burke writes: "To make any thing very terrible, obscurity seems in general to be necessary. When we know the full extent of any danger, when we can accustom our eyes to it, a great deal of the apprehension vanishes" (54).

19 *Ormond* presents a whole cast of secret witnesses, comprising Sophia Courtland (the narrator), a minor character called Baxter, and the villain, Ormond. The secret witnessing of Baxter and Ormond is more actively pursued than Arthur's and is in fact indistinguishable from curiosity. On secrecy in *Ormond*, see Levine, *Conspiracy and Romance*, ch. 1 (15–57).

20 Teresa Goddu (*Gothic America* 139n8) and Sean X. Goudie (*Creole America* 177) both emphasize that we do not know for certain whether the Thetford brothers' machinations have worked as planned. Goddu and Goudie suggest that the two con-men may have fallen victim to the one-upmanship of conspiratorial mulattos. However, this interpretation loses sight of the fact that only Welbeck is a victim of the scheme. Only indirectly will Thetford be a victim, too: he will perish from the fever.

21 The phrase is taken from "Walstein's School of History" – "Every man is encompassed by numerous claims, and is the subject of intricate relations" ("Walstein's School" 337) – and serves as the title of a study by Karen Weyler. In Weyler's reading, however, the social complexity of modernity – the fact that numerous claims are being made on the individual – is reduced to an expression of class and gender anxieties brought under control by the novel.

22 Norman Grabo has pointed out that in the plethora of incidental characters, *Arthur Mervyn* exceeds Brown's other mazelike novels, *Ormond* and *Edgar Huntly*. In *Arthur Mervyn*, the minor characters "gain more importance because each one is given an opinion, a point of view, or even a story, and because the network of their stories, implicit and explicit, constitutes the character of Arthur" (*Coincidental Art* 87).

23 Stacey Margolis notes that in *Arthur Mervyn*, Brown organizes characters by a principle of communicative proximity, tying together "those who carry around and recite each other's stories" (353). This leads her to argue, persuasively, that urban life as depicted by Brown "create[s] unexpected connections between individuals and unprecedented channels of communication" (355).

24 See, for instance, Goddu, *Gothic America*, Gould, "Race, Commerce," Mackenthun, *Fictions*, Levine, "Arthur Mervyn's Revolutions." For a non-metaphorical reading of the yellow fever, see Waterman, "Arthur Mervyn's Medical Repository."

25 This argument, focusing on the detrimental effects of the imagination, is at the core of Bryan Waterman's "Arthur Mervyn's Medical Repository."

26 Brown generally seems to have agreed with the consensus of rational medical discourse according to which the psychic turmoil incited by fear triggered the physical outbreak of the disease. As Philip Gould explains, "Eighteenth-century medical theory generally correlated physical, psychological, and moral health, and most medical writing on the yellow fever epidemic theorized that the mind's excessive passions (or what Rush called one kind of 'indirect debility') could stimulate the body's contagion into activity and thereby trigger the disease. Many argued that fevers, which were characterized by excessive blood circulation and a nervous pulse, should be combated by citizens' rational self-control" (164). Gould's larger point is that the medical discourse espoused an ideal of balance that also informed the critique of the free market, which was descried as excessive.

27 By thanatopolitics, I invoke Giorgio Agamben's notion of biopolitics (developed most extensively in *Homo Sacer* and *State of Exception*), which hinges on the reduction of the political subject to bare life. In this theory, the sovereign, in deciding over the state of exception, also decides over life and death of the

subject by being able to suspend the rule of law. I refer to Agamben's biopolitics as a thanatopolitics in order to distinguish it from Michel Foucault's biopolitics, which emphasizes the cultivation of life for the purposes of control. I adopt the distinction between Foucauldian biopolitics and Agamben's thanatopolitics from Rey Chow, "Sacrifice" 133.

28 The biopolitical security paradigm exemplified by Arthur, much like that described by Michel Foucault in his lectures *Security, Territory, Population* (his 1977–78 lecture course), elevates circulation and laissez-faire to the principles of life to be guarded and cultivated by security. But unlike Foucault's theorization, Arthur's biopolitics of security does not aim at normalization and thereby turn into a means of governmental rule. Understood as a redefinition of virtue, laissez-faire circulation is an unruly process that subjects the compelled agent to contingency and disease and resists categorization, such as sick and healthy, that would allow for the securing of life from disease based on statistically calculated probabilities.

29 On the history of the adventurer, see Michael Nerlich, who points out that "the essential hallmark that distinguishes [the modern adventurer] from the classical conception is that adventures are undertaken on a *voluntary* basis, they are *sought out* (*la quête de l'aventure*, 'the quest for adventure'), and this quest and hence the adventurer himself are glorified" (5).

30 See Wood, "Interests and Disinterestedness" and *Empire of Liberty*, esp. 218–227, for examples of how Antifederalists accused the Federalists of falling short of their professed disinterestedness.

31 In the "Introduction" to their essay collection *Revising Charles Brockden Brown*, Philip Barnard, Mark Kamrath, and Stephen Shapiro attempt to denigrate the insistence on irony and ambiguity in Brown's writings by linking it to liberal modernism and the New Criticism. In its stead, they uphold a position that links republicanism with postmodernism. From that perspective, "the turn from liberalism to republicanism" appears as aligned with a turn "from irony to sentiment and Gothic" (xiv).

32 See, for instance, Justus, "Arthur Mervyn, American," Brancaccio, "Studied Ambiguities: Arthur Mervyn and the Problem of the Unreliable Narrator," Bell, "'The Double-Tongued Deceiver': Sincerity and Duplicity in the Novels of Charles Brockden Brown," Hedges, "Charles Brockden Brown and the Culture of Contradictions," Elliott, "The Burden of the Past" (ch. 6 of his *Revolutionary Writers*), and Christophersen, "*Arthur Mervyn*: Sickness, Success, and the Recompense of Virtue" (ch. 5 of his *The Apparition in the Glass*).

33 Among the early readings, no other article came to the verdict "guilty" with as much conviction as James Russo's "Chameleon of Convenient Vice," according to which Arthur is not really Arthur but a minor character named Clavering.

34 See Vogl, *Specter of Capital* 23–27, for the metaphorological history of the "invisible hand," which, for the Scholastics, still referred to God's hands directing earthly events. In Smith's usage, this theological layer of meaning had not entirely disappeared. Smith employed the metaphor not only for the power behind organizing the natural order of the economy but also for the manipulator of the cosmological order of nature.

35 In *Chance and the Eighteenth-Century Novel*, Jesse Molesworth has recently insisted on the incommensurability of the narrative logic of fiction and the ideals of order espoused by Enlightenment rationality, including probability theory. Drawing on Peter Brooks, Tony Tanner, and D. A. Miller, he argues that "plot emerges ... as a series of delays, deferrals, and avoidances, with the narrative pleasure of plotting existing only so long as its ultimate desire remains unfulfilled" (6). Molesworth rightly reminds us that there is no plot where there isn't "something happening" (5). An event happens when the established order is disrupted in one way or another. Most difficult to narrate (to the point of unnarratability) is the moment when nothing happens, that is, when everything goes according to plan.

3 Harriet Jacobs's Imagined Community of Insecurity

1 On abolitionism and the public sphere, see Fanuzzi, *Abolition's Public Sphere*; DeLombard, *Slavery on Trial*; and Caleb Smith, *The Oracle and the Curse*.
2 As Ulla Haselstein puts it, "By means of the affirmative citation of structural patterns [such as the sentimental novel], Jacobs accepts the official morality according to which it is the woman who is responsible for the illegitimate sexual act. But as this morality disregards the fact that black women are in no way protected against sexual abuse and are therefore deprived of the condition of possibility of leading a virtuous life, the result is a moral indictment of slavery" (*Gabe* 133, my trans.)
3 Lee also argues that by employing the language of risk calculation, slave narrators created another method besides sympathy of involving the reader in the narrative: "they invite their readers to identify with slaves not only through emotional sympathy (how would it feel to be a slave?) but also by participating vicariously in probabilistic decision making (what would I do in such circumstances?)" (97).
4 The idea of the slave as indebted became most pronounced in debates about the meaning of the right of possession. In the mid-nineteenth century, legal commentators increasingly pointed out that the possession in the slave did not encompass the totality of the person or the slave's soul, but only the slave's labor. Once this point was stressed, the slave was clearly defined as owing his labor. At the same time, however, southern legal practice generally did not stop at claiming the slave's labor. As legal historian Thomas Morris argues in his seminal study of slavery and the law, "As slavery was increasingly and passionately condemned during the nineteenth century, proslavery apologists tried to narrow the claim to property rights in slaves to a claim to their labor, and this was joined with a claim to obedience. But slaves as property were closer to the description of Blackstone that the owner of property was allowed 'not the immediate use only, but the very substance of the thing to be used.' More than simply the labor of the slave was claimed as a property right, but, in nonlegal discourse, the more the system came under attack the more Southern whites defended their system and the less they seemed to claim" (*Southern Slavery* 62).

5 As members of the revolutionary generation had routinely referred to their "enslavement" for describing their subjection to the British crown, Jacobs's reference to Henry can be read as a reappropriation of enslavement. However, as Frank Kelleter points out, in revolutionary discourse "slavery" had a limited meaning that did not explicitly refer to chattel slavery: "being a slave here meant not being the master of the laws under which one lived" (669). This also suggests that, in the view of the revolutionary generation, the fact that so many of the Founding Fathers were slaveholders did not necessarily pose a contradiction to their struggle against being enslaved by the British.

6 In this regard, it is of consequence that in some slave jurisdictions, slaves were treated as real estate rather than as chattel personal. As Thomas Morris writes, "could slaves be defined as realty or as chattels? Given the mobility and the humanity of slaves, the answer may seem obvious, but it is not, even though scholars normally refer to slaves as 'chattels personal'" (*Southern Slavery* 64). Morris discusses several slave codes from the late eighteenth century to the mid-nineteenth century that defined slaves as real estate (among them Virginia, Kentucky, and Arkansas) and concludes that while legal definition had no impact on the status of the slave, it "did concern, for example ... the rules that would apply to them if their owner died without a will" (65). Treating slaves as chattel rather than real property was favored by free-market economists: "political economists, such as Louisa McCord and J. D. B. De Bow, leading proponents of a laissez-faire market, expressly rejected the idea that slaves should be attached to the soil or be exempt from sale for payment of debts" (65).

7 As Jeannine DeLombard writes, "the portrait of the kneeling, half-naked black man ... matched many Northerners' mental image of 'The Slave.' That image had its material origins in the seal that British pottery manufacturer and reformer Josiah Wedgwood had begun producing for the Society for the Abolition of the Slave Trade in the winter of 1787–88. ... [V]ersions of the Wedgwood seal bore the slogan, 'Am I Not a Man and a Brother?' Reproduced on everything from sugar bowls, snuff boxes, and figurines to handkerchiefs, brooches, and hairpins, Wedgwood's image had become on both sides of the Atlantic a familiar sentimental icon of the innocent, suffering slave" (35–36).

8 It also needs to be noted that risk for the slave is never an individualized act. Risks are understood to be shared with other members of the slave community, particularly the family members closest to the slave. Linda is keenly aware of this when she considers what the repercussions of her flight might be for her children. She makes the decision to escape the moment she is informed that they will be sent to the Flint plantation to be "broken in" (in the case of her son) and raised up to become a valuable object of sexual consumption (in the case of her daughter), hoping that her absence will induce the Flints to get rid of the annoyance of having to care for them.

9 For scholarly literature on the higher law, see particularly Crane, *Race, Citizenship, and Law*, and Nabers, *Victory of Law*. For a narrative history of the higher law discourse in the much publicized court cases of the 1850s, see Lubet, *Fugitive Justice*.

10 Jennifer Fleischner argues that the most important models for Jacobs are not the female family members, but rather her father Elijah and her brother John (William), both of whom exemplify the determination for active resistance (see *Mastering Slavery* 64).

11 In this regard *Incidents* stands in striking contrast to Solomon Northup's *Twelve Years A Slave*. Calling on the reader's sympathy, Northup describes how Patsey, a "favorite slave" like Jacobs, is broken down by her master. Having been brutally flogged, the young woman undergoes a radical transformation: "She no longer moved with that buoyant and elastic step – there was not that mirthful sparkle in her eyes that formerly distinguished her. The bounding vigor – the sprightly, laughter-loving spirit of her youth, were gone. She fell into a mournful and desponding mood, and oftentimes would start up in her sleep, and with raised hands, plead for mercy" (258).

12 Jacobs does not stage the power of slavery to break down individual slaves. Slavery's most pernicious effect, instead, becomes visible in those who break the ties of racial solidarity. Linda is twice forced to relocate because of her neighbor's slave Jenny, who cannot be trusted with the knowledge of Linda's secret presence. Moreover, Linda relates as particularly threatening an invitation extended by her grandmother to the constable and a free black man who "tried to pass himself off for white. … Every body knew he had the blood of a slave father in his veins; but for the sake of passing himself off for white, he was ready to kiss the slaveholders' feet" (865).

13 While Linda emphasizes the confusing effect of the city, Arthur Mervyn marvels at the splendor of the buildings on Market Street: "you may be prompted to smile when I tell you that, in walking through this avenue, I, for a moment, conceived myself transported to the hall 'pendent with many a row of starry lamps and blazing crescents fed by naphtha and asphaltos.' That this transition from my homely and quiet retreat had been effected in so few hours wore the aspect of miracle or magic" (*Arthur Mervyn* 22). But the difference between Linda's and Arthur's impressions is smaller than it may seem. As the editors of the Hackett edition point out, Arthur quotes loosely from John Milton's *Paradise Lost*, Book I; "the quotation foreshadows a context of urban corruption and vicious, subterranean struggles within market society" (23).

14 The *National Era*'s writer here participates in a rich discourse on the intelligence of fugitives, which Jeffrey Hole has eloquently explored in "Enforcement on a Grand Scale: Fugitive Intelligence and the Literary Tactics of Douglass and Melville." Hole investigates possible relations between literary writing and resistant tactics of fugitives that he locates "in the structuring of plots and ordering of narrative, in imagining the conditions of possibility, in discovering and making use of topoi and tropes, in eliciting hegemonic or subaltern historical memory, in performing various styles of persuasion or subterfuge, and in evincing implicit or explicit theories of conflict" (217).

15 This involves reconceptualizing the public sphere as a space of communication not primarily rational (as Fanuzzi – following the Habermasian tradition – would have it) but affect-laden.

16 William Wells Brown, for instance, uses the topos to highlight a moment of extraordinary fear. Unable to trust his master who sends him to an auction, putatively to be "hired out," Brown endeavors to make available his own fear to the reader by putting it beyond words: "I am at a loss for language to express my feelings on that occasion. Although my master had told me that he had not sold me, ... I did not believe him ... until I had been to New Orleans, and was on my return" (*Narrative* 389). On the topos of the inexpressible, see Richards, *Distancing English*.

17 Jeannine DeLombard has remarked that abolitionist rhetoric, built on the trope of the "trial" of public opinion, often presupposed that whites were speaking on behalf of blacks, making it difficult for the black abolitionist to "depict himself or herself as either victim of or witness to the crime of slavery" (*Slavery* 26). "Distinguishing between the roles of black and white abolitionists in this manner contributed to the larger process in which white activists endorsed ideas of racial equality and racial difference simultaneously" (26). The constellation of the sentimental slave narrative is related to that analyzed by DeLombard: if the slave narrative was presumed to address a white readership that was sympathetic to the slave's plight, yet also essentially different from the slave, how could the slave narrative make room for an implied black reader who did not answer to the simultaneity of racial equality and racial difference? As I argue in the remainder of this chapter, Jacobs solves this issue in two ways: she sets the official addressee next to one that is addressed obliquely and "unofficially." Second, she creates a community of insecurity that includes whites and blacks and thus writes into being a transracial addressee who can no longer imagine himself or herself as racially equal and different simultaneously. The whole point of her rhetorical strategy will be to move back and forth between these two solutions.

18 As Simon Dalby explains, "The traditional notions of a security dilemma refer to the observation that military preparations in one state, made in the name of providing for protection of a population, often have the unintended consequence of alarming policy makers in other states. Increased power in one state makes other state policy makers react by taking military and political actions to protect their state against the possibilities of military threat from the first state" (13).

19 Though Garrison turned away from non-violence only shortly before the Civil War, he had, as Cleves writes, "used anti-Jacobin language to assail slavery, slaveholders, and antiabolitionists ... from the very beginning of his abolitionist career through the Civil War" (*Reign* 236). The point here is that anti-Jacobinism was on the face of it nonviolent – which is why the violence of slavery was seen as the death toll of civilization – but the step from bemoaning southern lynch law to fantasizing about a retaliatory northern lynch law was never far off.

20 As we can glean from Cleves, *Reign of Terror* 247–268, Jacobs was in the company of most prominent African American abolitionists – among them William Wells Brown, William C. Nell, Henry Highland Garnet, and Frederick

Douglass – in making use of the idiom of the reign of terror. Reporting the violent resistance of fugitives in Christiana, Pennsylvania, *Frederick Douglass' Paper* drew out the implication of this approach as early as 1851: "the reign of terror," the writer argued, forced people either to flee to Canada or "to shoulder our musket for revolutionizing our own" (qtd. in Cleves, *Reign of Terror* 268).

21 One should note the special relevance of the political escalation of the 1850s for Jacobs's decision to become a writer at all. As Jean Fagan Yellin writes, "Responding to Jacobs's concerns in the tense atmosphere in which the Kansas-Nebraska Act functionally destroyed the Missouri Compromise and the North sent fugitive slaves back into southern slavery, Amy Post suggested that Jacobs could contribute to the movement by telling the story of her life" (Yellin, *Harriet Jacobs Family Papers*, Vol. 1, 189).

22 It should be emphasized that while New York in the 1850s was a more dangerous place for fugitives than New England, Jacobs's insistence throughout the text that the 1850 Fugitive Slave Law also spelled out the "fall" of Massachusetts makes New York, in this instance, stand for the North as a whole.

23 One might speculate whether Mrs. Bruce would have been willing to send her child along with Linda if it had been a boy (and would thus have been endowed with the full set of citizenship rights). But important for the rhetorical analysis that interests me here is the fact that Jacobs does not to mention the child's gender in this passage at all.

24 Of her three letters to the *New York Tribune*, only two survive. The first letter Jacobs signed "A Fugitive Slave" (Yellin, *Family Papers*, Vol. 1, 200).

25 Although the term "Jim Crow" is often associated with the post-Reconstruction era, Jacobs already uses it in its familiar meaning: "Being in servitude to the Anglo-Saxon race, I was not put into a Jim Crow car, on our way to Rockaway, neither was I invited to ride through the streets on the top of trunks in a truck; but every where I found the same manifestations of that cruel prejudice, which so discourages the feelings, and represses the energies of the colored people" (920).

26 In part, Jacobs's focus on what I earlier termed "the official addressee" has to do with the institutional frame of the slave narrative. But the merely oblique appearance of her social embeddedness among African Americans also serves to shield these friends and acquaintances from public exposure. This ties in with the suppression of places and the invention of pseudonyms throughout the text. Both Child, in her introduction, and Jacobs, in her preface, claimed to be responsible for these protective textual measures. In addition, Child explained in a letter to John Greenleaf Whittier: "I use fictitious names in the book; first, lest the Southern family, who secreted Linda some months, should be brought into difficulty; secondly, lest some of her surviving relatives at the South should be persecuted; and thirdly, out of delicacy to Mrs. Willis, who would not like to have her name bandied about in the newspapers, perhaps to the injury of her husband's interests, and certainly to the injury of his feelings" (Child, *Collected* 48:1300; qtd. in Tricomi 225).

27 I thank Carla Peterson for suggesting this point to me. I am moreover indebted to her for sharpening my awareness of the importance of Jacobs's extended cast.
28 John Brown, a white militant abolitionist who had become nationally known for having killed five proslavery proponents in Pottawatomie, Kansas, in 1856, became an even greater celebrity in 1859, when he conducted what became known as "John Brown's Raid on Harpers Ferry." With the support of sixteen whites and five blacks, Brown took the US arsenal at Harpers Ferry, Virginia, hoping to incite a slave resurrection. The arsenal was taken back by Virginia militia and US marines two days later; during and after the raid, Brown's group killed four and lost ten men. Brown became a martyr figure of the abolitionist movement and soon thereafter a cultural hero of the North.
29 See Bruce Mills, Albert Tricomi, and, most recently, Caleb Smith. Tricomi is paradigmatic when he writes, "Child directed [the manuscript] away from the combustible militarism of John Brown's October 1859 raid on Harpers Ferry, against which the country was still recoiling, and foregrounded those melodramatic and sentimental parts illustrating the destruction of families and especially the sexual victimization of girls and women under slavery, along with the devastating effects this abuse brought to their grieving mothers" (219).

4 Willa Cather and the Security of Radical Contingency

1 In his explanatory notes for the Willa Cather Scholarly Edition of the novel, James Woodress suggests that "the time of the third book is probably about when Cather was writing the novel, 1923–24" (346). Because Cather heavily fictionalizes her historical sources, the timing of "Tom Outland's Story" is somewhat unclear. As "discoverer" of the Blue Mesa, Tom Outland is partially modeled on Richard Wetherill, who explored Mesa Verde with fellow cowboy Charlie Mason in 1888 (see Harrell, *From Mesa Verde* 46). This date is supported by the fact that soon after, during Tom's trip to Washington, DC, he meets with officials who are preparing for an "International Exposition" in Paris (*Professor's House* 243); this seems to be an allusion to the Universal Exposition of 1889 in Paris, though it could also refer to the Universal Exposition of 1900, also in Paris. This latter date is supported by the fact that during the first summer that Tom and his friend Roddy spend together as cowboys, Roddy is said to follow "the great injustices of his time" in the newspapers, among them the Dreyfus affair – a rather vague time marker, since the affair lasted from 1894 to 1906 (212). But whatever the exact year of Tom's time on the mesa, what matters is that it goes back in time roughly thirty years. This aligns Cather's novel with a basic convention of regionalism – as Tom Lutz remarks, this time interval had become "a standard for local color writers" (*Cosmopolitan Vistas* 108). Cather, in fact, adheres to it strictly in the opening sentence of *O Pioneers!* (139) and broadens it to "thirty or forty years" in that of *A Lost Lady* (3). The interval of thirty years (give or take) measures the distance between youth and middle age, and thus renders the return to the rural region as a return to youth.

2 Susan Stewart's influential *On Longing*, originally published in 1984 and reissued in 1993, pointedly expresses a view that continues to be widely shared in current critical theory. She speaks of "the social disease of nostalgia" (23) that imposes narrative structures and their attending closure on "'lived' history" (22). As a consequence, nostalgia becomes deeply ideological, a ruse that helps perpetuate the idealizations operative in the reproduction of power: "Nostalgia, like any form of narrative, is always ideological: the past it seeks has never existed except as narrative, and hence, always absent, that past continually threatens to reproduce itself as a felt lack" (23). My own reading is by no means entirely divorced from Stewart's analytic grid: In Cather's text, I will argue, history and nostalgia are roughly opposing poles; however, the conceptualization of history to which Cather hints at the end of her novel draws on an open-endedness made perceivable precisely by nostalgia.

3 In *Willa Cather in Context*, Guy Reynolds defends Cather against the charge of being out of touch with the realities of her time; instead, he makes the case for "a 'progressive' Cather, a writer liberally attuned to the broad currents of early twentieth-century American life – race, immigration and multiculturalism" (11). More recently, Sarah Wilson argues that "while nostalgia is a powerful force in Cather's novels, we must now recognize that it is often parried by an equally powerful historicist skepticism" ("Fragmentary" 571). Her reading of *The Professor's House* effectively negates the force of nostalgia and instead aims to establish the "formal and thematic density of Cather's commitment to historicism" (571). By contrast, several critics working in the field of queer studies have begun to reappraise Cather's identification with the "backward" as a strategy to counter the future-fixated temporality of heteronormativity, and have thus begun to critically reclaim precisely her nostalgia. See particularly Nealon, "Affect-Genealogy," and Love, *Feeling Backward*.

4 As this wording suggests, my argument is broadly in alignment with Svetlana Boym's influential proposal to revise the overwhelmingly negative image of nostalgia by distinguishing between two kinds of nostalgia, which she calls "restorative" and "reflective": "Restorative nostalgia stresses *nostos* and attempts a transhistorical reconstruction of the lost home. Reflective nostalgia thrives in *algia*, the longing itself, and delays the homecoming – wistfully, ironically, desperately.... Restorative nostalgia protects the absolute truth, while reflective nostalgia calls it into doubt" (*Future of Nostalgia* xviii). Boym's take on nostalgia is in some sense liberating, but it does build on a problematic binary: Her distinction is so value-laden (restorative is bad, reflective is good) that the reappraisal of nostalgia seems won somewhat too cheaply. Not surprisingly, for instance, virtually the only clear-cut case of restorative nostalgia is found in overt political ideologies of nationalism. Just about any piece of fiction, on the other hand, comfortingly fits into the category of "reflective nostalgia."

5 Richard Brodhead (*Cultures* 175) has characterized Cather as "stubbornly resistant to the modernism that made a master in her day" (by "master," Brodhead refers to what he perceives as an organizing category of the literary field), and Michael North (*Reading* 3) invokes – without fully subscribing to it – Edmund Wilson's verdict that "her work had been rendered obsolete by *Ulysses*." On

the other hand, several critics have insisted on Cather's integration into modernism. In *Willa Cather's Modernism: A Study of Style and Technique*, Jo Ann Middleton claims – unpersuasively – that Cather experimented no less than other modernists, even if she "took the path of simplicity rather than that of obscurity" (43). Only marginally more convincing is Richard Millington's argument, in "Willa Cather's American Modernism," that her fiction is preoccupied with the making of meaning and thus "free[s] her characters from the forms of emplotment that the tradition of the Victorian novel had designated for them" (64–65). Kelsey Squire pairs *The Professor's House* with *The Great Gatsby* (also published in 1925) to show that both Cather and Fitzgerald are proponents of a "modern regionalism" characterized by a "modern experience of place," in which "'love of place,' attachment, and market value" are in tension with one another ("'Jazz Age' Places" 54). This leads Squire to argue, convincingly, that modern regionalism presents "the attempt to learn to live in exile, . . . that through knowing one's place, exile can be endured" (62). Squire seems to suggest that Cather's works express a longing for the premodern world while accepting the dispersal effected by modernity – a split attitude that may itself be described as modernist.

6 In "Unwrapping the Mummy: Cather's Mother Eve and the Business of Desire," John Swift offers a subtle rumination on the ethical ramifications of the figure of Eve for the act of interpretation, particular with regard to gender relations.

7 The archeological record, in fact, puts into question Cather's starting point that the cliff city provided a degree of security that allowed the Pueblo communities to dedicate themselves to the higher pursuits of life. If Pueblo dwellers erected the Cliff Palace of Mesa Verde for the purposes of security, this does not suggest that their civilization flowered peacefully, but rather that it was the necessity of defense that made them relocate there. As Kuckelman explains: "In the mid-thirteenth century, in the final decades before the region was completely depopulated, many people relocated from their small, scattered farmsteads to nearby canyon rims, cliff overhangs, and other defensible places. . . . This clustering of people could have been both an offensive and a defensive, safety-in-numbers strategy. . . . These settlements . . . boasted excellent defensive properties: they were difficult to see from a distance, complicated to reach, and strategically dangerous to attack" ("Ancient Violence" 129).

8 Foote's emphasis on heterogeneity and difference has also been pursued in several parallel strands of research, ranging from the feminist readings of Judith Fetterley and Majorie Pryse, who argue, in their coauthored *Writing Out of Place*, for the genre's "creation of a space for female difference" (79), to the most recent cosmopolitan approaches. In *Cosmopolitan Vistas*, Tom Lutz, for instance, maintains that regionalism's implied readers and authors push for ever more inclusive moral and aesthetic positions, which transcend the limits of its rural and urban characters alike, while Philip Joseph aims to recover a literary regionalism peopled with subjects who "insist on shaping modern history, not exempting themselves from it" (*Regionalism in a Global Age* 10) and who thus articulate alternative public spheres opposed to the corporate market culture which has come to dominate national debate.

9 See, for instance, Squire, "'Jazz Age' Places," Joseph, "*Regionalism in a Global Age*," and Lutz, "Cather and Regional Imagination."
10 The influence of naturalism on Cather has been traced most meticulously in relation to her early journalistic writings and her novels up to *Song of the Lark*. Amy Ahearn points out that the tradition of naturalism also linked her to the aspiration to compose the Great American Novel: "Cather self-consciously positions herself as one of the Great American Novelists by adopting naturalistic conventions for her writing" ("Full-Blooded Writing" 144). In his magisterial study of the "Great American Novel," Lawrence Buell also discusses *Song of the Lark*, and he, too, comments on Cather's indebtedness to naturalism. Noting "*Lark*'s ... investment in the saga of youthful ambition realizing itself," he remarks that "though not ranked among naturalists like London and Dreiser, Cather shares their fascination with assertive characters driven by a combination of internal energies and larger socioenvironmental forces" (*Dream* 134).
11 This is not to suggest that we do not find examples of the tragic return to the rural site of youth in Cather's oeuvre. To take just one of several examples from her early career, in "The Sculptor's Funeral," from 1905, a small frontier town is stifled by the materialist mediocrity of its leading citizens, while in the metropolis, creative minds have the freedom to achieve lasting triumphs of the human spirit. In this constellation, Jim Laird's decision to return home to practice law, instead of following his friend Harvey Merrick in the audacious endeavor of becoming "a great man" (47), leads to his depressing defeat. Recalling his youthful aspirations on the night before Harvey's funeral does not give Jim renewed hope for future possibilities, but sends him into a drunken stupor and soon into the coffin.
12 In his detailed tracing of Cather's fictional adaptation of the historical Mesa Verde, David Harrell has shown that the Smithsonian was, *pace* Cather, very much committed to preserving Native American artifacts. See also Matthias Schubnell's findings: "Between 1867 and 1884, ... the institution's accession catalog recorded 45,000 specimens of a total of 75,000 items received during this period. ... Indeed, the collecting by the Smithsonian reached such proportions that it threatened the artistic production by individual tribes" ("From Mesa Verde to Germany" 38).
13 At the end of §79 of *Being and Time*, Heidegger discusses the notion of "there is" ("es gibt") in relation to the temporality of *Dasein* and the "taking care of time." Heidegger uses the phrase "there is" precisely to emphasize the public and collective character of the "now" of *Dasein*, and contrasts it to the sense of private time given to oneself as the finite time of life. In the revised version of the Stambaugh translation (2010) the passage reads as follows: "The 'now' expressed is spoken by each one in the publicness of being-with-one-another-in-the-world. The time interpreted and expressed by any particular Dasein is thus also always already *made public* as such on the basis of its ecstatic being-in-the-world. Since everyday taking care understands itself in terms of the 'world' taken care of, it knows the 'time' that it takes for itself *not as its own*, but rather heedfully *exploits* the time that 'there is,' the time with which

the *they* reckons. But the publicness of 'time' is all the more compelling the more factical Dasein *explicitly takes care* of time by expressly taking it into account" (391).

14 The type of possession I am describing as "non-transitive" may at first glance be difficult to reconcile with the idea of "filial piety" Tom reads about "in the Latin poets" (253). John Swift, in "Memory, Myth, and *The Professor's House*," suggests that possession here equals being possessed: "To be possessed is to be a son, affiliated and filiated, situated in the stable, defining matrix of the family, and what Tom discovers on the mesa stands as a regressively won replacement for his missing biological family" (305). But familial affiliation may in fact be the best image for a type of possession in which possessor and possessed become interchangeable, in which possession strictly speaking does not have an object but is rather constituted by a shared being-in-the-world.

15 Cather highlights Tom's affinities with the Mesa Verdeans in his sensibility to the sun's sacred quality. As archeologists Winston Hurst and Jonathan Till explain: "Ancient Mesa Verdeans used the land and the sky as a vast and intricate calendar to guide them in their scheduling of ceremonies and to remind them of the proper times for planting, harvesting, and hunting" ("Mesa Verdean Sacred Landscapes" 82). In contrast to the Mesa Verdeans, for Tom the sacredness of the sun becomes divorced from all worldly functionality.

16 In a psychoanalytic reading of nostalgia, one might argue that Tom's story of his solitary experience on the Blue Mesa encapsulates the nostalgic's utopia of returning to a maternal union before the separation of the symbolic and nature. This line of thought is pursued in Greg Forter's perceptive reading of the novel. According to Forter, "what is at stake is the psychically 'primitive' condition in which the infant feels itself merged with the mother. *The Professor's House* imagines this state as an introjected register of experience that, inasmuch as it remains internally accessible to adults, can counter the alienations of modernity with a prealienated unity, and that therefore serves as the source for authentic (non-alienated) creativity" (147). Forter makes use of the psychoanalytic notion of an originary state of union in order to highlight the novel's preoccupation with a temporal position *before*. The drawback of the psychoanalytic rendition of this state, it seems to me, is its tendency to perceive the state of union as the *telos* of desire, and the breaking in of time as necessary loss. What I aim to capture with the term "radical contingency" is different precisely in this regard: the state of being before life is not marked by a desire for union and stasis, with the gaze turned inward, but by a desire for having the full range of life's possibilities ahead of oneself, with the gaze turned outward (literally toward the sun). Instead of ever coming closer, however, the future in the state of radical contingency remains distant like the sun, emitting light. Time becomes spatialized energy. For an earlier psychoanalytic reading, in which the sun becomes equated (in Freudian fashion) with the strong Father, see Swift, "Memory" 305.

17 Swift makes a similar point by drawing on Mircea Eliade's theory of the myth-seeking characteristic in human behavior. In his reading, Tom's narrative

accomplishes the work of myth, which is the work of transporting us back to the moment of creation and beginning: "Myth speaks of and from a time beyond human chronological time, and – for Eliade – the cultural purpose of recovering, recounting, or re-enacting mythic experience is the therapeutic reconnection of the diminished world-in-time to that significant 'strong time' of its beginning" ("Memory" 302).

18 Louise Poresky has detailed the similarities between both novels most meticulously. In light of her findings she suggests that Woolf indeed modeled her novel on Cather's. Her list includes the following convergences: "Both refer to a house in their titles and have multiple houses in their stories, both have a professor and his family at the center of the story and an expedition at the center of the plot, both have a main character gazing out a window at a body of water, both take place during World War I, both are constructed out of three parts, and both have a portrait waiting to be completed" ("Cather and Woolf" 69–70). Though it is enticing to speculate whether these similarities point to a conscious response by Woolf to Cather, the differences between the two novels are ultimately more striking. Where Cather creates a mood of nostalgia, Woolf's tracking the processes of consciousness is too much involved in the present to create a similar effect. Typically, Woolf packs into the present moment of narration plural memories located at different points in the past along with several simultaneous perceptions of the present. *To the Lighthouse* comes closest to *The Professor's House* in its middle section, "Time Passes," when the housekeeper, Mrs. McNab, enters the deserted house, filled with relics of a life seemingly abruptly interrupted, and remembers the bygone preWar times with the Ramsays. Despite Woolf's overall investment in the present, however, a kernel of nostalgia – of the knowingness about the loss that comes with the progression of time – is at work in her novel as well, creating a rather distant similarity to Cather's. Martin Hägglund is right in noting that Woolf does not render the present "timeless," but rather as filled with the anticipation of its becoming obsolescent: "On the one hand, Woolf has a celebrated ability to depict moments of time in their unique texture ... On the other hand, Woolf also depicts the relentless negativity of time that destroys the moments to which it gives rise. It would be a mistake to oppose these two types of temporality to one another. Rather, the violent passage of time is at work even in the most immediate and fully experienced moment" (*Dying* 56–57).

19 Steven Trout has noted the irony that "Outland's 'apparatus' will be removed from its academic context, hauled off from the modest institution that Outland chose over Johns Hopkins, in order to serve as an advertisement masquerading as a memorial. Moreover, this transferal of artifacts from the public sector to the private echoes Fechtig's raid on the treasures of the Blue Mesa" (*Memorial Fictions* 175).

20 Though Tom's story is told in the first person, Cather renders vague who is actually speaking. Tom's story is embedded within St. Peter's remembering their time together during one summer of male-male bliss – a memory of one

summer nestled inside the memory of another summer. This suggests that the first person we read may be St. Peter repeating in direct speech, and perhaps paraphrasing or even altering, what Tom told him. Susan Rosowski offered a subtle description: "In turning to Outland for his second youth years ago, St. Peter had found a surrogate, and in evoking his memory now, he gives himself up to the memory so completely that the surrogate (Outland) and the speaker (St. Peter) merge" (*Voyage* 132–133).

21 See Cather's own emphasis on the old house in a letter from January 1939: "[Tom] and the atmosphere he brought with him became really a part of the house – that is, of the old house which the Professor could not altogether leave" (*Letters* 567).

22 In "Willa Cather's *The Professor's House*: Sleeping with the Dead," Lisa Marie Lucenti argues that for the Professor, the result of striving for timelessness is becoming self-entombed: St. Peter "aims to sleep with or into his own death" (243).

23 I adopt this reference from Merrill Maguire Skaggs, who writes that Augusta's name "suggests the 'Roman' who defined an Augustan age. That epoch symbolizes peace (the Pax Romana), practical improvements (roads and architecture), and the Augustan literature known for its restraint" (*After the World* 81).

24 Cather wrote Frost a note making explicit the reference: "This is really a story of 'letting go with the heart' but most reviewers seem to consider it an attempt to popularize a system of philosophy" (Sergeant, *Memoir* 215). John J. Murphy notes that "the phrase 'letting go with the heart' is from 'Wild Grapes,' which was published the year before *The Professor's House* in Frost's *New Hampshire* collection (1924). In it a female persona recalls being suspended in the air when picking grapes from a vine growing on a birch.... She compares letting go with the hands to letting go with the heart and mind; she confesses never yet having to let go with the mind and hopes never to have to let go with the heart" ("Holy Cities" 61–62).

25 Walter Benn Michaels's influential reading of Cather's novel (in his study of the 1920s, *Our America*) is based on this binary. In *Our America*, Michaels reads the novel as exemplary of the emergence of a nativist ideology that conceptualized a pluralism based on the unassimilability of the immigrant (in this case, of Louie Marsellus, the Jew) alongside the appropriation of the Native American as the ur-American. In Michaels's reading, Cather's novel exemplifies the fact that in the 1920s Americans began to identify with the trope of the vanishing Indian so that American identity itself became narrated as being in the process of vanishing, polluted in its racial purity by the incoming hordes of foreigners. As forceful as Michaels's reading is, it depends on reducing the novel to its surface level and thus requires ignoring its inner dynamics of revisionism.

26 See, for instance, Eve Kosofsky Sedgwick, who ends her essay on Cather by a reflection on "Berengaria." She writes that "Berengaria was the wife of Richard the Lion-Hearted, who was known for preferring to her intimacy that of men, including, legendarily, his young minstrel" ("Cather and Others" 174).

27 James Watt writes that "Praise of Saladin as an individual was a feature of work by contemporaries of Scott, such as Charles Mills, as well as of histories by Hume and Gibbon" ("Scott, the Scottish Enlightenment" 106), and further fleshes out the context of Scott's self-positioning: "One of the things that makes *The Talisman* such a fascinating novel is that it was written at a time when the counter-revisionist reaction against Enlightenment historians was in full swing" (107).
28 Cather had tried to come to terms with the Great War's lure of heroism before, in *One of Ours*, from 1922, portraying a Midwestern country lad who prefers an early heroic death in the trenches over the numbing provinciality of Midwestern farm life – a preference treated with mild irony, but by no means unequivocally condemned by the narrator. Not surprisingly, the novel provoked a spiteful and chauvinistic comment by Hemingway. In an exchange with Edmund Wilson, Hemingway ridiculed Cather: "You were in the war weren't you? Wasn't that last scene in the lines wonderful? Do you know where it came from? The battle scene in *Birth of a Nation*. I identified episode after episode, Catherized. Poor woman she had to get her war experience somewhere" (qtd. in Wilson, *Shores of Light* 118). Michael North suggests changing the terms of the debate over *One of Ours* by shifting Claude's interest from the war to France, turning Claude effectively into a member of the American expatriates. On this reading, Cather provoked the modernists' ire not because she differed from their convictions, but because her Claude is uncannily similar to them, especially in his taking on an aesthetic concern with domesticity – a concern marked so far as feminized: "In short, *One of Ours* is not at all what Hemingway said it was, the story of a woman's battle envy; rather, it is the story of a man's envy of muslin dresses and pretty flowers, and this is what made it so disconcerting for Hemingway's generation" (*Reading* 186). This interpretation, however, has difficulties accounting for Claude's fascination with military vigor, which, even before the war, he mounts against the deadening effects of the value of security: "This security was what was the matter with everybody; that only perfect security was required to kill all the best qualities in people and develop the mean ones.... Safety, security; if you followed that reasoning out, then the unborn, those who would never be born, were the safest of all; nothing could happen to them" (1024).
29 Ann Fisher-Wirth has suggestively noted that, "however briefly, Louie presents a counter to St. Peter's despair, as well as an alternative to Tom's solitary, essentially ascetic idealism: the alternative of worldliness and eros, which is always suspect and flawed but can also be noble. In Cather's perhaps unconscious revaluation of Louie, *The Professor's House* teaches itself one way to go forward" ("Anasazi Cannibalism" 25).
30 Attempts were made early on, however. John Gillingham writes that the "historian Ralph of Diceto traced Richard's ancestry through Edith to the Anglo-Saxon kings of Wessex, the line of Alfred the Great and Cerdic, and then, through them, back to Woden and Noah" (Gillingham, *Richard I* 24). Hugh Thomas more generally points out that beginning with King Richard's reign

the Norman nobility began to be accepted as English: "Clearly writers were coming to think of a distinct, straightforwardly English nobility in Richard's reign" (Thomas, *The English* 80).

31 T. Austin Graham, in "Blood on the Rock: Cather's Southwestern History," has speculated that St. Peter's history of the "Spanish Adventurers" – about which the reader learns very little – "probably takes a sober view of its eponymous adventurers, and a sympathetic one of the Native Americans they encountered, killed, displaced, enslaved, and converted" (50). The reasons he provides, however, cannot account for the romantic framework that allows St. Peter to treat conquest as a heroic feat of outstanding, rule-breaking individuals. Graham is right in pointing out that St. Peter's work is aligned by Cather less with academic historiography than with the historical novel (which makes St. Peter a kind of professional adventurer himself) (54). But this only heightens the suspicion that the Professor's life work is the opposite of "sober" regarding its heroes. My point is not, however, to accuse Cather of an imperialist attitude, but rather to suggest that her protagonist comes to confront his unexamined beliefs in the course of the novel.

5 Cold War Liberalism and Flannery O'Connor's "The Displaced Person"

1 Mark Neocleous lists a number of earlier occurrences of the term "national security," among them the National Security League, a nativist organization formed in 1914, and articles on foreign policy by Edward Mead Earle and Walter Lippman from the late 1930s and early 1940s. He concludes that "what is significant is that although the term appears in these [earlier] texts there is little substantive analysis of what it is or might mean" (*Critique* 209n2).

2 On this point, see Neocleous: "The most forceful advocate of the concept, Navy Secretary James Forrestal, commented that 'national security' can only be secured with a broad and comprehensive front, and made a point of adding that 'I am using the word *security* here consistently and continuously rather than *defense*' ... 'I like your words *national security*,' one Senator commented" (*Critique* 76).

3 The emerging academic field of International Relations was an exception in this regard. Here, "realism" became a clearly defined approach, or school, whose most influential proponent was Hans Morgenthau. Vibeke Schou Tjalve and Michael C. Williams have shown that Morgenthau's intellectual position is close to that of Reinhold Niebuhr's and Arthur Schlesinger's (Niebuhr, in fact, directly influenced Morgenthau). But whereas Schlesinger held onto the term "liberalism," Morgenthau substituted it with "realism" (see their "Re-Thinking the Logic of Security").

4 Amanda Anderson has recently emphasized the degree to which mid-century liberalism adopted a moderately pessimistic outlook on life and thus articulated a sharp divergence from eighteenth-century liberalism, which was organized around characterizations such as "optimistic" and "blissfully

progressive." Like myself, Anderson sees liberalism's turn toward the skeptical as a political critique that should not be hastily brushed aside by the notion that liberalism disavowed its own investment in power struggles: "Liberalism in this twentieth-century form is thus precisely a rejection of the progressive optimism that was seen to mark nineteenth-century liberalism and its heir, twentieth-century radicalism. In this sense, a certain noncommunist liberalism aims to preserve the democratic project against considerable dangers as manifested on both the right and the left" ("Character and Ideology" 217). See also Anderson's "The Liberal Aesthetic."

5 In "Cold War Liberalism and the Problem of Security," I have offered a reading of the literary criticism of Trilling, Schlesinger, and Chambers with regard to security and insecurity. For a related argument, see Steven Belletto's *No Accident, Comrade!* (2011). Belletto demonstrates "how the concept of chance became politicized during the Cold War" (4). As he shows, intellectuals and writers, including Margaret Mead, Herbert Marcuse, and Sidney Hook, mounted chance, understood as "the absence of planning or intention" (14), as a defense against political totalitarian regimes that were seen as eradicating freedom through meticulous planning of every aspect of life. Belletto's main interest lies in the paradoxical challenge the commitment to chance posed for the literary writer. In the hands of postwar novelists beholden to the values of chance and uncertainty, chance had to be built into literary narrative in a controlled and intentional manner. "Narrative chance," he therefore concludes, "is marked always by its inability to achieve the same sort of freedom possible in real life" (26). While Belletto productively uses this paradox as a starting point for tracing how American literary writers thought through the relation of chance and narrative, that paradox becomes much less pressing if "chance" and "accident" are conceptualized alongside the aesthetic liberal values of uncertainty and ambiguity – values that were intended to enable a struggle with difficulty that would then lead to freedom. Namwali Serpell, in her recent appraisal of the literary ethics of uncertainty (which, in her framing, grows out of "the agonistic, unsettling experience over time" made possible by reading literature [9]) reengages the writings of Trilling and (more substantially) Empson. The historical anchor for her project is thus a moment "at midcentury [when uncertainty] was being declared as the very source of literature's ethical value" (11). Like "narrative chance," literary uncertainty must be designed by the author, but its actualization by the reader outstrips authorial intention or planning.

6 This line of thought finds expression, for instance, in Campbell, *Writing Security*, and Dillon, *Politics of Security*, even if Dillon himself draws on Nietzsche in order to move beyond the conventional framework of security studies.

7 In *The Prestige of Violence* (2011), Sally Bachner argues that post-1960s American literature obsessively turned to violence, but in a manner that proclaimed violence to lie beyond the grasp of language, in a nonsymbolizable realm of "the real." Bachner effectually proposes that the rendering of violence as inexpressible (in literature and theory) served an ideological purpose,

though she uses a Bourdieuian framework, rather than that of ideology critique, to conceptualize it:

> I argue that the fascination with violence that underwrites fiction and theory of the period is an index of the discomfort that privileged Americans feel by virtue of the fact that they are at once citizens of a relatively peaceful and prosperous society and the inhabitants of a larger, much less peaceful and prosperous world.... The structural opposition between violence and conventional language, and the foregrounding of a violence guaranteed by its material absence at the center of American life, enables a deeply therapeutic and illusory reckoning with that violence. It converts the typical perception of violence held by members of the nation's dominant class – that it cannot be directly experienced, that it is most present in its absence, that it evades conventional discourse – into a truth about violence itself. (5)

In positing a single underlying contradiction as the cause for the emergence of the "prestige of violence," she foregoes the possibility of paying attention to more nuanced and specific contexts of, and rationales for, the valorization of violence in postwar American literature. As I aim to show here, O'Connor – whom Bachner does not consider, as O'Connor predates the era on which she focuses – helped raise the prestige of violence through the attempt to distinguish herself from what she perceived as mainstream liberalism. However, the use of violence in her fiction could only resonate so well in American literary culture because violence was already central to Cold War liberalism's articulation of a concept of tragic democracy. If there is a contradiction underlying the prestige of violence at that historical moment, it is the contradictory adherence of liberalism to insecurity and mastery.

8 In her early work, we find instances in which the alternative to the secular order of security is provided by a religious outlook of insecurity that is less sacramental than explicitly otherworldly. This is particularly true for the asceticism of Hazel Motes of *Wise Blood*, who blinds himself and thus visually denies his situatedness in material creation.

9 Frederick Asals writes that "Psychologically, at least, Flannery O'Connor seems to have been an inveterate 'Manichean'" (*Imagination* 120). Similarly, Frederick Crews states that "O'Connor's own Manichaeism expresses itself not only in the portrayal of an undignified human species but also in an emphasis on redemption so uncompromising as to be dubiously Christian in spirit (*Critics* 155). Harold Bloom contends that "O'Connor's fictive universe [is] essentially Gnostic" ("Introduction" 5). As Bloom writes, "In the Gnostic formulation, creation and fall were one and the same event, and all that can save us is a certain spark within us, a spark that is no part of the creation but rather goes back to the original abyss. The grandeur or sublimity that shines through the ruined creation is a kind of abyss radiance, whether in Blake or Carlyle or the early Eliot or in such novelistic masters of the grotesque as Faulkner, West, and O'Connor" (5).

10 Asals, in his usual acuteness, similarly argues that "the tendency of the metaphoric activity in Flannery O'Connor's later fiction is to move toward two poles at once, to strain away from the vision of a distinctively humanistic center. One

impulse in her writing is downward, an absorption of the human to the realm of things, of animals and objects; the contrary drive is upward, a touching of the human with the grotesque luminosity of the divine" (*Imagination* 67).

11 Admittedly, there are exceptions to this, though in these world politics gets discussed much more briefly than in "The Displaced Person." In "A Good Man Is Hard to Find," for instance, the Grandmother voices her misgivings about the Marshall Plan: "The old lady said that in her opinion Europe was entirely to blame for the way things were now. She said the way Europe acted you would think we were made of money and Red Sam said it was no use talking about it, she was exactly right" (142).

12 The resonances with regionalism's (conflicted) embrace of the rural as the antidote to modernization are obvious. In this light, Cather and O'Connor can be read together as two authors who affirmed the rural region's ability to provide for a space of antimodern security, and who simultaneously reconceptualized the experience of security as consisting of uncertainty and insecurity.

13 In his works *A Sociology for the South* (1854), and *Cannibals All!* (1857), Fitzhugh linked a critique of capitalism to proslavery paternalism, arguing that slavery was the most effective protection against capitalism's brutality of (labor) competition, particularly for blacks, who he claimed to be child-like.

14 Since the irony of this image consists in aligning Mrs. Shortley with the Displaced Person, it is not only the concentration camp that is evoked here, but the DP refugee camp as well. This double reference is the story's first notable suggestion that the two are linked in a way that cannot be accounted for by Mrs. Shortley's political and historical ignorance. After all, the narrating voice describing this image cannot be mixed up with the character's perception since the image describes that character's dead body. We hear, then, the story's first echo of Hannah Arendt's argument, developed in *The Origins of Totalitarianism*, that the internment camp is "the only practical substitute for a nonexistent homeland" – a substitute that, in light of the dysfunctionality of the nation-state system, may in principle become the fate of any human being (284).

15 As I point out in my discussion of Harriet Jacobs, before the emancipation of slavery, some slave jurisdictions treated slaves as real estate rather than chattel personal. As Thomas Morris explains, this made no difference with regard to the status of the slave, but it did affect, "for example … the rules that would apply to them if their owner died without a will" (*Southern Slavery* 65).

16 For Arendt, this genuine political community did not – could not – take the form of the nation-state, since the expansive nation-state produced minorities unprotected by a nationally conceived community. Judith Butler emphasizes that it was the point of Arendt's critical practice "to underscore the political paradoxes of the nation-state. For instance: if the nation-state secures the rights of citizens, then surely the nation-state is a necessity; but if the nation-state relies on nationalism and invariably produces massive numbers of stateless people, it clearly needs to be opposed. And: if the nation-state is opposed, then what, if anything, serves as its alternative?" (*Parting Ways* 131).

17 This "accident" recalls the more explicit roadside accident that will lead to the encounter with The Misfit in "A Good Man Is Hard to Find." As Belletto points out, in that story "the fully capitalized word 'ACCIDENT' draws attention to itself typographically and conceptually; as an example of narrative chance, it demands to be interpreted both as the unexpected, unintended accident, and as a key part of the story's design, the event that allows The Misfit and grandmother to come together" (*No Accident* 27). These two meanings of "accident" are at work in the tractor scene of "The Displaced Person" as well, though the emphasis is more strongly on the design of cosmic harmony, which is attributed as much to the author as to God.

18 I am thinking here of Judith Butler's notion of cohabitation, which she develops, in *Parting Ways*, through her engagement with Arendt and which "emerges in part from a condition of exile" (153). In Butler's reading of Arendt, only a state apparatus can guarantee rights and thus protect the individual. But the nation-state inevitably produces stateless – and therefore utterly unprotected – minorities. Therefore, what is needed is some kind of formalized polity that would guarantee the rights of the entire heterogeneous population. The solution could only reside in some sort of federalism that is open to heterogeneity and plurality. This form of political constellation, Butler suggests, must itself be based on displacement, or exile. Only if the polity shares an ethos of displacement does a cohabitation of the pluralized polity become possible. It would be tempting to read the conception of displacement as our shared ontological position in O'Connor's story alongside Butler and Arendt – but as far as I can see, O'Connor ontologizes displacement by spiritually allegorizing it. This cuts short the ways in which displacement can become a political ethos and thus the basis of a genuine community of cohabitation. In fact, I suggest that her aesthetics of rage denigrates such attempts as hopelessly liberal.

19 O'Connor minced no words about her attempt to direct the violence of her stories at her readers. In her essay "The Fiction Writer and His Country," she wrote, "The novelist with Christian concerns will find in modern life distortions which are repugnant to him, and his problem will be to make these appear as distortions to an audience which is used to seeing them as natural; and he may well be forced to take ever more violent means to get his vision across to this hostile audience.... [Y]ou have to make your vision apparent by shock – to the hard of hearing you shout, and for the almost-blind you draw large and startling figures" ("Fiction Writer" 805–806). To a degree, O'Connor resounds the convictions of Cold War intellectuals like Lionel Trilling, who wrote in his essay "On the Teaching of Modern Literature" that works of literature "were manifestly contrived to be not static and commemorative but mobile and aggressive, and one does not describe a quinquereme or a howitzer or a tank without estimating how much damage it can do" (388). But what sets O'Connor apart from Trilling is the language of religious warfare. Whereas for Trilling it is the work of literature itself that is best described in military terms, for O'Connor it is Christian concerns that must be fought for with the weapons of literature.

20 Christa Buschendorf has remarked that in almost all of O'Connor's stories, the characters' limits of vision are counteracted by the narrator's description of wide-angle landscapes that encompass the sky. Though it is generally the case that this kind of upward gaze is seen by the characters themselves, the description of the widened view emphasizes the narrator's voice. Therefore, the cosmic long shot serves the purpose of underscoring – and transcending – the characters' limitations (see *Mit Kinderaugen* 108). On this point, see also J. O. Tate, "Flannery O'Connor's Counterplot." In "The Displaced Person," symbols (the peacock, the sun) fulfill the function of the view toward the sky.

21 Or, as the serial killer remarks at the end of "A Good Man is Hard to Find" upon shooting the endlessly blabbering grandmother: "She would of been a good woman … if it had been somebody there to shoot her every minute of her life" (153).

22 The impression of self-hatred is confirmed by the recently released journal she kept beginning in 1946, while studying at the Iowa Writers' Workshop. Here, O'Connor routinely practices a rigorous self-critique, praying to "Dear God" to not merely improve her, but to "help me push myself aside" (*A Prayer Journal* 3). Her art poses a particular challenge to her, since artistic creation runs the risk of arrogating the power of divine creation. In a particular variant of what I have called above the "agency dilemma," she thus has to literally transfer authorship of her own literary work to God: "Don't let me ever think, dear God, that I was anything but the instrument for Your story – just like the typewriter was mine" (11).

23 For an analysis of this kind of double, see Asals, *Imagination*, ch. 3, 95–123.

24 It may appear as if this structure of affect could be explained with the help of René Girard's theory of sacrificial violence as developed, for instance, in *Violence and the Sacred* (1972) and *Things Hidden since the Foundation of the World* (1978). Despite superficial similarities to what I am describing, I resist the invocation of Girard as I do not share his notion of primordial, mimetic rivalry that routinely gets deflected onto a scapegoat (a dynamic which, for Girard, is only overcome with God's sacrifice of his son). My point is not that reader and narrator are always in a conflict of mimetic desire that leads to violence, but that O'Connor, through her narrator, mounts a theologically motivated critique that includes the reader and herself. I should add that recently, Girard has become a popular way for O'Connor's Christian readers to account for the violence of her texts while insisting on the piousness of her fiction. See particularly Srigley, "The Violence of Love" and O'Gorman, *Peculiar Crossroads*. For a stringent critique of Girard, see White, "Ethnological 'Lie' and Mythical 'Truth'."

25 This explains how the critique of security-as-rationality could evolve, in the hands of Hans Morgenthau, into the first influential school of "security studies" in International Relations – a school that labeled itself "realism" and soon became associated with the military buildup of the Cold War, although it never gave up, as Michael Williams has argued with great aplomb about Morgenthau, its commitment to skepticism (see *Realism Reconsidered*, a recent essay collection on Morgenthau edited by Williams).

6 In the Future, Toward Death

1 The publication of *Zero K* (2016) came too late for that novel to be considered in this chapter. In *Zero K*, DeLillo deepens his engagement with the questions of mortality (by turning immortality into the novel's explicit theme) and authentic existence, and he makes explicit his concern with Heidegger's philosophy of existence (and its troubled embeddedness in history) when he has his protagonist reflect on Heidegger's famous passage, "'Man alone exists. Rocks are, but they do not exist. Trees are, but they do not exist. Horses are, but they do not exist'" (*Zero K* 213). I briefly return to *Zero K* in my epilogue.
2 In fact, he was not the only postmodernist who spontaneously interpreted the attacks as a check on the predominance of simulation and virtuality. Jean Baudrillard, similarly, saw the terrorist attack as "an act that restores an irreducible particularity in the middle of a generalized exchange system" ("Spirit" 135).
3 This has been suggested by Hamilton Carroll. See his "'Like Nothing in this Life': September 11 and the Limits of Representation in Don DeLillo's *Falling Man*."
4 Here it becomes obvious that engaging the future for DeLillo is not just a philosophical question pertaining to the actual and the virtual, but a matter of power. This logic also underlies *Falling Man*, where the American loss of control over the future is linked by one character to the loss of imperial control. "They [the terrorists] strike a blow to this country's dominance. They achieve this, to show how a great power can be vulnerable" (46). Control over the future is tantamount to the capacity to actively shape the world. The weaker party is forced into passive endurance – a position whose temporality consists in having to experience the future as fate.
5 A "haircut" is also a technical term in finance, but here the meaning is ultimately the opposite: it refers to the difference between the market value of an asset and the amount for which it can be used as a collateral. The size of the haircut depends on the riskiness of the asset; a "haircut," in other words, is a preemptive safety measure against risk. Thus, taken in the colloquial sense, Packer's getting a haircut suggests that he is courting loss; understood in the technical sense, he is insuring himself against it. The novel, as I will argue, exploits this very ambiguity. I thank Christian Kloeckner for pointing out the different meanings of the phrase to me.
6 In using this phrase, DeLillo explicitly equates Packer's world with the pre-9/11 world as he had presented it in "Ruins." Recall that there, too, he had described the pre-9/11 dispensation as being "summoned … to live permanently in the future" (33). What I emphasize in this chapter, however, is that Packer's world may seem and feel as if belonging to a previous epoch, but in providing insights into the confluence of finance capitalism and the prevalence of the logic of security, the novel in fact addresses our still current era of late capitalism.
7 Both movies (as well as Belfort's memoirs that provide the source for *Wolf*) operate on the assumption that success is only possible by breaking the rules. Nonetheless, their behavior is marked as explicitly illegal and is punished by the legal justice system (if in an unjustly lenient way, in Belfort's case). The idea that only "insiders" can make it does not change the fact that Gekko's and Belfort's behavior breaks the rules of the system and diverges from the norm. Indeed, it is their outlaw status that qualifies them to act as the heroes of their stories.

8 Philip Nel provides a concise overview of DeLillo's deep engagement with Joyce (and other modernists) throughout his novels (see "DeLillo and Modernism"). DeLillo has claimed that it is through Joyce that he "learned to see something in language that carried a radiance, something that made me feel the beauty and fervor of words" (DeLillo, "Art of Fiction").
9 In Tennyson's poem, Ulysses calls on his mariners to venture on yet another voyage. But his language is heavy with uncertainty: "Come, my friends,/ 'T is not too late to seek a newer world./ ... It may be that the gulfs will wash us down:/ It may be we shall touch the Happy Isles" (90).
10 Cowart writes, "Like Odysseus, who sojourns with Circe, Calypso, and Nausicaa before reaching Penelope, Packer dallies with Didi Fancher, his bodyguard Kendra Hays, and ... 'his chief of finance,' Jane Melman, before the long-desired and long-postponed sexual encounter with his wife" (*Don DeLillo* 220).
11 Wood's primarily stylistic critique ultimately leads him to claim that "The effect of this eager, puppyish, scrambling language, when it runs after contemporary technologies and forces, is to rob DeLillo of whatever critique he might have intended. Indeed, it is hard to discern if DeLillo does have critique in mind, so boisterously lost is his prose. He seems to want to cover postmodernity in happy licks" ("Traffic"). Updike, by contrast, comes to the conclusion that DeLillo' novel suffers from his overidentification with the novel's poor, as a result of which DeLillo allegedly denies Packer any humanity.
12 The term "postmodern sublime" is Joseph Tabbi's. See his study of the same title. For Tabbi, the "excessive production of technology itself" is the "successor[] to the omnipotent 'nature' of nineteenth-century romanticism" in that it "represent[s] a magnitude" that "at once attracts and repels the imagination" (16).
13 As Amy Hungerford, an influential proponent of this position, puts it, "Glossolalia, the Latin mass, small talk, the ritual of conversation or of the sentence – this is how DeLillo imagines fiction as a religious meditation in which language is the final enlightenment" (377).
14 It would moreover reappear in *Falling Man* (2007).
15 DeLillo first explored the fluid distinction between monologue and dialogue in *Players* (1977). The main characters, Lyle and Pammy Wyant, share what is almost a private language – a vernacular of intimacy and boredom – which consequently does not have to be spoken in its completeness. As DeLillo himself reflects in a 1993 interview, "I concentrated on dialogue most deeply in *Players*. It's hyperrealistic, spoken by urban men and women who live together, who know each other's speech patterns and thought patterns and finish each other sentences or don't even bother because it isn't necessary" (DeLillo, "The Art of Fiction").
16 Further examples of the genre David Zimmerman calls "titan novel" include Jack London's *Burning Daylight* (1910), Robert Herrick's *Memoirs of An American Citizen* (1905), Abraham Cahan's *The Rise of David Levinsky* (1917), and Harold Frederic's *The Market-Place* (1898) (see Zimmerman, "Novels of Business"). On Dreiser, see particularly Walter Benn Michaels, *Gold Standard*,

ch. 2. Michaels stresses that events in *The Financier* "persistently exhibit nature not primarily as an organizing force dedicated to the survival of the fittest but as the ultimate measure of life's instability, the 'mystic chemistry' that embodies the 'insecurity and uncertainty of life'" (76) – which Cowperwood desires with erotic abandon. On *The Financier*, see also Zimmerman, *Panic!*, ch. 5.

17 See Updike, "One-Way Street," Shippey, "Cooling Connections," Greif, "Bonfire of the Verities," Caldwell, "Bonfire on Inanities," Mentzinger, "A Ride." For a collection of review summaries, see http://perival.com/delillo/cosmopolis_media.html. Among academic critics, Jerry Varsava ("The 'Saturated Self'") and Eric Heyne ("Death of an American Supervillain") also follow lines of arguments that see Packer as a larger-than-life figure resonant with the tradition of financier representations roughly sketched out above. Heyne extends this tradition by placing Packer in the context of superhero comics. Reading DeLillo's aesthetics in the context of comics is suggestive because so much of *Cosmopolis* is self-consciously cast in exaggerations and clichés. Packer, however, is hardly a supervillain.

18 As Alison Shonkwiler has rightly remarked, Packer is part of an "über-elite" that is highly generic and thus provides a counterpoint to the "individual objects of Wolfean satire" ("Financial Sublime" 260).

19 The quote is taken from *City of God*, book 13, ch. 11. Augustine's chapter headline reads "Whether one can both be living and dead at the same time" (*City* 531).

20 Heidegger discusses authenticity (*Eigentlichkeit*) and "being-toward-death" in the first chapter of Division 2 of *Being and Time* (see particularly §47–53, trans. Macquarrie and Robinson 281–311). I am not claiming an influence of Heidegger on DeLillo here but merely a resonance. DeLillo's indebtedness to a broadly defined existentialist tradition more overtly goes back to Kierkegaard. In *Falling Man*, for instance, Lianne reflects at length on her college reading of Kierkegaard. *Point Omega*, moreover, takes liberties with the Jesuit philosopher Pierre Teilhard de Chardin, who is sometimes considered a Christian existentialist. The larger confluences between the contemporary imagination of security and a return to existentialism would require a separate study.

21 Heidegger writes, "The ownmost possibility, which is non-relational, not to be outstripped, and certain, is *indefinite* as regards its certainty" (*Being and Time*, trans. Macquarrie and Robinson 310).

22 In "From Virtue to Virtual," Russell Scott Valentino reads the novel as suggesting "that the conceptual thread from the bodily foundations of virtue to the absent body of virtuality shows, on one hand, a gradual de-corporealization of value in modern life and, on the other, a range of human reactions to the increasing centrality of this 'symbolic public order' from euphoria to anxiety to madness" (144). Packer, he argues, is a "*kosmou polites* [who] recognizes neither the representative nor the fact of the *res publica*" (153). Considering that Packer's numbness in the time of risk results in part from his isolation, becoming ready to begin "the business of living" would indeed have to make room for some form of socially embedded being. Yet the only collective that Packer

can envision is the corporation made up of conformity and competition. His notion of the embedded individual reverts to "jockeying junior executives," in short, to the organization man.

Epilogue

1 See, for instance, a good portion of the contributions to the recent special issue *Security Studies and American Literary History* (edited by David Watson) in *American Literary History*. See my response for a longer discussion ("Aestheticizing Insecurity").
2 The most explicit version of the argument for affirmation is found in Timothy Melley's article "Security, Secrecy, and the Liberal Imaginary," which builds on his study, *The Covert Sphere*. Melley argues with great aplomb that the treatment of security in popular fiction and film provides fantasies of agency useful for a public whose critical, democratic input has been diminished by the secrecy of the security state: "The genre's celebration of individual agency is often part of a masculinist fantasy that compensates for the terror of becoming a feminized ward of the security state" ("Security" 165). Melley ascribes the ideological function of literature to popular genres. He sets artistic postmodern novels apart from popular texts by granting them a critical function, achieved through a "postmodern epistemological skepticism" (*Covert* 147), which "is both a symptom of state secrecy and a powerful commentary on it" (146). I take exception to Melley's assessment neither regarding the ideological work done by many popular texts, nor regarding the capacity for critique he ascribes to authors like DeLillo, but rather in regard to the binary construction of cooptation versus critique. This leaves the category of appeal unaccounted for, with the result that appeal can appear only on the side of the ideologically co-opted text. In effect, appeal comes to mean ideological co-optation; by the same token, a text that has not been co-opted can be "powerful" only in its capacity to critically comment on ideological constellations. For an argument that is related to Melley's (though concerned exclusively with the popular), see Susan Faludi's book *The Terror Dream*. Faludi argues that in response to the terror attacks of September 11, 2001, Americans reverted to popular myths in which a starkly gendered division between a helpless female victim and a heroic male protector became the blueprint for figuring the relation between citizens and political leaders.
3 For a helpful delineation of the development from social to national security in the United States, see Neocleous, *Critique of Security*, chapter 3. In *The Sympathetic State*, Michele Landis Dauber has demonstrated that the welfare state during the Great Depression became an acceptable idea only once FDR's administration invoked the tradition of disaster relief. Social security, Dauber's argument implies, was built – like national security and homeland security later on – on the logic of the emergency.
4 I take the term "desire for catastrophe" from Eva Horn, *Zukunft als Katastrophe*. Horn adopts the phrase from Pierre-Henry Jeudy's *Le désir de catastrophe*. She applies it not to Anthropocene discourse but to the Cold War security

rationality underlying the "Mutual Assured Destruction" doctrine, in which she recognizes the perversely appealing fantasy of collective mass death: "The desire for catastrophe underlying the cold war seems to circle around a constantly conjured and constantly disavowed fantasy: All people will die at the same time. Death no longer confronts the individual with his or her individual finitude; death is no longer unjust. No one can be survived by anyone else" (n.p., my trans.).

Bibliography

Acker, Kathy. *Empire of the Senseless*. New York: Grove Press, 1988.
Agamben, Giorgio. *Homo Sacer: Sovereign Power and Bare Life*. Trans. Daniel Heller-Roazen. Stanford: Stanford University Press, 1998.
   State of Exception. Trans. Kevin Attell. Chicago: University of Chicago Press, 2005.
Ahearn, Amy. "Full-Blooded Writing and Journalistic Fictions: Naturalism, the Female Artist and Willa Cather's *The Song of the Lark*." *American Literary Realism* 33.2, Special Issue: Willa Cather (Winter 2001): 143–156.
Altheide, David L. *Terrorism and the Politics of Fear*. Lanham: AltaMira, 2006.
Amoore, Louise. *The Politics of Possibility: Risk and Security Beyond Probability*. Durham: Duke University Press, 2013.
Amoore, Louise, and Marieke de Goede, eds. *Risk and the War on Terror*. London: Routledge, 2008.
Anderson, Amanda. "Character and Ideology: The Case of Cold War Liberalism." *New Literary History* 42.2 (Spring 2011a): 209–229.
   "The Liberal Aesthetic." *Theory After 'Theory.'* Ed. Jane Elliott and Derek Attridge. New York: Routledge, 2011b. 249–61.
Angus, Ian. *Facing the Anthropocene: Fossil Capitalism and the Crisis of the Earth System*. New York: Monthly Review Press, 2016.
Anker, Elisabeth R. *Orgies of Feeling: Melodrama and the Politics of Freedom*. Durham: Duke University Press, 2014.
Appleby, Joyce. *Capitalism and a New Social Order: The Republican Vision of the 1790s*. New York: NYU Press, 1984.
Arendt, Hannah. *The Origins of Totalitarianism*. Cleveland: Meridian Books, 1958.
Aristotle. *The Poetics of Aristotle*. Ed. and trans. S. H. Butcher. London: Macmillan, 1895.
Armstrong, Tim. *The Logic of Slavery: Debt, Technology, and Pain in American Literature*. New York: Cambridge University Press, 2012.
Asals, Frederick. *Flannery O'Connor: The Imagination of Extremity*. Athens: University of Georgia Press, 1982
Augustine. *The City of God*. Vol. 1. Ed. Marcus Dods. Edinburgh: T. & T. Clark, 1884.
Bachner, Sally. *The Prestige of Violence: American Fiction, 1962–2007*. Athens: University of Georgia Press, 2011.

Bacon, Jon Lance. *Flannery O'Connor and Cold War Culture*. New York: Cambridge University Press, 1993.
Bailyn, Bernard. *The Ideological Origins of the American Revolution*. Cambridge, MA: Belknap Press of Harvard University Press, 1992.
Baker, Jennifer. *Securing the Commonwealth: Debt, Speculation, and Writing in the Making of Early America*. Baltimore: Johns Hopkins University Press, 2005.
Barnard, Philip, Mark Kamrath, and Stephen Shapiro. "Introduction." *Revising Charles Brockden Brown: Culture, Politics, and Sexuality in the Early American Republic*. Ed. Philip Barnard, Mark Kamrath, and Stephen Shapiro. Knoxville: University of Tennessee Press, 2004. ix–xxi.
Barnard, Philip and Stephen Shapiro. "Introduction." *Charles Brockden Brown, Arthur Mervyn, or, Memoirs of the year 1793*. Ed., intr. and notes Philip Barnard and Stephen Shapiro. Indianapolis: Hackett, 2008. ix–xliv.
Baudrillard, Jean. "The Spirit of Terrorism." *Telos* 121 (Fall 2001): 134–142.
Bauman, Zygmunt. *Liquid Modernity*. Cambridge: Polity, 2000.
Beck, Ulrich. *Risk Society: Towards a New Modernity* [1986]. London: Sage, 1992.
  World at Risk. Cambridge: Polity Press, 2009.
Bell, Michael Davitt. "'The Double-Tongued Deceiver': Sincerity and Duplicity in the Novels of Charles Brockden Brown." *Early American Literature* 9.2 (Fall 1974): 143–163.
Belletto, Steven. *No Accident, Comrade: Chance and Design in Cold War American Narratives*. New York: Oxford University Press, 2011.
Benjamin, Walter. "Theses on the Philosophy of History." *Illuminations*. Ed. and intr. Hannah Arendt. Trans. Harry Zohn. New York: Schocken, 1968. 253–264.
Bercovitch, Sacvan. *The American Jeremiad*. Madison: University of Wisconsin Press, 1978.
Bernoulli, Jacob. *The Art of Conjecturing*, together with "*Letter to a Friend on Sets in Court Tennis*" [*Ars Conjectandi*, 1713]. Trans. Edith Dudley Sylla. Baltimore: Johns Hopkins University Press, 2006.
Bernstein, Peter L. *Against the Gods: The Remarkable Story of Risk*. New York: Wiley, 1996.
Bertodano, Helena. "And Quiet Goes the Don." *The Daily Telegraph* (May 13, 2003). http://www.telegraph.co.uk/culture/donotmigrate/3594421/And-quiet-goes-the-Don.html
Bleikasten, André. "The Heresy of Flannery O'Connor." *Critical Essays on Flannery O'Connor*. Ed. Melvin J. Friedman and Beverly Lyon Clark. Boston: G. K. Hall, 1985. 138–158.
Bloom, Harold. "Introduction." *Flannery O'Connor – New Edition. Bloom's Modern Critical Views*. Ed. Harold Bloom. New York: Infobase, 2009. 1–8.
Bonneuil, Christophe and Jean-Baptiste Fressoz. *The Shock of the Anthropocene. The Earth, History, and Us*. Trans. David Fernbach. New York: Verso, 2016. Ebook.
Bourke, Joanna. *Fear: A Cultural History*. London: Virago, 2005.
Boxall, Peter. *Don DeLillo: The Possibility of Fiction*. London: Routledge, 2006.
Boym, Svetlana. *The Future of Nostalgia*. New York: Basic Books, 2001.

Brancaccio, Patrick. "Studied Ambiguities: *Arthur Mervyn* and the Problem of the Unreliable Narrator." *American Literature* 42.1 (1970): 18–27.

Bröckling, Ulrich. *Das unternehmerische Selbst: Soziologie einer Subjektivierungsform*. Frankfurt am Main: Suhrkamp, 2007.

Brodhead, Richard. *Cultures of Letters: Scenes of Reading and Writing in Nineteenth-Century America*. Chicago: University of Chicago Press, 1993.

Brooks, Peter. *Reading for the Plot: Design and Intention in Narrative*. Oxford: Clarendon Press, 1984.

Brown, Charles Brockden. "The Difference between History and Romance." *Arthur Mervyn, or, Memoirs of the Year 1793* [1799/1800]. With related texts. Ed., intr. and notes Philip Barnard and Stephen Shapiro. Indianapolis: Hackett, 2008. 340–343.

"The Editor['s] Address to the Public." *Literary Magazine* 1.1 (October 1803): 3–6. *The Charles Brockden Brown Electronic Archive and Scholarly Edition*. www.brockdenbrown.cah.ucf.edu

"The Man at Home. No. III." *Weekly Magazine* 1.3 (February 1798): 65–67. *The Charles Brockden Brown Electronic Archive and Scholarly Edition*. www.brockdenbrown.cah.ucf.edu

"The Man at Home. No. XI." *Weekly Magazine* 1.11 (April 1798): 320–323. *The Charles Brockden Brown Electronic Archive and Scholarly Edition*. www.brockdenbrown.cah.ucf.edu

"Walstein's School of History." *Arthur Mervyn, or, Memoirs of the Year 1793* [1799/1800]. With related texts. Ed., intr. and notes Philip Barnard and Stephen Shapiro. Indianapolis: Hackett, 2008. 331–339.

Arthur Mervyn, or, Memoirs of the Year 1793 [1799/1800]. With related texts. Ed., intr. and notes Philip Barnard and Stephen Shapiro. Indianapolis: Hackett, 2008.

Ormond; Or, the Secret Witness [1799]. Ed. Mary Chapin. Petersborough: Broadview Press, 1999.

Brown, William Wells. *Narrative of William W. Brown* [1847]. *American Slave Narratives*. Ed. William L. Andrews and Henry Louis Gates Jr. New York: Library of America, 2000.

Buell, Lawrence. *The Dream of the Great American Novel*. Cambridge, MA: The Belknap Press of Harvard University Press, 2014.

Burgess, Peter. *The Ethical Subject of Security*. London: Routledge, 2011.

Burke, Edmund. *Philosophical Enquiry* [1757]. Ed., intr., and notes Adam Phillips [Oxford World's Classics]. Oxford: Oxford University Press, 1998.

Burroughs, Stephen. *Memoirs of the Notorious Stephen Burroughs* [1798]. Boston: Charles Gaylord, 1835.

Buschendorf, Christa. *Mit Kinderaugen: Zur Perspektivtechnik bei William Faulkner, Carson McCullers und Flannery O'Connor*. Würzburg: Königshausen und Neumann, 1988.

Butler, Judith. *Parting Ways: Jewishness and the Critique of Zionism*. New York: Columbia University Press, 2012.

Buzan, Barry, Ole Waever, and Jaap de Wilde. *Security: A New Framework for Analysis*. Boulder: Lynne Rienner, 1998.

Caldwell, Gail. "Bonfire of Inanities." *Boston Globe* (April 6, 2003, C6).
Cameron, Catherine M. "Leaving Mesa Verde." *The Mesa Verde World: Explorations in Ancestral Puebloan Archaeology*. Ed. David Grant Nobel. Santa Fe: School of American Research Press, 2006. 139–147.
Campbell, David. *Writing Security: United States Foreign Policy and the Politics of Identity*. Minneapolis: University of Minnesota Press, 1992.
Campbell, David, and Michael Dillon, eds. *The Political Subject of Violence*. Manchester: Manchester University Press, 1993.
Campe, Rüdiger. *The Game of Probability: Literature and Calculation from Pascal to Kleist* [2002]. Trans. Ellwood H. Wiggins, Jr. Stanford: Stanford University Press, 2012.
Carroll, Hamilton. "'Like Nothing in this Life': September 11 and the Limits of Representation in Don DeLillo's *Falling Man*." *Studies in American Fiction* 40.1 (Spring 2013): 107–130.
Cather, Willa. "'Joseph and His Brothers'." *Not Under Forty* [1936]. *Stories, Poems, and Other Writings*. Ed. Sharon O'Brien. New York: Library of America, 1992. 859–871.
"148 Charles Street." *Not Under Forty* [1936]. *Stories, Poems, and Other Writings*. Ed. Sharon O'Brien. New York: Library of America, 1992. 838–848.
"Mesa Verde." *Denver Times*, January 31, 1916.
The Professor's House. Willa Cather Scholarly Edition. Lincoln: University of Nebraska Press, 2002. 327–334.
"The Novel Démeublé." *Not Under Forty* [1936]. *Stories, Poems, and Other Writings*. Ed. Sharon O'Brien. New York: Library of America, 1992. 834–837.
A Lost Lady [1923]. *Later Novels*. Ed. Sharon O'Brien. New York: Library of America, 1990.
My Ántonia [1918]. *Early Novels and Stories*. Ed. Sharon O'Brien. New York: Library of America, 1987.
Not Under Forty [1936]. *Stories, Poems, and Other Writings*. Ed. Sharon O'Brien. New York: Library of America, 1992
O Pioneers! [1913]. *Early Novels and Stories*. Ed. Sharon O'Brien. New York: Library of America, 1987.
One of Ours [1922]. *Early Novels and Stories*. Ed. Sharon O'Brien. New York: Library of America, 1987.
The Professor's House [1925]. *Later Novels*. Ed. Sharon O'Brien. New York: Library of America, 1990.
"The Sculptor's Funeral" [1905]. *Early Novels and Stories*. Ed. Sharon O'Brien. New York: Library of America, 1987.
The Selected Letters of Willa Cather. Ed. Andrew Jewell and Janis Stout. New York: Knopf, 2013.
Cawelti, John G. *Apostles of the Self-Made Man*. Chicago: University of Chicago Press, 1965.
Chow, Rey. "Sacrifice, Mimesis, and the Theorizing of Victimhood (A Speculative Essay)." *Representations* 94.1 (Spring 2006): 131–149.
Christophersen, Bill. *The Apparition in the Glass: Charles Brockden Brown's American Gothic*. Athens: University of Georgia Press, 1992.

Cleves, Rachel Hope. "'Savage Barbarities!' Slavery, Race, and the Uncivilizing Process in the United States." *Civilizing and Decivilizing Processes: Figurational Approaches to American Culture.* Ed. Christa Buschendorf, Astrid Franke, Johannes Voelz. Newcastle: Cambridge Scholars, 2011. 103–122.
  The Reign of Terror in America: Visions of Violence from Anti-Jacobinism to Antislavery. New York: Cambridge University Press, 2009.
Clymer, Jeffory A. *America's Culture of Terrorism: Violence, Capitalism, and the Written Word.* Chapel Hill: University of North Carolina Press, 2003.
Cohen, Gerald Daniel. *In War's Wake: Europe's Displaced Persons in the Postwar Order.* New York: Oxford University Press, 2012.
Coleridge, Samuel Taylor. *Coleridge's Shakespeare Criticism*, vol. 1. Ed. Thomas Middleton Rayson. London: Constable, 1960.
Conze, Werner. "Sicherheit, Schutz." *Geschichtliche Grundbegriffe: Historisches Lexikon zur politisch-sozialen Sprache in Deutschland.* 8 vols. Ed. O. Brunner, W. Conze, and R. Kosselleck. Stuttgart: Klett, 1972–1997. 5: 831–862.
Cowart, David. *Don DeLillo: The Physics of Language* [2002]. Savannah: University of Georgia Press, 2012.
  "The Lady Vanishes: Don DeLillo's *Point Omega*." *Contemporary Literature* 53.1 (Spring 2012): 31–50.
Crane, Gregg. *Race, Citizenship, and Law in American Literature.* New York: Cambridge University Press, 2002.
Crews, Frederick. *The Critics Bear It Away: American Fiction and the Academy.* New York: Random House, 1992.
Dalby, Simon. "Contesting an Essential Concept: Reading the Dilemmas in Contemporary Security Discourse." *Critical Security Studies: Concepts and Cases.* Ed. Keith Krause and Michael C. Williams. Minneapolis: University of Minnesota Press, 1997. 3–31.
Daston, Lorraine. "Fortuna and the Passions: Chance, Culture, and the Literary Text." Ed. Thomas M. Kavanagh. *Michigan Romance Studies* 14 (1994): 25–47.
Dauber, Michele Landis. *The Sympathetic State: Disaster Relief and the Origins of the American Welfare State.* Chicago: University of Chicago Press, 2012.
Davidson, Cathy. *Revolution and the Word.* Oxford: Oxford University Press, 1986.
Däwes, Birgit. *Ground Zero Fiction: History, Memory and Representation in the American 9/11 Novel.* Heidelberg: Winter, 2011.
DeLillo, Don. "In the Ruins of the Future: Reflections on Terror and Loss in the Shadow of September." *Harper's* December 2001: 33–40.
  "The Art of Fiction No. 135." An Interview with Adam Begley. *Paris Review* 128 (1993). Web.
  Americana [1971]. New York: Penguin, 1989.
  Cosmopolis. New York: Scribner, 2003.
  End Zone [1972]. New York: Penguin, 1986.
  Falling Man. New York: Scribner, 2007.
  Point Omega. New York: Scribner, 2010.
  The Names [1982]. New York: Vintage 1989.
  Underworld [1997]. New York: Scribner, 2003.
  White Noise [1985]. New York: Penguin, 1986.

Zero K: A Novel. New York: Scribner, 2016.
DeLombard, Jeannine Marie. *Slavery on Trial: Law, Abolitionism, and Print Culture*. Chapel Hill: University of North Carolina Press, 2007.
Delumeau, Jean. *Sin and Fear: The Emergence of a Western Guilt Culture, 13th–18th Centuries*. New York: St. Martin's Press, 1990.
Derrida, Jacques. "The Law of Genre." *Critical Inquiry* 7.1 (Autumn 1980): 55–81.
Dillon, Michael. "Security, Race and War." *Foucault on Politics, Security, and War*. Ed. Michael Dillon and Andrews Neal. New York: Palgrave Macmillan, 2008. 166–196.
Politics of Security: Towards a Political Philosophy of Continental Thought. London: Routledge, 1996.
Dillon, Michael, and Andrews Neal, eds. *Foucault on Politics, Security, and War*. New York: Palgrave Macmillan, 2008.
Douglass, Frederick. *Narrative of the Life of Frederick Douglass, and American Slave* [1845]. *American Slave Narratives*. Ed. William L. Andrews and Henry Louis Gates Jr. New York: Library of America, 2000.
Eliot, T. S. "Tradition and Individual Talent." *Perspecta* 19 (1982): 36–42.
Elliott, Emory. *Revolutionary Writers: Literature and Authority in the New Republic, 1725–1810*. New York: Oxford University Press, 1982.
Emerson, Ralph Waldo. "Circles." *Essays, First Series. The Collected Works of Ralph Waldo Emerson*. Ed. Alfred R. Ferguson, Joseph Slater, Douglas Emory Wilson, Ronald A. Bosco, et al. 10 vols. Cambridge, MA: The Belknap Press of Harvard UP, 1971–2013. II: 177–190.
Ernest, John. *Liberation Historiography: African American Writers and the Challenge of History, 1794–1861*. Chapel Hill: University of North Carolina Press, 2004.
Esposito, Elena. "Beyond the Promise of Security: Uncertainty as Resource." *Security and Liberalism*. Ed. Johannes Voelz. *Telos* 170 (Spring 2015): 89–108.
Die Fiktion der wahrscheinlichen Realität. Frankfurt am Main: Suhrkamp, 2007.
Ewald, François. "Insurance and Risk." *The Foucault Effect: Studies in Governmentality: With Two Lectures by and an Interview with Michel Foucault*. Ed. Graham Burchell, Colin Gordon, and Peter Miller. Chicago. University of Chicago Press, 1991. 197–210.
"Two Infinities of Risk." *The Politics of Everyday Fear*. Ed. Brian Massumi. Minneapolis: University of Minnesota Press, 1993. 221–228.
Ezzy, Douglas. "Theorizing Narrative Identity: Symbolic Interactionism and Hermeneutics." *The Sociological Quarterly* 39.2 (1998): 239–252.
Faludi, Susan. *The Terror Dream: Fear and Fantasy in Post-9/11 America*. New York: Metropolitan Books, 2007.
Fanuzzi, Robert. *Abolition's Public Sphere*. Minneapolis: University of Minnesota Press, 2003.
Felski, Rita. *The Uses of Literature*. Malden: Blackwell, 2008.
Fetterley, Judith, and Marjorie Pryse. *Writing Out of Place: Regionalism, Women, and American Literary Culture*. Urbana: University of Illinois Press, 2003.
Fisher-Wirth, Ann. "Anasazi Cannibalism: Eating Eden." *Willa Cather and the American Southwest*. Ed. John N. Swift and Joseph R. Urgo. Lincoln: University of Nebraska Press, 2002. 22–30.

Fitzhugh, George. *A Sociology for the South: Or, the Failure of Free Society.* Richmond: A. Morris, 1854.
Cannibals All! Or, Slaves Without Masters [1857]. Cambridge, MA: Belknap Press of Harvard University Press, 1960.
Fleischner, Jennifer. *Mastering Slavery: Memory, Family, and Identity in Women's Slave Narratives.* New York: NYU Press, 1996.
Fluck, Winfried. *Das kulturelle Imaginäre: eine Funktionsgeschichte des amerikanischen Romans, 1790–1900.* Frankfurt am Main: Suhrkamp, 1997.
"The Imaginary and the Second Narrative: Reading as Transfer." *The Imaginary and Its Worlds: American Studies after the Transnational Turn.* Ed. Laura Bieger, Ramón Saldívar, Johannes Voelz. Hanover: University Press of New England, 2013. 237–264.
Foote, Stephanie. *Regional Fictions: Culture and Identity in Nineteenth-Century American Literature.* Madison: University of Wisconsin Press, 2001.
Forter, Greg. *Gender, Race, and Mourning in American Modernism.* Cambridge: Cambridge University Press, 2011.
Foster, Hal. *The Return of the Real: The Avant-Garde at the End of the Century.* Cambridge, MA: MIT Press, 1996.
Foucault, Michel. *Security, Territory, Population. Lectures at the Collège de France, 1977–78.* Ed. Michel Senellart, trans. Graham Burchell. New York: Palgrave Macmillan, 2007.
Frederick Douglass' Paper. "Abolition in Missouri." December 2, 1853. *African American Newspapers.* Web.
Gallagher, Catherine. "The Rise of Fictionality." *The Novel*, Vol. 1: *History, Geography, and Culture.* Ed. Franco Moretti. Princeton: Princeton University Press, 2006. 336–363.
Garland, Hamlin. *Main-Travelled Roads* [1891]. Rev. and expanded edition. New York: Harper and Row, 1922. Reprint: University of Nebraska Press, 1995.
Garrison, William Lloyd. *The New "Reign of Terror" in the Slaveholding States, for 1859–1860.* Anti-Slavery Tracts, No. 4, New Series. New York: American Anti-Slavery Society, 1860.
Gillingham, John. *Richard I.* New Haven: Yale University Press, 1999.
Girard, René. *Things Hidden Since the Foundation of the World* [1978]. Trans. Stephen Bann (Books II & III) and Michael Metteer (Book I). Stanford: Stanford University Press, 1987.
Girard, René. *Violence and the Sacred* [1972]. Trans. Patrick Gregory. Baltimore: Johns Hopkins University Press, 1977.
Glassner, Barry. "Narrative Techniques of Fear Mongering." *Social Research* 71.4 (Winter 2004): 819–826.
The Culture of Fear: Why Americans Are Afraid of the Wrong Things. New York: Basic Books, 1999.
Goddu, Teresa A. *Gothic America: Narrative, History, and Nation.* New York: Columbia University Press, 1997.
Godwin, William. "Of History and Romance." Appendix A of William Godwin, *Caleb Williams.* Ed. Gary Handwerk and A. A. Markley. Toronto: Broadview Press, 2000. 453–467.

Caleb Williams. Ed. Gary Handwerk and A. A. Markley. Toronto: Broadview Press, 2000. 453–467.

Enquiry Concerning Human Justice, and Its Influence on Morals and Happiness [1798]. Volume 1. London: J. Watson, 1842.

Goede, Marieke de. *Speculative Security: The Politics of Pursuing Terrorist Monies*. Minneapolis: University of Minnesota Press, 2012.

Gooch, Brad. *Flannery: A Life of Flannery O'Connor*. New York: Little, Brown, 2009.

Goudie, Sean X. *Creole America: The West Indies and the Formation of Literature and Culture in the New Republic*. Philadelphia: University of Pennsylvania Press, 2006.

Gould, Philip. "Race, Commerce, and the Literature of Yellow Fever in the Early National Philadelphia." *Early American Literature* 35.2 (2000): 157–186.

Grabo, Norman S. *The Coincidental Art of Charles Brockden Brown*. Chapel Hill: University Press of North Carolina, 1981.

Graham, T. Austin. "Blood on the Rock: Cather's Southwestern History." *American Literary History* 28.1 (2016): 46–68.

Gray, Richard. *After the Fall: American Literature Since 9/11*. Chichester: Wiley-Blackwell, 2011.

Greif, Mark. "Bonfire of the Verities." *The American Prospect* (April 2003): 54–55.

Hacking, Ian. *The Emergence of Probability*. Cambridge: Cambridge University Press, 1975.

Hägglund, Martin. *Dying For Time: Proust, Woolf, Nabokov*. Cambridge, MA: Harvard University Press, 2012.

Halttunen, Karen. *Confidence Men and Painted Women: A Study of Middle-Class Culture in America, 1830–1870*. New Haven: Yale University Press, 1982.

Hamilton, John T. *Security: Politics, Humanity, and the Philology of Care*. Princeton: Princeton University Press, 2013.

Hamilton, Ross. *Accident: A Philosophical and Literary History*. Chicago: University of Chicago Press, 2007.

Harrell, David. *From Mesa Verde to The Professor's House*. Albuquerque: University of New Mexico Press, 1992.

Haselstein, Ulla. *Die Gabe der Zivilisation: Kultureller Austausch und literarische Textpraxis, 1682–1861*. München: Fink, 2000.

Hedges, William. "Charles Brockden Brown and the Culture of Contradictions." *Early American Literature* 9.2 (Fall 1974): 107–142.

Heidegger, Martin. *Being and Time* [1927]. Trans. John Macquarrie and Edward Robinson. Oxford: Blackwell, 1962.

Being and Time [1927]. Trans. Joan Stambaugh. Rev. and with a foreword by Dennis J. Schmidt. Albany: SUNY Press, 2010.

Heise, Ursula. *Imagining Extinction: The Cultural Meanings of Endangered Species*. Chicago: University of Chicago Press, 2016.

Henry, Katherine. *Liberalism and the Culture of Security: The Nineteenth-Century Rhetoric of Reform*. Tuscaloosa: University of Alabama Press, 2011.

Heyne, Eric. "'A Bruised Cartoonish Quality': The Death of an American Supervillain in Don DeLillo's *Cosmopolis*." *Critique: Studies in Contemporary Fiction* 54.4 (2013): 438–451.
Hicks, Granville. "Bright Incidents." Review of Cather, *Shadows on the Rock*. *Forum and Century* 86.2 (August 1931): vi–viii.
Hole, Jeffrey. "Enforcement on a Grand Scale: Fugitive Intelligence and the Literary Tactics of Douglass and Melville." *American Literature* 85.2 (June 2013): 217–246.
Homeland Security Advisory System Task Force. "Report and Recommendations." September 2009. www.dhs.gov/xlibrary/assets/hsac_final_report_09_15_09.pdf
Horn, Eva. *Zukunft als Katastrophe*. Frankfurt am Main: Fischer, 2014. Ebook.
Houen, Alex. *Terrorism and Modern Literature from Joseph Conrad to Ciaran Carson*. Oxford: Oxford University Press, 2002.
Hungerford, Amy. "Don DeLillo's Latin Mass." *Contemporary Literature* 47.3 (2006): 343–380.
Jacobs, Harriet. *Incidents in the Life of a Slave Girl* [1861]. *American Slave Narratives*. Ed. William L. Andrews and Henry Louis Gates Jr. New York: Library of America, 2000.
James, William. "What Is an Emotion?" *Mind* 9.34 (April 1884): 188–205.
Jameson, Fredric. *Postmodernism, or, the Cultural Logic of Late Capitalism*. Durham: Duke University Press, 1991.
Jeudy, Pierre-Henry. *Le désir de catastrophe*. Paris: Aubier, 1990.
Jewett, Sarah Orne. *The Country of the Pointed Firs* [1896]. *Novels and Stories*. Ed. Michael Davitt Bell. New York: Library of America, 1994.
Joseph, Philip. *American Literary Regionalism in a Global Age*. Baton Rouge: Louisiana State University Press, 2007.
Joyce, James. *Ulysses* [1922]. London: Penguin, 2000.
Justus, James H. "Arthur Mervyn, American." *American Literature* 42.3 (1970): 304–324.
Kalyvas, Andreas, and Ira Katznelson. *Liberal Beginnings: Making a Republic for the Moderns*. New York: Cambridge University Press, 2008.
Kaplan, Amy. "Nation, Region, and Empire." *Columbia History of the American Novel*. Ed. Emory Elliott. New York: Columbia University Press, 1991. 240–266.
Kaufmann, Franz-Xaver. *Sicherheit als soziologisches und sozialpolitisches Problem*. Stuttgart: Enke, 1973.
Keller, Julia. "After the Attack, Postmodernism Loses Its Glib Grip." *Chicago Tribune* (September 27, 2001). http://articles.chicagotribune.com/2001-09-27/features/0109270018_1_postmodernism-military-personnel-field-in-southwestern-pennsylvania.
Kelleter, Frank. *Amerikanische Aufklärung: Sprachen der Rationalität im Zeitalter der Revolution*. Paderborn: Ferdinand Schöningh, 2002.
Kimmage, Michael. *The Conservative Turn: Lionel Trilling, Whittaker Chambers, and the Lessons of Anti-Communism*. Cambridge, MA: Harvard University Press, 2009.

Koselleck, Reinhart. "'Space of Experience' and 'Horizon of Expectation': Two Historical Categories." *Futures Past: On the Semantics of Historical Time* [1979]. Trans. and intr. Keith Tribe. New York: Columbia University Press, 2004. 255–275.

Kuckelman, Kristen A. "Ancient Violence in the Mesa Verde Region." *The Mesa Verde World: Explorations in Ancestral Puebloan Archaeology*. Ed. David Grant Nobel. Santa Fe: School of American Research Press, 2006. 127–135.

Larson, John L. *The Market Revolution in America: Liberty, Ambition, and the Eclipse of the Common Good*. New York: Cambridge University Press, 2010.

Lee, Maurice S. *Uncertain Chances: Science, Skepticism, and Belief in Nineteenth-Century American Literature*. New York: Oxford University Press, 2012.

Lentricchia, Frank, and Jody McAuliffe. *Crimes of Art and Terror*. Chicago: University of Chicago Press, 2003.

Levine, Robert S. "Arthur Mervyn's Revolutions." *Studies in American Fiction* 12 (1984): 145–160.

Conspiracy and Romance: Studies in Brockden Brown, Cooper, Hawthorne, and Melville. Cambridge: Cambridge University Press, 1989.

Levy, Jonathan. *Freaks of Fortune: The Emerging World of Capitalism and Risk in America*. Cambridge, MA: Harvard University Press, 2012.

Linke, Uli, and Danielle Taana Smith, eds. *Cultures of Fear: A Critical Reader*. London: Pluto Press, 2009.

Looby, Christopher. *Voicing America: Language, Literary Form, and the Origins of the United States*. Chicago: University of Chicago Press, 1996.

Lotman, Yuri M. "The Origin of Plot in the Light of Typology." Trans. Julian Graffy. *Poetics Today* 1.1–2 (Autumn 1979): 161–184.

Universe of the Mind: A Semiotic Theory of Culture. Trans. Ann Shukman. Bloomington: Indiana University Press, 1990.

Love, Heather. *Feeling Backward: Loss and the Politics of Queer History*. Cambridge, MA: Harvard University Press, 2007.

Lubet, Steven. *Fugitive Justice: Runaways, Rescuers, and Slavery on Trial*. Cambridge, MA: Belknap Press of Harvard University Press, 2010.

Lucenti, Lisa M. "Willa Cather's *The Professor's House*: Sleeping with the Dead." *Texas Studies in Literature and Language* 41.3 (Fall 1999): 236–261.

Luhmann, Niklas. *Risk: A Sociological Theory*. Berlin: Walter DeGruyter, 1991.

Lupton, Deborah. *Risk*. London: Routledge, 1999.

Lutz, Tom. "Cather and the Regional Imagination." *The Cambridge History of the American Novel*. Gen. ed. Leonard Cassuto, assoc. ed. Clare Virginia Eby and Benjamin Reiss. Cambridge: Cambridge University Press, 2011. 437–451.

Cosmopolitan Vistas: American Regionalism and Literary Value. Ithaca: Cornell University Press, 2004.

Mackenthun, Gesa. *Fictions of the Black Atlantic in American Foundational Literature*. London: Routledge, 2004.

Madison, James, Alexander Hamilton, and John Jay. *The Federalist with Letters of "Brutus."* Ed. Terence Ball. New York: Cambridge University Press, 2003.

Margolis, Stacey. "Network Theory circa 1800: Charles Brockden Brown's Arthur Mervyn." *Novel: A Forum on Fiction.* 45.3 (Fall 2012): 343–367.

Marinetti, F. T. "An Open Letter to the Futurist Mac Delmarle" ["Lettera aperta al futurista Mac Delmarle," 1913]. Trans. Doug Thompson. *Critical Writings.* Ed. Günther Berghaus. New York: Farrar, Straus and Giroux, 2006. 104–106.

Maritain, Jacques. *Art and Scholasticism* [1920] and *The Frontiers of Poetry.* Trans. Joseph W. Evans. New York: Charles Scribner's Sons, 1962.

Marshall, Kate. "What Are the Novels of the Anthropocene? American Fiction in Geological Time." *American Literary History* 27.3 (September 2015): 523–538.

Martinez-Bonati, Felix. *Fictive Discourse and the Structures of Literature: A Phenomenological Approach.* Trans. Philip W. Silver. Ithaca: Cornell University Press, 1981.

Massumi, Brian. "Fear (The Spectrum Said)." *positions* 13.1 (Spring 2005): 31–48.

 ed. *The Politics of Everyday Fear.* Minneapolis: University of Minnesota Press, 1993.

Meister, Chad. "The Problem of Evil." *The Cambridge Companion to Christian Philosophical Theology.* Ed. Charles Taliferro and Chad Meister. New York: Cambridge University Press, 2010. 152–169.

Melley, Timothy. "Security, Secrecy, and the Liberal Imaginary." *Security and Liberalism.* Ed. Johannes Voelz. *Telos* 170 (Spring 2015): 149–167.

 The Covert Sphere: Secrecy, Fiction, and the National Security State. Ithaca: Cornell University Press, 2012.

Mencken, H. L. "The Sahara of the Bozart." H. L. Mencken, *The American Scene: A Reader.* Ed. Huntington Cairns. New York: Knopf, 1977. 157–168.

Mentzinger, Bob. "A Ride Across Manhattan, with Don DeLillo as Chaffeur." *New Haven Register* (April 20, 2003).

Merton, Robert K. "The Unanticipated Consequences of Purposive Social Action." *American Sociological Review* 1 (1936): 894–904.

Michaels, Walter Benn. *Our America: Nativism, Modernism, and Pluralism.* Durham: Duke University Press, 1995.

 The Gold Standard and the Logic of Naturalism. Berkeley: University of California Press, 1987.

Middleton, Jo Ann. *Willa Cather's Modernism: A Study of Style and Technique.* Rutherford; London: Fairleigh Dickinson University Press; Associated University Presses, 1990.

Mihm, Stephen. *A Nation of Counterfeiters: Capitalists, Con Men, and the Making of the United States.* Cambridge, MA: Harvard University Press, 2007.

Millington, Richard. "Willa Cather's American Modernism." *The Cambridge Companion to Willa Cather.* Ed. Marilee Lindeman. New York: Cambridge University Press, 2005. 51–65.

Mills, Bruce. "Lydia Maria Child and the Endings to Harriet Jacobs's *Incidents in the Life of a Slave Girl.*" *American Literature* 64.2 (June 1992): 255–272.

Molesworth, Jesse. *Chance and the Eighteenth-Century Novel: Realism, Probability, Magic.* New York: Cambridge University Press, 2010.

Montaigne, Michel de. "That to Philosophize is to Learn to Die" [1572–74]. *The Complete Works: Essays, Travel Journals, Letters*. Trans. Donald M. Frame. New York: Alfred A. Knopf (Everyman's Library), 2003. 67–82.

Morris, Thomas. *Southern Slavery and the Law, 1619–1860*. Chapel Hill: University of North Carolina Press, 1996.

Münkler, Herfried. "Strategien der Sicherung: Welten der Sicherheit und Kulturen des Risikos. Theoretische Perspektiven." *Sicherheit und Risiko: Über den Umgang mit Gefahr im 21. Jahrhundert*. Ed. Herfried Münkler, Matthias Bohlender, Sabine Meurer. Bielefeld: Transcript, 2010. 11–34.

Murphy, Andrew. *Prodigal Nation: Moral Decline and Divine Punishment from New England to 9/11*. Oxford: Oxford University Press, 2009.

Murphy, John J. "Holy Cities, Poor Savages, and the Science Culture: Positioning *The Professor's House*." *Willa Cather and the American Southwest*. Ed. John N. Swift and Joseph R. Urgo. Lincoln: University of Nebraska Press, 2002. 55–68.

Nabers, Deak. *Victory of Law: The Fourteenth Amendment, the Civil War, and American Literature, 1852–1867*. Baltimore: Johns Hopkins University Press, 2006.

Nealon, Christopher. "Affect-Genealogy: Feeling and Affiliation in Willa Cather." *American Literature* 69.1 (March 1997): 5–37

Nel, Philip. "DeLillo and Modernism." *The Cambridge Companion to Don DeLillo*. Ed. John N. Duvall. New York: Cambridge University Press, 2008. 13–26.

Neocleous, Mark. *Critique of Security*. Edinburgh: Edinburgh University Press, 2008.

Nerlich, Michael. *Ideology of Adventure: Studies in Modern Consciousness, 1100–1750*. 2 volumes. Minneapolis: University of Minnesota Press, 1987.

Niebuhr, Reinhold. *The Irony of American History* [1952]. Chicago: University of Chicago Press, 2008.

Norris, Frank. *The Pit: A Story of Chicago* [1903]. New York: Penguin, 1994.

North, Michael. *Reading 1922: A Return to the Scene of the Modern*. New York: Oxford University Press, 1999.

Northup, Solomon. *Twelve Years a Slave* [1853]. Mineola: Dover, 2000.

O'Connor, Flannery. "A Circle in the Fire." *A Good Man Is Hard to Find, and Other Stories*. 232–251.

A Good Man Is Hard to Find, and Other Stories [1955]. *Collected Works*. Ed. Sally Fitzgerald. New York: Library of America, 1988.

"A Good Man Is Hard to Find." *A Good Man Is Hard to Find, and Other Stories*. 137–153.

A Prayer Journal. Ed. W. A. Sessions. New York: Farrar, Straus & Giroux, 2013.

"A Stroke of Good Fortune." *A Good Man Is Hard to Find, and Other Stories*. 184–196.

"A Temple of the Holy Ghost." *A Good Man Is Hard to Find, and Other Stories*. 197–209.

Everything That Rises Must Converge [1965]. *Collected Works*. Ed. Sally Fitzgerald. New York: Library of America, 1988.

"Everything That Rises Must Converge." *Everything That Rises Must Converge*. 485–500.

"Good Country People." *A Good Man Is Hard to Find, and Other Stories.* 263–284.
"Greenleaf." *Everything That Rises Must Converge.* 501–524.
"Judgment Day." *Everything That Rises Must Converge.* 676–695.
Letters. Collected Works. Ed. Sally Fitzgerald. New York: Library of America, 1988.
"Revelation." *Everything That Rises Must Converge.* 633–654.
"The Artificial Nigger." *A Good Man Is Hard to Find, and Other Stories.* 210–231.
"The Catholic Novelist in the Protestant South." *Stories and Occasional Prose. Collected Works.* Ed. Sally Fitzgerald. New York: Library of America, 1988. 853–864.
"The Comforts of Home." *Everything That Rises Must Converge.* 573–594.
"The Displaced Person." *A Good Man Is Hard to Find, and Other Stories.* 285–327.
"The Enduring Chill." *Everything That Rises Must Converge.* 547–572.
"The Fiction Writer and His Country." *Stories and Occasional Prose. Collected Works.* Ed. Sally Fitzgerald. New York: Library of America, 1988. 801–806.
"The Geranium." *Stories and Occasional Prose. Collected Works.* Ed. Sally Fitzgerald. New York: Library of America, 1988. 701–713.
"The Lame Shall Enter First." *Everything That Rises Must Converge.* 595–632.
The Violent Bear It Away [1960]. *Collected Works.* Ed. Sally Fitzgerald. New York: Library of America, 1988.
Wise Blood [1952]. *Collected Works.* Ed. Sally Fitzgerald. New York: Library of America, 1988.
O'Gorman, Farrell. *Peculiar Crossroads: Flannery O'Connor, Walker Percy, and Catholic Vision in Postwar Southern Fiction.* Baton Rouge: Louisiana State University Press, 2004.
Orians, Harrison G. "Censure of Fiction in American Romances and Magazines 1789–1810." *PMLA* 52 (1937): 195–215.
Pells, Richard. *The Liberal Mind in a Conservative Age: American Intellectuals in the 1940s and 1950s.* New York: Harper and Row, 1985.
Pocock, J. G. A. *The Machiavellian Moment: Florentine Political Thought and the Atlantic Republican Tradition.* Princeton: Princeton University Press, 1975.
  "Virtues, Rights, and Manners: A Model for Historians of Political Thought." *Virtue, Commerce, and History. Essays on Political Thought and History, Chiefly in the Eighteenth Century.* Cambridge: Cambridge University Press, 1985. 37–50.
Poresky, Louise A. "Cather and Woolf in Dialogue: *The Professor's House* and *To the Lighthouse*." *Papers on Language and Literature* 44.1 (Winter 2008): 67–86.
Ransom, John Crowe. "Reconstructed but Unregenerate." *Twelve Southerners, I'll Take My Stand: The South and the Agrarian Tradition* [1930]. Ed. Louis D. Rubin, Jr. Baton Rouge: Louisiana State University Press, 1977. 1–27.
Reynolds, Guy. *Willa Cather in Context: Progress, Race, Empire.* New York: St. Martin's, 1996.
Richards, Page. *Distancing English: A Chapter in the History of the Inexpressible.* Columbus: Ohio State University Press, 2009.
Ricoeur, Paul. "Life: A Story in Search of a Narrator." *A Ricoeur Reader: Reflection and Imagination.* Ed. Mario J. Valdés. Toronto: University of Toronto Press, 1991. 425–37.

"Narrative Time." *Critical Inquiry* 7.1 (Autumn 1980): 169–190.
"The Hermeneutical Function of Distanciation." *From Text to Action: Essays in Hermeneutics, II*. New York: Continuum, 2008. 72–85.
Ritter, Joachim, ed. *Historisches Wörterbuch der Philosophie*. 13 volumes. Darmstadt: Wissenschaftliche Buchgesellschaft, 1971–2007.
Robin, Corey. *Fear: The History of a Political Idea*. Oxford: Oxford University Press, 2004.
Rosenblatt, Roger. "The Age of Irony Comes to an End." *Time* (September 24, 2001). http://content.time.com/time/magazine/article/0,9171,1000893,00.html
Rosenblum, Nancy. *Another Liberalism: Romanticism and the Reconstruction of Liberal Thought*. Cambridge, MA: Harvard University Press, 1987.
Rosowski, Susan J. *The Voyage Perilous: Willa Cather's Romanticism*. Lincoln: University of Nebraska Press, 1986.
Rubin, Louis. Introduction. *Twelve Southerners, I'll Take My Stand: The South and the Agrarian Tradition* [1930]. Ed. Louis D. Rubin, Jr. Baton Rouge: Louisiana State University Press, 1977. xi–xxxv.
Russo, James R. "The Chameleon of Convenient Vice: A Study of the Narrative of Arthur Mervyn." *Studies in the Novel* 11. 4 (Winter 1979): 381–405.
Schaub, Thomas Hill. *American Fiction in the Cold War*. Madison: University of Wisconsin Press, 1991.
Scheiding, Oliver. *Geschichte und Fiktion: Zum Funktionswandel des frühen amerikanischen Romans*. Paderborn: Ferdinand Schöningh, 2003.
Schlesinger, Jr., Arthur. *The Vital Center: The Politics of Freedom*. Boston: Houghton Mifflin, 1949.
Schrimm-Heins, Andrea. "Gewissheit und Sicherheit. Geschichte und Bedeutungswandel der Begriffe certitudo und securitas. Teil 1." *Archiv für Begriffsgeschichte* 34 (1991): 123–213.
"Gewissheit und Sicherheit. Geschichte und Bedeutungswandel der Begriffe certitudo und securitas. Teil 2." *Archiv für Begriffsgeschichte* 35 (1992): 115–213.
Schubnell, Matthias. "From Mesa Verde to Germany: The Appropriation of Indian Artifacts as Part of Willa Cather's Cultural Critique in *The Professor's House*." *Willa Cather and the American Southwest*. Ed. John N. Swift and Joseph R. Urgo. Lincoln: University of Nebraska Press, 2002. 31–42.
Scott, Sir Walter. *The Talisman*. 1825. Edinburgh: Adam and Charles Black, 1863.
Scranton, Roy. *Learning to Die in the Anthropocene: Reflections on the End of a Civilization*. San Francisco: City Lights, 2015.
Sedgwick, Eve Kosofsky. "Willa Cather and Others." *Tendencies*. London: Routledge, 1994. 165–174.
Sellers, Charles G. *The Market Revolution: Jacksonian America, 1815–1846*. New York: Oxford University Press, 1991.
Sergeant, Elizabeth Shepley. *Willa Cather, a Memoir*. Philadelphia: Lippincott, 1953.
Serpell, Namwali C. *Seven Modes of Uncertainty*. Cambridge, MA: Harvard University Press, 2014.
Shapiro, Michael J. *Reading the Postmodern Polity: Political Theory As Textual Practice*. Minneapolis: University of Minnesota Press, 1992.

Shapiro, Stephen. *The Culture and Commerce of the Early American Novel: Reading the Atlantic World-System*. University Park: Pennsylvania State University Press, 2008.
Shippey, Tom. "Cooling Connections." *The Times Literary Supplement* (May 2, 2003), 23.
Shonkwiler, Alison. "Don DeLillo's Financial Sublime." *Contemporary Literature* 51.2 (Summer 2010): 246–282.
Simmel, Georg. "The Adventurer" [1911]. *On Individuality and Social Forms: Selected Writings*. Ed. and Intr. Donald N. Levine. Chicago: University of Chicago Press, 1971. 187–198.
Skaggs, Merrill Maguire. *After the World Broke in Two: The Later Novels of Willa Cather*. Charlottesville: University Press of Virginia, 1990.
Skinner, Quentin. *Machiavelli: A Very Short Introduction*. Oxford: Oxford University Press, 1981.
Smith, Adam. *An Inquiry into the Nature and Causes of the Wealth of Nations*. 2 vols. Ed., intr., notes Edwin Cannan. London: Methuen, 1904.
Smith, Caleb. *The Oracle and the Curse: A Poetics of Justice From the Revolution to the Civil War*. Cambridge, MA: Harvard University Press, 2013.
Somers, Margaret. "The Narrative Constitution of Identity: A Relational and Network Approach." *Theory and Society* 23.5 (1994): 605–649.
Squire, Kelsey. "'Jazz Age' Places: Modern Regionalism in Willa Cather's *The Professor's House*." *Cather Studies* 9 (2011): 45–66.
Srigley, Susan. "The Violence of Love: Reflections on Self-Sacrifice through Flannery O'Connor and René Girard." *Religion & Literature* 39.3 (Autumn 2007): 31–45.
Stearns, Peter. *American Fear: The Causes and Consequences of High Anxiety*. New York: Routledge, 2006.
Stewart, Susan. *On Longing: Narratives of the Miniature, the Gigantic, the Souvenir, the Collection* [1984]. Durham: Duke University Press, 1993.
Stigler, Stephen M. *The History of Statistics: The Measurement of Uncertainty Before 1900*. Cambridge, MA: The Belknap Press of Harvard University Press, 1986.
Svendsen, Lars. *A Philosophy of Fear*. London: Reaktion Books, 2008.
Swift, John N. "Memory, Myth, and 'The Professor's House'." *Western American Literature* 20.4 (Winter 1986): 301–314.
  "Unwrapping the Mummy: Cather's Mother Eve and the Business of Desire." *Willa Cather and the American Southwest*. Ed. John N. Swift and Joseph R. Urgo. Lincoln: University of Nebraska Press, 2002. 13–21.
Swift, Simon. *Hannah Arendt*. New York: Routledge, 2009.
Tabbi, Joseph. *Postmodern Sublime: Technology and American Writing From Mailer to Cyberpunk*. Ithaca: Cornell University Press, 1995.
[Tate, Allen.] "Introduction: A Statement of Principles." *Twelve Southerners, I'll Take My Stand: The South and the Agrarian Tradition* [1930]. Ed. Louis D. Rubin, Jr. Baton Rouge: Louisiana State University Press, 1977. xxxvii–xlviii.
Tate, Allen. "Remarks on the Southern Religion." *Twelve Southerners, I'll Take My Stand: The South and the Agrarian Tradition* [1930]. Ed. Louis D. Rubin, Jr. Baton Rouge: Louisiana State University Press, 1977. 155–175.

Tate, J. O., Jr. "Flannery O'Connor's Counterplot." *Southern Review* 16.4 (1980): 869–878.
Taylor, Charles. "The Politics of Recognition." *Multiculturalism: Examining the Politics of Recognition*. Ed. Amy Gutmann. Princeton: Princeton University Press, 1994. 25–74.
  A Secular Age. Cambridge: Belknap Press of Harvard University Press, 2007.
Tennyson, Lord Alfred. *Poems. Selections*. Everyman's Library. New York: Knopf, 2004.
The National Era. "Our Readers Must Excuse Us For Troubling Them With So Long ..." February 8, 1849. *African American Newspapers*. Web.
  "Reign of Terror in Virginia – The Remedy." December 1, 1859. *African American Newspapers*. Web.
  "Slave Insurrection Movements." December 18, 1856. *African American Newspapers*. Web.
Thomas, Hugh M. *The English and the Normans: Ethnic Hostility, Assimilation, and Identity, 1066–c.1220*. Oxford: Oxford University Press, 2003.
Thoreau, Henry David. *Walden* [1854]. *Henry David Thoreau: A Week on the Concord and Merrimack Rivers, Walden, The Maine Woods, Cape Cod*. Notes by Robert F. Sayre. New York: Library of America, 1985.
Tjalve, Vibeke Schou, and Michael C. Williams. "Re-Thinking the Logic of Security: Liberal Realism and the Recovery of American Political Thought." *Security and Liberalism*. Ed. Johannes Voelz. *Telos* 170 (Spring 2015): 46–66.
Tocqueville, Alexis de. *Democracy in America*. Ed. Eduardo Nola, trans. James T. Schleifer. Indianapolis: Liberty Fund, 2010.
Tricomi, Albert. "Harriet Jacobs's Autobiography and the Voice of Lydia Maria Child." *ESQ* 53.3 (2007): 217–252.
Trilling, Lionel. "On the Teaching of Modern Literature." *The Moral Obligation to Be Intelligent: Selected Essays*. Ed. Leon Wieseltier. New York: Farrar, Straus & Giroux, 2000. 381–401.
  "Willa Cather" [1936]. *Willa Cather: Modern Critical Views*. Ed. Harold Bloom. New York: Chelsea House. 7–13.
Trout, Steven. *Memorial Fictions: Willa Cather and the First World War*. Lincoln: University of Nebraska Press, 2002.
U.S. Department of the Navy. "U.S. NAVY SHIPS—USS *Imperator* (ID # 4080)." www.history.navy.mil/photos/sh-usn/usnsh-i/id4080.htm
Updike, John. "One-Way Street." *The New Yorker* (March 31, 2003), 102–103.
Valentino, Russell Scott. "From Virtue to Virtual: Don DeLillo's *Cosmopolis* and the Corruption of the Absent Body." *Modern Fiction Studies* 53.1 (Spring 2007): 140–162.
Varsava, Jerry. "The 'Saturated Self': Don DeLillo on the Problem of Rogue Capitalism." *Contemporary Literature* 46.1 (Spring 2005): 78–107.
Voelz, Johannes. "Aestheticizing Insecurity: Response to Security Studies and American Literary History," a special issue of *American Literary History*, ed. by David Watson. *American Literary History* 29.3 (2017): 615–624.
  "Cold War Liberalism and the Problem of Security." *REAL: Yearbook of Research in English and American Literature* 30 (2014): 255–281.

"The Aspiration for Impossible Security: Revisiting Liberal Political Thought." *Security and Liberalism*. Ed. Johannes Voelz. *Telos* 170 (Spring 2015): 23–45.
Vogl, Joseph. *The Specter of Capital*. Trans. Joachim Redner and Robert Savage. Stanford: Stanford University Press, 2015.
Warner, Michael. *The Letters of the Republic: Publication and the Public Sphere in Eighteenth-Century America*. Cambridge, MA: Harvard University Press, 1990.
Waterman, Bryan. "Arthur Mervyn's Medical Repository and the Early Republic's Knowledge." *American Literary History* 15.2 (2003): 213–247.
Republic of Intellect: The Friendly Club of New York City and the Making of American Literature. Baltimore: Johns Hopkins University Press, 2007.
Watt, James. "Scott, the Scottish Enlightenment, and Romantic Orientalism." *Scotland and the Borders of Romanticism*. Ed. Leith Davis, Ian Duncan, and Janet Sorensen. Cambridge: Cambridge University Press, 2004. 94–112.
Weyler, Karen A. *Intricate Relations: Sexual and Economic Desire in American Fiction, 1789–1814*. Iowa City: University of Iowa Press, 2004.
White, Hayden. "Ethnological 'Lie' and Mythical 'Truth'." Review of René Girard, *Violence and the Sacred*. *Diacritics* 8.1 (Spring 1978): 2–9.
"The Value of Narrativity in the Representation of Reality." *The Content of the Form: Narrative Discourse and Historical Representation*. Baltimore: Johns Hopkins University Press, 1987. 1–27.
Williams, Michael C., ed. *Realism Reconsidered: The Legacy of Hans Morgenthau in International Relations*. New York: Oxford University Press, 2007.
Williams, Michael C., and Vibeke Schou Tjalve. "Re-Thinking the Logic of Security: Liberal Realism and the Recovery of American Political Thought." *Security and Liberalism*. Ed. Johannes Voelz. *Telos* 170 (Spring 2015): 46–66.
Williams, Raymond. *The Country and the City*. New York: Oxford University Press, 1975.
Wilson, Edmund. *The Shores of Light: A Literary Chronicle of the Twenties and Thirties*. New York: Farrar, Straus and Young, 1952.
Wilson, Sarah. "Fragmentary and Inconclusive Violence: National History and Literary Form in The Professor's House." *American Literature* 75.3 (September 2003): 571–99.
Wood, Gordon S. *Empire of Liberty: A History of the Early Republic, 1789–1815*. New York: Oxford University Press, 2005.
"Interests and Disinterestedness in the Making of the Constitution." *Beyond Confederation*. Ed. Richard Beeman, Stephen Botein, and Edward C. Carter II. Chapel Hill: University of North Carolina Press, 1987. 69–109.
The Creation of the American Republic, 1776–1787. Chapel Hill: University of North Carolina Press, 1998.
Wood, James. "Traffic." *The New Republic* (April 14, 2003), 30–33.
Woodress, James, with Kari A. Ronning. Explanatory Notes. Willa Cather, *The Professor's House*. Willa Cather Scholarly Edition. Lincoln: University of Nebraska Press, 2002. 337–384.
Yellin, Jean Fagan. *Harriet Jacobs: A Life*. New York: Basic Civitas Books, 2004.
Yellin, Jean Fagan, ed. *The Harriet Jacobs Family Papers*. 2 vols. Chapel Hill: University of North Carolina Press, 2008.

Zimmerman, David A. "Novels of American Business, Industry, and Consumerism." *The Cambridge History of the American Novel*. Gen. ed. Leonard Cassuto, assoc. ed. Clare Virginia Eby and Benjamin Reiss. New York: Cambridge University Press, 2011. 409–424.

Panic! Markets, Crises, and Crowds in American Fiction. Chapel Hill: University of North Carolina Press, 2006.

Zweig, Stefan. *The World of Yesterday: An Autobiography* [1942]. Lincoln: University of Nebraska Press, 1964.

Index

adventure, 55, 112, 124–25, 184. *See also* Brown, Charles Brockden; Cather, Willa; narrative
Agamben, Giorgio, 199n27
aggression. *See* insecurity; O'Connor, Flannery and violence
Ahearn, Amy, 209n10
American naturalist novel, 169–70
Amoore, Louise, 181–82
Anderson, Amanda, 214n4
Angus, Ian, 186
Anker, Elisabeth, 190n10
anthropocene, 126, 186–88
Appleby, Joyce, 195n1
Arendt, Hannah, 144–45, 217n14
Aristotle, 20–21, 70, 193n27, 196n11
Armstrong, Tim, 69, 77
Augustine, 13
authenticity. *See* death

Bachner, Sally, 215n7
Baker, Jennifer, 195n3
Barnard, Philip, 200n31
Bauman, Zygmunt, 164
Beck, Ulrich, 191n14
Belletto, Steven, 215n5, 218n17
Bernoulli, Jacob, 41, 197n13
Bonneuil, Christophe, 186
Bourdieu, Pierre, 194n29
Boxall, Peter, 178
Boym, Svetlana, 207n4
Brodhead, Richard, 104, 106, 207n5
Brooks, Peter, 24
Brown, Charles Brockden, 2, 19, 24, 34–64, 195n4
  Arthur Mervyn, 4, 16, 18, 34, 35, 38–64, 178, 184, 203n13
  "The Difference between History and Romance", 21, 40
  Edgar Huntly, 192n20, 199n22
  and fictionality, 41, 64
  literary theory, 39
  "The Man At Home", 38
  Ormond, 38, 46, 199n22
  on virtue, 40
  "Walstein's School of History", 39, 41, 199n21
Brown, John, 87, 94, 206n28
Brown, William Wells, 204n16
Buell, Lawrence, 209n10
Burgess, Peter, 189n2
Burke, Edmund, 46, 198n18
Burroughs, Stephen, 59–60
Butler, Judith, 218n18
Buzan, Barry, 194n29

Cameron, Catherine M., 103
Campe, Rüdiger, 192n20
Cather, Willa, 2, 14, 96–104, 207n3, 208n7, 211n18
  A Lost Lady, 124, 206n1
  and adventurism, 124–25
  Death Comes for the Archbishop, 96
  and modernism, 98–100
  and naturalism, 103, 109, 209n10
  and nostalgia, 97–98, 108
  "The Novel Démeublé", 113
  and regionalism, 104–08
  "The Sculptor's Funeral", 209n11
  My Ántonia, 102
  Not Under Forty, 98–99, 101
  O Pioneers!, 206n1
  The Professor's House, 4, 6, 27, 96–98, 100–04, 108–27, 184, 213n29
  Shadows on the Rock, 96
  Song of the Lark, 209n10
Child, Lydia Maria, 205n26
Civil War, 91
Cleves, Rachel Hope, 87, 204n19, 204n20
Cold War, 129–32
  intellectuals, 129, 131, 154
  liberalism, 132, 133
  and violence, 133–34
Coleridge, Samuel Taylor, 193n25
conjecture, 40, 46, 57

Cowart, David, 163, 176, 185
Crane, Gregg, 88
cultural semiotics, 25–26

Dalby, Simon, 204n18
de Montaigne, Michel, 186–87
de Wilde, Jaap, 194n29
death, 184
 and authenticity, 174–75, 176, 177
DeLillo, Don, 2, 14, 16
 Cosmopolis, 5, 6, 160–61, 162–65, 166–80, 184
 Falling Man, 159–60
 and futurity, 158–60, 164–65, 166–67, 170–71, 179–80
 "In the Ruins of the Future", 157, 158
 and materiality of signs, 165–66
 The Names, 165
 and pain, 176–77
 Point Omega, 160, 185
 and temporality, 163–64
 White Noise, 166
 Zero K, 185
DeLombard, Jeannine, 202n7, 204n17
Derrida, Jacques, 193n24
Displaced Persons, 137
Doppelgänger, 175–76
Douglass, Frederick, 69
Dreiser, Theodore, 169–70
dystopia, 12

Eliot, T. S., 99
Emerson, Ralph Waldo, 3, 174
empowerment. *See* fictionality and imaginary empowerment
Esposito, Elena, 198n16
existentialism, 174. *See also* philosophy of existence

Faludi, Susan, 223n2
Fanuzzi, Robert, 83
fear, 8, 32, 199n26
 culture of, 8
 and security, 11
 as a temporal emotion, 10
Felski, Rita, 31
Fetterley, Judith, 208n8
Fewkes, Jesse Walter, 103
fictionality, 20–23, 66
 and imaginary empowerment, 30–32
 rise of, 19
finance capitalism, 60, 157
 end of, 158
 and futurity, 161–62
 in popular culture, 162
 and time, 166–67

financial hero, 170
Fisher-Wirth, Ann, 213n29
Fleischner, Jennifer, 203n10
Fluck, Winfried, 29, 198n17
Foote, Stephanie, 105, 208n8
Forter, Greg, 210n16
fortune, 38, 50
Foucault, Michel, 191n14, 194n29, 200n27, 200n28
Fressoz, Jean-Baptiste, 186
futurity, 10, 51, 125, 183–84, 185–86. *See also* Anthropocene; DeLillo, Don; finance capitalism

Gallagher, Catherine, 19, 20–22, 28–29
Garland, Hamlin
 Main-Travelled Roads, 106–08
Garrison, William Lloyd, 87, 204n19
Gillingham, John, 213n30
Girard, René, 219n24
Glassner, Barry, 190n5
Goddu, Teresa, 199n20
Godwin, William, 46, 58, 197n12
Goudie, Sean, 199n20
Gould, Philip, 199n26
Grabo, Norman, 48
Graham, T. Austin, 214n31

Hägglund, Martin, 10, 13, 211n18
Halttunen, Karen, 18, 192n18
Hamilton, John, 11, 13, 103, 190n9
Hamilton, Ross, 193n27
Harrell, David, 209n12
Haselstein, Ulla, 201n2
Hawthorne, Nathaniel, 192n20
Hegel, Georg Wilhelm Friedrich, 24, 74
Heidegger, Martin, 111, 174, 175, 190n8, 209n13
Henry, Katherine, 196n7
Hicks, Granville, 97
Homer
 Odyssey, 162–63
Horn, Eva, 223n4
Hurst, Winston, 210n15

I'll Take My Stand!, 139–41
imaginary. *See* fictionality
insecurity, 173–74. *See also* threat
 acceptance of, 154
 and aggression, 148–55
 affective, 81–83
 constituting community, 5, 7, 65, 86–95
 economic, 138, 139–43, 145
 as enabling condition, 2, 5–8, 146, 155, 183, 184
 and freedom, 76
 political, 139, 143–45
 religious, 134, 145–48, 154

as thrill, 172–73
and uncertainty, 11–12, 17, 52, 183

Jacobs, Harriet, 2, 14, 16, 18, 19, 65–66, 184, 202n5, 204n17, 205n26
   black readership of, 93
   Incidents in the Life of a Slave Girl, 4, 5, 65, 71–77, 80–95
   rhetorics of, 66, 94
   topos of incommensurability, 84–86, 91
   topos of the inexpressible, 83–84, 204n16
James, William, 9
Jameson, Frederic, 164
Jewett, Sarah Orne, 106
   The Country of the Pointed Firs, 106
Joseph, Philip, 208n8

Kalyvas, Andreas, 196n5
Kamrath, Mark, 200n31
Kaplan, Amy, 104
Katznelson, Ira, 196n5
Kennan, George, 132
Kierkegaard, Søren, 156, 174, 222n20
Koselleck, Reinhart, 191n11
Kosofsky Sedgwick, Eve, 212n26
Kuckelman, Kristen A., 208n7

Lee, Maurice, 68
Leibniz, Gottfried Wilhelm, 197n13
Levy, Jonathan, 70
Lotman, Yuri, 25–27, 30, 33, 38
Lucenti, Lisa Marie, 212n22
Luhman, Niklas, 191n14
Lutz, Tom, 100, 206n1, 208n8

Machiavelli, Niccolo, 37
Madison, James, 36
management
   risk, 16
   security, 160, 161
Mandeville, Bernard, 61
Margolis, Stacey, 199n23
Marinetti, Filippo Tommaso, 100
Maritain, Jacques, 156
Marshall, Kate, 186
Massumi, Brian, 8–10
Melley, Timothy, 223n2
Melville, Herman, 192n20
Michaels, Walter Benn, 212n25
Middleton, Jo Ann, 208n5
Mihm, Stephen, 22
Millington, Richard, 208n5
Morgenthau, Hans, 214n3, 219n25
Morris, Thomas, 201n4, 202n6
mortality. *See* death; security

Münkler, Herfried, 15
Murphy, John J., 212n24

Nabers, Deak, 88
narrative, 24–25, 97. *See also* adventure; plot
   intruding figure, 137
   mobile character, 26
naturalism, 107–08. *See also* American naturalist novel; Cather, Willa
Neocleous, Mark, 214n1, 214n2
Nerlich, Michael, 200n29
Niebuhr, Reinhold, 130, 154
9/11, 157
   as rupture, 158, 159
Norris, Frank, 169–70
North, Michael, 207n5, 213n28
Northup, Solomon, 203n11
nostalgia, 6, 97, 98, 104–06, 115, 127, 207n2, 210n16. *See also* Cather, Willa; regionalism
   and modernism, 99–100

O'Connor, Flannery, 2, 4, 14, 156
   "The Catholic Novelist in the Protestant South", 135, 150
   "The Displaced Person", 137–54, 184
   "The Fiction Writer and His Country", 6
   and religion, 134–36
   and the South, 151
   and violence, 133–34, 135, 136, 137, 139, 146, 148, 153
Odysseus-figure, 162–63
Orians, Harrison, 20

pain. *See* DeLillo, Don
Pells, Richard, 130
philosophy of existence, 174–75. *See also* existentialism
plot, 24–25, 38. *See also* narrative
Pocock, John Greville Agard, 194n1, 195n3, 196n6
Poresky, Louise, 211n18
Proust, Marcel, 99
Pryse, Marjorie, 208n8

regionalism, 104–08, 117–18. *See also* Cather, Willa
   and nostalgia, 105
religion. *See* insecurity; O'Connor, Flannery
republicanism, 34–38, 61
   individualism, 45
   virtue, 35, 38, 42, 61
Reynolds, Guy, 207n3
Ricoeur, Paul, 25, 29, 193n24
risk, 68, 160, 173–74
   of death, 69
   economic, 61, 162
   logics of, 14–16, 172, 181–82
   and personhood, 70

risk (cont.)
  shared, 202n8
  time of, 161–71, 175
Rosowski, Susan, 212n20
Russo, James, 200n33

Sartre, Jean-Paul, 174
Scheiding, Oliver, 198n17
Schlesinger, Arthur, 130, 154
Schubnell, Matthias, 209n12
Scott, Walter
  The Talisman, 121, 122
Scranton, Roy, 186–87
secular modernity
  critique of, 134, 154
security. *See also* threat
  age of, 1, 13
  and agency, 12–13, 30, 32, 43, 50, 54–55, 60
  and capitalism, 14, 15, 16, 61–62, 138, 139, 172
  Christian understanding of, 146
  and Cold War, 154, 156
  and the Cold War, 129–32
  as cultural practice, 22–23
  and democracy, 17, 19, 181
  dialectics of, 129–30
  divine, 135
  as enabling condition, 12
  etymology of, 4, 11
  and insecurity, 2–8, 138
  and liberalism, 196n7
  logics of, 15, 172, 181
  and mortality, 179–80
  and the nation state, 144–45
  national, 129–30, 131, 154, 156
  normativity of, 88
  nostalgic, 97–98, 104
  as orderliness, 2, 12, 15, 26–27
  pervasiveness of, 4, 32
  in public discourse, 32, 129
  as radical contingency, 111–14, 127, 210n16
  as rationality, 131, 133, 136
  and risk, 160
  sciences of, 189n2
  and secularity, 13–14
  as social construct, 194n29
  time of, 171–80
  and uncertainty, 6, 11–12, 14–15, 160
Serpell, Namwali, 192n22
Shapiro, Stephen, 200n31
Shelley, Mary, 47
Simmel, Georg, 184
Skaggs, Merrill Maguire, 212n23
Skinner, Quentin, 37
slavery
  and civilization, 90
  fugitives, 68, 79, 91

insecure property, 77–78
politics of, 5, 74, 79
slave narratives, 78, 83, 84
and subjectivity, 76
Smith, Adam, 61
Southern Renascence, 139–41
  slavery, 140
speculation, 21
  financial, 157, 159–60, 161, 167
Squire, Kelsey, 208n5
Stewart, Susan, 207n2
Svendsen, Lars, 10
Swift, John, 208n6, 210n14, 210n17

Taylor, Charles, 13
Teilhard de Chardin, Pierre, 156, 185, 222n20
temporality. *See* DeLillo, Don; futurity; risk; security
terrorism, 1, 3–4, 156
thanatopolitics, 52–53, 199n27
Thomas, Hugh, 213n30
Thoreau, Henry David, 6, 12
threat, 3, 181, 183, 184. *See also* insecurity; security
  and possibility, 183
Till, Jonathan, 210n15
time. *See* DeLillo, Don; futurity; risk; security
timelessness, 30, 162
Tocqueville, Alexis de, 17
transgression, 30, 54
Tricomi, Albert, 206n29
Trilling, Lionel, 97, 131, 154
Trout, Steven, 211n19

uncertainty. *See* insecurity; risk; security; threat

Valentino, Russel Scott, 222n22
violence. *See* O'Connor, Flannery; Cold War
virtue, 50
Vogl, Joseph, 163

Waever, Ole, 194n29
Wall Street, 162, 170
Watt, James, 213n27
White, Hayden, 24
Williams, Raymond, 104
Wilson, Edmund, 207n5
Wilson, Sarah, 207n3
The Wolf of Wall Street, 162, 170
Wolfe, Tom, 170
Wood, Gordon, 194n1, 195n3
Woodress, James, 206n1
Woolf, Virginia, 98, 114, 211n18

Yellin, Jean Fagan, 205n21

Zweig, Stefan, 189n1

RECENT BOOKS IN THIS SERIES (*continued from page iii*)

156. JOANNA FREER
     Thomas Pynchon and American Counterculture
155. DOMINIC MASTROIANNI
     Politics and Skepticism in Antebellum American Literature
154. LENA HILL
     Visualizing Blackness and the Creation of the African American Literary Tradition
153. GAVIN JONES
     Failure and the American Writer
152. MICHAEL ZISER
     Environmental Practice and Early American Literature
151. ANDREW HEBARD
     The Poetics of Sovereignty in American Literature, 1885–1910
150. TIM ARMSTRONG
     The Logic of Slavery: Debt, Technology, and Pain in American Literature
149. CHRISTOPHER FREEBURG
     Melville and the Idea of Blackness: Race and Imperialism in Nineteenth-Century America
148. JUSTINE S. MURISON
     The Politics of Anxiety in Nineteenth-Century American Literature
147. DORRI BEAM
     Style, Gender, and Fantasy in Nineteenth-Century American Women's Writing
146. HSUAN L. HSU
     Geography and the Production of Space in Nineteenth-Century American Literature
145. YOGITA GOYAL
     Romance, Diaspora, and Black Atlantic Literature
144. MICHAEL W. CLUNE
     American Literature and the Free Market, 1945–2000
143. KERRY LARSON
     Imagining Equality in Nineteenth-Century American Literature

142. LAWRENCE ALAN ROSENWALD
Multilingual America: Language and the Making of American Literature

141. ANITA PATTERSON
Race, American Literature and Transnational Modernisms

140. THEO DAVIS
Formalism, Experience, and the Making of American Literature in the Nineteenth Century

Lightning Source UK Ltd.
Milton Keynes UK
UKHW010851130722
405777UK00007B/248